WITHDRAWN

Media Product Portfolios: Issues in Management of Multiple Products and Services

Edited by
Robert G. Picard

LAWRENCE ERLBAUM ASSOCIATES, PUBLISHERS
2005   **Mahwah, New Jersey**   **London**

Camera ready copy for this book was provided by the author.

Lawrence Erlbaum Associates, Inc., Publishers
10 Industrial Avenue
Mahwah, New Jersey 07430
www.erlbaum.com

Cover design by Kathryn Houghtaling Lacey

Library of Congress Cataloging-in-Publication Data

Media product portfolios : issues in management of multiple products and services / edited by Robert G. Ricard.
      p. cm.

Includes bibliographical references and index.

ISBN 0-8058-5589-0 (alk. paper)
1. Mass media—Management. 2. Mass media—Economic aspects.
    I. Picard, Robert G.
P96.M34M42 2005
302.23'068—dc22   2005040134
                                       CIP

Contents

Preface

Media product portfolios are rapidly becoming the predominant shared characteristic of media companies worldwide. The phenomenon involves firms from all kinds of media—newspapers, magazines, television, radio, cinema— and is found in enterprises ranging from small, local firms to large, globalized companies.

These developments raise significant questions and issues for media managers, employees, scholars, and social observers. Despite growing important of portfolio activities in media operations, they remain one of the least explored and most misunderstood aspects of media firms. The ability to comprehend their meaning and impact is significantly hampered by lack of knowledge.

This book breaks new ground by introducing the concepts of product portfolio management and applying them to media companies in a comprehensive manner. It draws from knowledge and methods of analyzing product portfolio management in other industries, applies that knowledge to media industries, and analyzes current practices in media firms.

The process and issues of portfolio strategy, development, and management are complex and wide ranging. The book explores the development of media product portfolios from an interdisciplinary perspective, providing insight from business, economic, organizational, and communication approaches. It is intended to help develop comprehension of methods of product portfolio development and management, to evaluate the effectiveness and challenges of media product portfolios, and to identify best practices in portfolio management.

The book explores why and how firms develop portfolios, how company strategy and organizational development relate to portfolios, the role of leaders in developing portfolio activities, economic and economic geography issues in portfolios, production issues, challenges in managing multiple products and operations, issues of marketing and branding issues in portfolios, personnel implications, and the unique challenges in the internationalization of media portfolio operations.

The authors combine theoretical concepts and analysis with the applied media business practices and then explore challenges of operating media firms and portfolios. It is richly illustrated with examples of media products, organizational structures, and issues involving media companies throughout the world. The authors explore expectations for portfolios, limitations of portfolios, and successes and failures in the operations of media product portfolios.

The book is the result of a coordinated effort of scholars in the U.S. and Europe to explore the characteristics, processes, challenges, and implications of media product portfolios. The process began with a seminal seminar on media product portfolios in at Jönköping International Business School, Jönköping University, Sweden, in 2003 and continued with the extensive research and study by authors of this volume.

It is hoped that the volume will bring greater attention and understand to the topic, improve analysis of companies and portfolios, and lead to better management practices in media firms.

Robert G. Picard

1
The Nature of Media Product Portfolios

Robert G. Picard
Jönköping International Business School

Product portfolios are created when companies begin producing and offering more than one product into the market. Effective management of companies with multiple products requires changes in the ways they were managed when they offered single products. As the size of the product portfolio grows, significant change is sometimes required in company strategy, organization, and administration, as well as in product development activities, marketing, and customer service.

An electrical appliance firm, for example, may manufacture a range of products including handsaws, toaster ovens, and portable radios. A plastics manufacturer may produce kitchenware, automobile components, and toys. Media firms, however, have historically focused on one product. Newspaper companies, for example, typically produced one newspaper, and radio broadcasters typically offered one channel of broadcasting. When they increased their products it was usually through replication of the initial product. The newspaper would launch or acquire a newspaper in another city and the radio firm would offer a second radio channel.

In recent years, that situation has changed. Media companies are increasingly developing broad product portfolios in response to market changes and convergence, as an effect of industry consolidation, and as a means of seeking economies of scale and scope. Media product portfolios are appearing in every media industry. Larger magazine firms publish hundreds of titles, broadcasting firms operate multiple channels, and newspaper firms produce multiple titles and different types of papers.

Cross-media portfolios are increasingly common in media companies. Some newspaper companies moved into the broadcasting sector, broadcasting companies have broadened their activities into program and motion picture production, and domestic portfolios are being expanded into international portfolios. Depending upon the organizational structures of these firms, they can be thought of as owning and managing media product portfolios and portfolios of media companies. A recent study of the six largest media firms, for example, shows that all are broad content-creation and development enterprises that provide content through different platforms and media (Albarran & Moellinger, 2002).

These changes are creating significant new managerial challenges. Managers with knowledge, skills, and experience in one media field are being given responsibilities for media with different economic, financial, and operational characteristics, and managers with skills operating one product line are suddenly asked to manage multiple products.

These changes are problematic because managers in media have typically been raised through the organizations without significant business education and with limited understanding of strategy and management and the issues associated with portfolio management. Even the literature of media management, including key texts, provides little recognition that product portfolios exist and tends to focus on managing media firms based on a single type and unit of media.

Understanding and managing portfolios of products are key challenges of media management in the 21st century and require an understanding of the rationales for, influences upon, and structures and operations of portfolios. Managing portfolios requires diligence and care. It is described as "a dynamic decision process...[in which] new projects are evaluated, selected, and prioritized; existing projects may be accelerated, killed, or deprioritized; and resources are allocated and reallocated to active projects" (Cooper, Edgett & Keinschmidt, 1998, p. 3). The goals of the process are to maximize the value of the portfolio, achieve and optimal balance among parts of the portfolio, and to ensure that the products reflect strategic priorities.

RATIONALE FOR PRODUCT PORTFOLIOS

A number of rationales exist for operating product portfolios, including risk reduction, managing life cycles, market exploitation, increasing the breadth of service, and efficiency.

Risk Reduction

Development of product portfolios is often undertaken as a means of lowering risks associated with operating firms. Creating a portfolio of products helps reduce risks of product failure, diminished demand, business cycles, market disruptions, or events that interfere with production and distribution. Such risks are amplified when firms are dependent on single products or operate in single geographic areas.

Print and broadcasting companies traditionally were active in only one media field but in the past three decades many firms have increasingly diversified their product range—primarily to other media products—as a means of reducing risks. As early as 1986, it was shown that media company portfolio development and diversification reduced resource dependence and their associated risks (Dimmick & Wallschlaeger, 1986). Audio recording, motion picture, and television programming production firms have long used portfolios to overcome risks due to the difficulties of forecasting creative product quality, consumer demand, and financial success.

Another rationale has been to stabilize company finances during contractions in the business cycle. Traditional print media companies, in particular, have diversified into broadcast and other media because print media revenues are far more affected by downturns than those of broadcast media (Picard, 2001a) and evidence exists that that diversification of media products reduces effects of recessions on company finances (Picard & Rimmer, 1999).

Managing Product Life Cycles

Fear of current and potential market changes and their effects on the primary product also leads to the development of portfolios. Given that products have individual life cycles, operating a portfolio of products at different states in life cycles is a means for maintaining company stability and achieving sustainability (Barksdale, 1982).

For example, since the mid-1990s, the majority of newspapers in Europe and North America have begun providing Internet products as a response to market and technological factors that appear to be leading their companies into the decline phase of the 300-year long newspaper life cycle. How that strategy has been operationalized has generally been dependent on the degree of risk perceived. Saksena and Hollified (2002), for example, have shown that in papers at which the Internet was viewed as seriously disruptive technology, managers developed Internet newspapers with more systematic thought and processes and created more comprehensive online products than those at papers where the Internet was viewed as less threatening to their survival.

Currently, major audio recording firms are entering joint ventures to provide online sales and distribution of songs in response to the disruption created to their existing business and potential end of the life cycle for physical recordings that was created by digitalization of audio products and distribution possibilities enabled by the Internet for both e-commerce in recordings, as well as unauthorized downloading.

Market Exploitation and Company Growth

Some portfolios develop because managers see market opportunities and seek for their companies to benefit through the provision of additional products. Acquiring benefits by exploiting such visible market opportunities and pursuing strategies for company growth are clear rationales for the development of many product portfolios.

In the 1970s and 1980s, for example, newspapers in North America and Europe began offering several types of free nondaily newspapers and advertising sheets to reach some categories of the print advertising market that did not use traditional dailies and to provide broader household distribution for advertising of large retailers (Thorn, 1987; Willis, 1988). These strategies created new revenue streams and supplemental uses for editorial material already produced by the daily. For many publishers, the movement into these total circulation newspapers and nonduplicating coverage newspapers represented their initial transition from a single product producer into a producer of a portfolio of products.

In recent years, a growing number of traditional paid daily newspaper publishers have increased their portfolios by moving into the free daily newspaper sector—not merely to defend the market position—but because they see it as a means of reaching a segment of readers not served by the paid product and for providing service to advertisers who do not use their paid daily product (Price, 2003; World Association of Newspapers, 2000).

Today, a number of European broadcasters are exploiting opportunities to create a portfolio channels in different European markets. Examples of these portfolios are seen in the operations of Modern Times Group's Viasat—which now has television operations in nine countries—and NRJ radio, which has radio stations and networks in nine countries.

Seeking new opportunities in the market is a relatively new phenomenon for most media firms and they typically lack formal processes and structures for managing new product development initiatives. The processes have been shown to contribute significantly to success of new products (Cooper & Kleinschmidt, 1995; Griffin, 1997). If media companies continue to adapt more entrepreneurial attitudes and seek to explore and launch a variety of new product and service activities, they may begin formalizing product development processes and research and development activities that have been previously absent.

Breadth of Market Service

Increasing contacts with customers and providing additional services is a focus of the development of some portfolios. The ability to provide multiple means of serving customers is seen as a critical means of developing loyalty.

The international cable television broadcaster Cable News Network (CNN), for example, operates a portfolio that began with a single cable network that was expanded into related headline and airport television channels, and then expanded into complementary Internet and mobile telephony services through which additional information and news updates are delivered.

In some countries, newspaper firms are operating Internet and mobile services, and have begun joint ventures with news operations of radio and television stations as a means of increasingly the frequency of their market contact with customers. This occurs because newspapers typically come into contact with their readers only 20 to 30 minutes a day and newspaper companies wish to increase the contacts and solidify their position as the primary news provider in the community.

The breadth of the portfolio and service provided can be analyzed by using a diversification index. Use of the index shows difference between degrees of diversification based on the contributions of different aspects of the portfolio to the company (Dimmick & Porco, 1990).

Efficiency

Operation of product portfolios is also a means of pursuing efficiency and advantages. This can occur through more efficient use of facilities and networks to achieve economies of scale and scope and by developing organizational structures that reduce transaction costs.

Creating a portfolio of similar media outlets—such as a portfolio of magazines—is a form of horizontal integration that may achieve efficiencies that reduce costs by exploiting benefits of economies of scale. Economies of scale are often product specific and related to cost efficiencies and capacity utilization of resources in a specific production facility (Teece, 1980, 1982), but they can also be achieved in multiple locations when some activities are combined to reduce average production price (Sherer & Ross, 1990). Doyle (2000) showed that various efficiencies in media do produce significant economies of scale and cost savings when portfolios of the same type of media products are constructed.

Strategic assets that allow resource sharing and competence transfers among products are also factor sin successful diversification (Markides & Williamson, 1996) because they make use of elements that create economies of scope. The publisher of a monthly magazine that has a distribution department that only operates at full capacity one week a month, for example, can achieve economies of scope in distribution by launching other titles to use the excess capacity in the remaining three weeks of each month.

Efficiencies can also be created by reducing costs throughout the value chain of media industries. The pursuit of these efficiencies has led to vertical integration in entertainment industries because they reduce transaction costs by creating a portfolio of value chain elements in which return is maximized across all functions (Gaustaud, 2002).

In the past decade, the practice of clustering media properties, a form of horizontal integration of operations in close proximity to each other, has emerged in attempts to gain efficiencies in operations of newspapers, broadcasting, and cable television operations (Ekelund et al., 2000; Lacy & Simon, 1987; Martin, 2003; Parsons, 2003). In such clusters, a broadcasting firm might seek to operate more than one radio station from a unified facility in which many production and support activities are consolidated, personnel can be shared, and cost savings achieved. Additional advantages may come from economies of scale (Doyle, 2000; Lacy & Simon, 1993; Sherer & Ross, 1990), economies scope (Teece, 1980), spatial economies (Dickens & Lloyd, 1990), or market advantages—such as lower costs of capital.

INFLUENCES ON MEDIA PORTFOLIOS

A variety of factors influence the type of product portfolios that can be or are established by media firms. These include both internal and exogenous influences that can be grouped into eight major categories (illustrated in Fig. 1.1): (1) company strategy; (2) company leadership and vision; (3) company structure; (4) company capacity and resources; (5) company culture; (6) market opportunities; (7) behavior of competitors; and (8) legal and policy controls. These influences determine what kinds of firms are included in portfolios.

Company strategy may narrow or broaden the portfolio it seeks to develop. Strategic choices involve building portfolios along related media product lines, complementary media product lines, unrelated media product lines, or unrelated products of another kind. These choices represent different forms of broad or narrow spectrums of diversification as classified by Varadarajan and Ramanujam (1987). A firm may choose to operate in only one media field, such as newspapers, and build a related media portfolio through horizontal integration and the operation of multiple newspapers. This strategy has been shown to enable media firms to gain market power, create synergy effects, and improve financial performance (Jung, 2003). Another firm may choose to

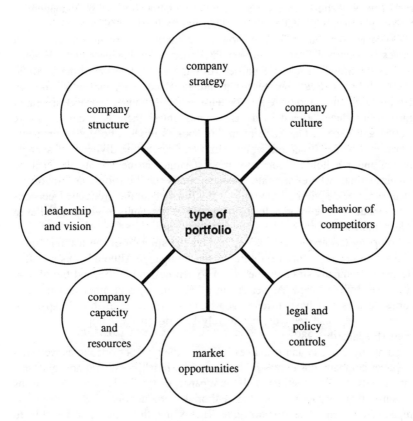

Fig. 1.1
Influences on the Type of Media Product Portfolios

operate complementary product lines such as television stations and a television program production company. Yet another may create a portfolio of unrelated media products and diversify into product lines such as newspapers, magazines, and broadcasting stations. In some cases, diversification may take the company outside of the media field and its supply networks, such as a newspaper firm that acquires or establishes a travel industry firm.

Studies of diversification in media firms indicate, however, that it may not produce efficiencies that improve company performance (Jung, 2003; Kolo & Vogt, 2003). Related diversification may produce efficiencies, but a high degree of unrelated diversification apparently does not. According to Jung (2003), broad diversification shows "a negative relationship with management effectiveness measures such as ROS, ROA, and ROI" (p. 245).

Company structure relates to how the company is organized, whether it operates as a unified firm or with separate independent business units. When a product portfolio is created in a unified firm, more coordination of the portfolio is likely. When separate business units are involved, each may offer its own portfolio of products and there may be tension between units and overlapping or competing products offered by different units unless there is strong corporate direction and control. Our concern in this book is product portfolios of media companies, whether structured within a unified firm, within divisions of a single firm, or under a holding company with separate business units. It must be recognized that where separate business units or divisions are involved, decisions are made within those units or divisions about the products. Decisions are also made at the corporate level about the business units, divisions, and even products themselves.

Company leadership and vision involves the strength of the leading figure and his or her vision of the future of the company. Although this is often reflected in company strategy, the vision sometimes can go beyond the official strategy set by the board. As set out in agency theory and other management theories, leaders may have different goals and desires for growth and expansion that provide personal rewards, not merely benefits to the company and it its owners (Eisenhardt, 1989).

Company capacity and resources influence the type of portfolio as well. If a newspaper company has excess printing capacity in its production house, it may create an advertising sheet, nondaily newspaper, or free daily paper as a means of using that capacity and the editorial, production, and distribution competencies within the organization. That same firm may not be able to establish or acquire a television station because it lacks managerial capacity or financial resources to support such a venture.

The third internal influence is company culture. The history, mission, and organizational behavior of a firm may constrain or direct the choices of portfolio that are possible. A firm that has been based in newspaper publishing with a long legacy of quality and social service orientation may encounter significant resistance to the establishment of a portfolio that includes a tabloid paper or television channel. A firm based in traditional media may have difficulties operating a portfolio that includes new media firms because of the differences in cultures and behavior.

The behavior of competitors may induce companies to develop or alter portfolios. This occurred in many nations as free newspapers were introduced and traditional publishers have moved to counter their entry by establishing their own free titles (Bakker, 2002; Picard, 2001b). Radio worldwide moved to establish portfolios that included online sites as a response to the entry of new online radio stations and streaming of audio signals by existing broadcasters.

Market opportunities can create conditions in which portfolio development becomes possible. In television, for example, the shift from analogue to digital terrestrial television has created the opportunity for many broadcasters to operate multiple channels. As a result, many public service channels in Europe are gaining 3 or 4 additional channels on which to broadcast additional programming. Many large commercial broadcasters have also acquired additional channels.

Media are among the most regulated industries—along with industries such as pharmaceuticals and finance—and for political and cultural rationales their ability to create portfolios are limited by special media ownership policies in many nations and general anti-cartel laws. In some nations owners of national channels are limited to one channel (or a DTTV multiplex) and in others the number of channels that may be owned in a city or in different cities is limited. Similarly cross-ownership limits constrain the development of portfolios. In the United Kingdom, for example, newspapers with more than 15% of the total national circulation are not allowed to own terrestrial television channels.

Because of the influences of internal and external factors, the types of media product portfolios that companies create vary widely.

ORGANIZATIONAL AND GEOGRAPHIC FACTORS IN MEDIA PRODUCT PORTFOLIOS

Organizational and geographic factors play important roles in the creation and operation of portfolios of all types (Fig. 1.2). The choices involve whether to operate the firms within the existing firm or to create a new organizational structure. Similarly, choices are made as to whether to operate within the same geographic market or in other markets

The choices made create different types of operations, with widely differing resource needs and market effects. Related media product lines, as indicated above, are built on a particular media type and can be produced using the same resources. An audio recording company, for example, offers recordings by a portfolio of artists and maintains a catalogue of recordings that can be reused in a variety of ways. Most major recording firms, however, have found it useful to expand that activity by launching or acquiring a portfolio of record labels, that is branded firms, which increase its overall product line but permit the labels to focus on specific genres or market segments even within the same geographic market. When this occurs, however, it becomes difficult to maintain integrated operations and there is a tendency to create subsidiary firms for different aspects

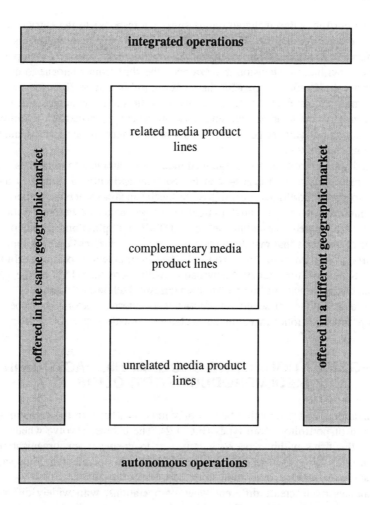

Fig. 1.2
Operational and Geographic Factors Affect Portfolio Choices and Operations

of the company's portfolio. The EMI Group, for example, includes autonomous labels such as Capitol Records, Virgin Records, EMI Classics, and Blue Note Records.

It has been argued that a television channel's programming should be conceptualized as assets and optimized as a product portfolio (Litman,

Srikhande & Ahn, 2000). Programs are selected to serve different audiences and carry different risks that are maximized across the viewing time to produce the optimal result for the company.

In another context, a firm that produces women's magazines might expand its portfolio by launching or acquiring sports or cultural magazines to reach a different audience and then integrate them within the publishing operations of a single company and then perhaps offer them in the same geographic market. In doing so, it would attempt to optimize its audience service without cannibalizing its existing customer base.

However, geographic expansion—especially international expansion—may require a different approach. Major magazine titles such as *Elle, Marie Claire, Playboy*, and *Cosmopolitan*, for example, have launched domestic editions of titles in many countries. Although these international magazine portfolios can be constructed as wholly owned publications, most firms find it more operationally effective to operate them autonomously or semi-autonomously through joint ventures or through licensing arrangements (Hafstrand, 1995).

International expansion in the magazine industry by European firms to the United States has been promoted by saturated domestic markets and efforts to understand and obtain contemporary practices and technologies not available in Europe (Bennett, 1999). International expansion is often a means of achieving product innovation as well as financial benefits (Hitt, 1997). Several recent studies indicated that market exploitation and innovation have been important in media firm internationalization (Gershon, 1997; Holtz-Bacha, 1997; van Kranenburg, Cloodt & Hagedoorn, 2001).

Internationalization, however, is accompanied by significant organizational change. Media firms operating in multiple national markets require complex organizational structures and operations that have been facilitated in recent years by improvements in telecommunications and information technologies and deregulatory policies. The development of multiple products, divisions, and subsidiaries to serve international markets has created a relatively new type of media firm, the transnational media corporation, according to Gershon (1997).

Operation of a portfolio of unrelated products also creates organizational complexity and difficulties in coordinating activities and gaining advantages across lines (Hill & Hoskisson, 1987; Hill, Hitt & Hoskisson 1992; Markides & Williamson, 1994). In multiproduct firms, the choice to diversify into unrelated products is often made as part of a risk-return trade-off in which lower returns are accepted in order to significantly reduce risk (Amihund & Lev, 1981; Amit & Livnat, 1988) Although the portfolios of media firms occasionally include unrelated products or services, it is rare that these are sought and they are most often found in family firms or in firms in which mergers and acquisitions have included unrelated properties that have not been divested.

ISSUES IN PORTFOLIO MANAGEMENT

Successful operation of portfolios requires companies to regularly analyze their portfolios and portfolio choices, to restructure their organizations and portfolios for effectiveness and efficiency when needed, and to adapt their portfolios to changing market conditions. Product portfolio operation also creates issues and complexities not encountered in single-product companies and these must be addressed if the benefits of portfolios are to be achieved.

PORTFOLIOS WITHIN PORTFOLIOS:
The Case of *GEO* Magazine

GEO magazine is one of the world's leading science, nature, and culture periodicals and is highly regarded for its high quality photography and the importance of its editorial material. After its launch in Germany, success of the title led its publisher to seek opportunities to capitalize on its strength and to increase revenues though creation of a portfolio of additional products around the title. These included GEO-branded specialty publications such as *GEO Saison* (a travel magazine), *Geo Wissen* (a science magazine), and *GEOlino* (a children's magazine). The portfolio includes GEO Online, DVDs and CDs containing content that builds on the brand of the published titles, and merchandise such as calendars and books containing the magazine's best photographs. The portfolio has been expanded internationally and *GEO* magazine is now published in France, Spain, South Korea, and Russia.

If one looks beyond *GEO* magazine and its related publications and products, one finds that the successful portfolio is itself part of a greater magazine portfolio operated by Grüner & Jahr through its German Magazines Division, Magazines France and USA Division, and International Magazines Division. These divisions publish a portfolio of 120 magazines titles in 11 countries, including publications in the business, parenting, fashion, public affairs, women's, and sports publishing segments. Although Grüner & Jahr is Europe's largest publishing company, with sales of nearly €3 billion annually, it is itself part of a larger portfolio of media companies held by Bertelsmann AG, which owns 75 percent of Grüner & Jahr's shares.

As this case illustrates, portfolios can be created simultaneously at the product, company, and business unit levels. Understanding portfolio strategies requires comprehension of strategy at those various levels. This is sometimes difficult in media firms that blur company, business unit, and corporate strategies.

At a very basic level, new issues of resource allocation arise and managers must ensure adequate resources to produce and support for all products. This includes not only financial resources but those of personnel and facilities. Because portfolios draw on a range of company resources, including management, production, marketing and sales, and distribution resources, it is critical to provide adequate cost accounting in order to be able to monitor the performance and make effective decisions about individual products in the portfolio (Allen, 2002; South & Oliver, 1998) and to organize the firm in a way that permits evaluation of categories of products in the company (Ezzmel, 1997, Nevaer & Deck, 1988).

The introduction of portfolio theory from investment analysis to product analysis has provided new ways to evaluate the significance and desirability of various elements of a product portfolio (Cardozo & Smith Jr., 1983; Leong & Lim, 1991; Sharpe, 2000). The concept is based on making risk-return analysis of products in the portfolio or products proposed for the portfolio, thus providing better decisions about capital investments, resource allocation, divestment, and product importance. In making decisions to add or cease a product line, risk as well as return issues should be considered, according to proponents of this approach (Cardozo & Wind, 1985).

It is rare that the products included in a portfolio have similar importance to a company. In many cases there are primary products and secondary products and companies must have clear understanding of their import and the implications of moving products up and down the importance scale. If the prioritization creates a change in business focus, or affects core activities, special care needs to be exercised. A number of methods exist for balancing the significance of alternative products in a portfolio (Proctor & Hassard, 1990).

One of the most widely accepted models for analyzing and understanding the attributes of products in portfolios is the growth/share matrix. The matrix allows strategic analysis based on the market shares of products and market growth, thus helping firms see the role of the products and to focus efforts and resources on those that are most important to company strategy and needs.

The matrix is based on four quadrants in which products are euphemistically named *stars*, *cash cows*, *problem children*, or *dogs*. Stars are high-growth products that generate a great deal of cash but also require a great deal of cash to maintain or increase share in the growing market. Cash cows have high market shares but low growth. These products generate a lot of cash but require little cash because the market is not growing; they are used to provide financial resources needed by the other types of products. Products considered a problem child require a lot of attention and a good deal of cash to build market share in the growing market. These are often new products or services not previously known to consumers. Dogs are products that are not achieving market success. Companies usually try to divest if another firm will buy them or cease production if they are unprofitable or use resources needed for other products.

In contemporary media firms with product portfolios, print media—especially established newspapers and magazines—are cash cows that are being used to fund problem child ventures in online, mobile, and other new media (Picard, 2003). Cable and satellite television and recently introduced commercial television have been stars for a number of firms in the past decade.

Importance, however, cannot be measured merely in monetary terms, but also in terms of strategy and resources. It has been shown that within the best companies, portfolio decisions tend to be made less on the basis of financial analysis methods and more using strategic methods (Cooper, Edgett, & Kleinschmidt, 1999). Nonquantitative criteria may support choices made not merely for profitability of products and the products operated under these conditions require different management (South & Oliver, 1998).

It may be necessary and desirable, for instance, to maintain a low profit or unprofitable product because of its contributions to the success of another product in the portfolio (Picard, 2003) or because it is the base product on which a brand has been established.

A newspaper, for example, may not be producing the greatest profits in a portfolio, but its editorial personnel may be the creators of the information carried on its Internet site and may provide the columns and features sold by a related news service. Similarly its production facilities may not reach profitability from printing the paper but provide the essential resource for a complimentary commercial printing activity.

In the operation of portfolios, issues of brand and branding become central. Questions of whether the additional products should be operated under the same brand as the initial product are central to strategy, and decisions about brands play important roles in the successful operations of firms (Barwise, 1992).

In media of all types, growth is becoming dependent on shifting brand awareness, acceptance, and trust among a portfolio of products and services (Galbi, 2001). Brands have been shown to be important in contemporary marketing of newspapers and related products (Wilkinson, 1998) and in television portfolios and value-added services (Todreas, 1999). Indeed, television and cable television firms appear to be using product extension onto the Internet primarily for informational purposes and to solidify brand loyalty, rather than significant exploitation of new market opportunities (Ha, 2002)

Brand transference is playing an important role in creating successful online operations for television channels adding Internet operations (Chan-Olmsted & Jung, 2001) and is an important competitive factor in financial news provision across platforms (Arrese & Medina, 2003). Leveraging established brands and extending them to other products must be carefully undertaken to ensure that the extensions are linked to the core concepts of the brand identity or the product that established the brand can be harmed.

In order to effectively manage portfolios, companies need to clearly understand the position of products within their markets, strategies, and performance needs (Wind & Mahanjan, 1981). The need is especially crucial when considering new products, killing products, or divesting products. Determining the correct breadth and depth of a portfolio involves balancing increased revenue from additional products against production and engineering costs, potential conflicts with other products, and market factors (Bordley, 2003). Because of the need to respond to media market changes, planning future products becomes critical. Companies need to focus on their futures and begin generating ideas, evaluating, and prioritizing potential products (Samli, 1996).

Media companies are now seeking to gain advantages and cost savings by integrating activities across their media products, and this presents significant issues in terms of inducements for product and business unit managers to take part in coordinated activities. It will also require media firms to find equitable ways to share the rewards of success that emanate from the cross-media activities among participating products, units, and managers.

The increased multidivisional activities are leading to more project-based activities in media firms and these will require new skills and understanding among staff and managers if they are to be effective. Existing research on new product development and cross-functional project teams shows that significant attention needs to be paid to ensuring the quality of project teams and fully involving team members so that their contributions are not neglected by others members, project leaders, and senior management (Barczak & Wilemon, 2003; Hoegel, Parboteeah & Gemuenden, 2003) and that inevitable tensions and conflicts due to differing objectives and goals, cultures, and perspectives do not interfere with creativity or success of the new product (Gobeli, Koenig & Bechinger, 1998; Thomas & Schmidt, 1976). Although media companies have used limited project-based approaches for product improvement and new product projects in the past, the team-based approaches required for cross-media and cross-business unit projects will be far more complex and involve greater investments so that greater attention to strategy, direction, oversight, and processes will be needed.

WHAT THIS BOOK WILL DO

Despite the growth of media portfolios, little literature exists about the underlying benefits and rationales of these portfolios, organizational needs and requirements, and the effectiveness of strategies. This book will explore these issues, focusing attention on how the type of portfolio affects management and performance of media portfolios, on differing strategies and requirements for various types of portfolios, and on how companies develop and improve their portfolios.

Chapters explore differences in requirements for leaders of companies with single products and portfolios, the roles of geography and economic geography in effective portfolio management and firm performance, and means for analyzing the effect of portfolios on firms' performance. Authors deal with issues raised by typical accounting methods and practices applied to media portfolios and the need to develop and manage technological platforms for cross-media portfolios.

The effects of portfolios on companies of differing size, methods for effectively handling marketing and cross-promotion of products, and issues arising from the internationalization of portfolios are also explored.

The need for understanding portfolios and how to manage them in media firms is growing daily as media companies pursue strategies of cross-media activity, vertical and horizontal integration, and diversification. This book provides a context for those activities and the issues that scholars and managers should consider as portfolios continue to change the media environment.

REFERENCES

Albarran, A. & Moellinger, T. (2003). The top six communication industry firms: structure, performance, and strategy. In R.G. Picard (ed.), *Media firms: Structures, operations, and performance* (pp. 103–122). Mahwah, NJ: Lawrence Erlbaum Associates.

Albarran, A. & Porco, J. (1990). Measuring and analyzing diversification of corporations involved in pay cable, *Journal of Media Economics*, *3*(2), 3–14.

Allen, T. (2002). Are your products profitable? *Strategic Finance*, *83*(9), 32–38 (March).

Amihud, Y. & Lev, B. (1981). Risk reduction as a managerial motive for corporate mergers, *Bell Journal of Economics*, *12*, 605–617.

Amit, R. & Livnat, J. (1988). Diversification and the risk-return trade-off, *Academy of Management Journal*, *31*(1), 154–166.

Arrese, A. & Medina, M. (2003). Competition between new and old media in economic and financial news markets. In R. G. Picard (ed.), *Media firms: Structures, operations, and performance* (pp. 59–75). Mahwah, NJ: Lawrence Erlbaum Associates.

Bakker, P. (2002). Free daily newspapers—Business models and strategies. *JMM—International Journal on Media Management, 4*(3), 180–187.

Barczak, G. & Wilemon, D. (2003). Team member experiences in new product development: Views from the trenches, *R&D Management, 33*(5), 463.

Barksdale, H. C. (1982). Portfolio analysis and the product life cycle. *Long Range Planning, 15*(6), 74–84.

Barwise, P. (1992). Brand portfolios. *European Management Journal, 10*(3), 277–286.

Bennett, J. (1999) Discovering America again. *Folio: Magazine for Magazine Management, 18*, 53–59 (September 30).

Bordley, R. (2003). Determining the appropriate depth and breadth of a firm's product portfolio. *Journal of Marketing Research, 40*, 39–52.

Cardozo, R. N. & Smith Jr., D. K. (1983). Applying financial portfolio theory to product portfolio decisions: An empirical study. *Journal of Marketing, 47*, 110–119 (Spring).

Cardozo, R. N. & Wind, J. (1985). Risk return approach to product portfolio strategy. *Long Range Planning, 18*(2), 77–86.

Chan-Olmsted, S. M. & Jung, J. (2001). Strategizing the net business: How the U.S. television networks diversify, brand, and compete in the internet age, *JMM—International Journal on Media Management, 3*(4), 213–225.

Cooper, R., Edgett, S. & Kleinschmidt, E. (1998). *Portfolio Management for New Products.* Reading, MA: Perseus Books.

Cooper, R. G. & Kleinschmidt, E. J. (1995). Benchmarking the firm's critical success factions in new product development, *The Journal of Product Innovation Management, 12*(5), 374–391.

Cooper, R., Edgett, S. & Kleinschmidt, E. (1999). New product portfolio management: Practices and performance. *The Journal of Product Innovation Management, 16*(4), 333–352.

Dickens, P. & Lloyd, P. (1990). *Location in space: Theoretical perspectives on economic geography.* New York: HarperCollins.

Dimmick, J. & Wallschlaeger, M. (1986). Measuring corporate diversification: A case study of new media ventures by television network parent companies, *Journal of Broadcasting and Electronic Media, 30,* 1–14.

Doyle, G. (2000). The economics of monomedia and cross-media expansion: A study of the case favouring deregulation of TV and newspaper ownership in the U.K. *Journal of Cultural Economics, 24*(1), 1–26.

Eisenhardt, K. (1989). Agency theory: An assessment and review. *Academy of Management Review, 14*(1), 57–74.

Ezzamel, M. (1997). *Business unit and divisional performance measurement.* Academic Press, 1997.

Galbi, D. (2001). The new business significance of branding, *JMM— International Journal on Media Management, 3*(4), 192–198.

Gaustsad, T. (2002). Joint product analysis in the media and entertainment industries: Joint value creation in the Norwegian film sector. In R. G. Picard (ed.), *Media firms: Structures, operations, and performance* (pp. 9–26. Mahwah, NJ: Lawrence Erlbaum Associates.

Gershon, R. (1997). *The transnational media corporation.* Mahwah, NJ: Lawrence Erlbaum Associates.

Gobeli, D., Koenig, H. & Bechinger, I. (1998). Managing conflict in software development teams: A multilevel analysis, *The Journal of Product Innovation Management, 15,* 423–435.

Griffin, A. (1997). PDMA research on new product development practices: updating trends and benchmarking best practices. *The Journal of Product Innovation Management, 14*(6), 429–458.

Ha, L. (2002). Enhanced television strategy models: A study of TV web sites, *Internet Research*, *12*(3), 235–248.

Hafstrand, H. (1995). Consumer magazines in transition: A study of approaches to internationalization, *Journal of Media Economics*, *8*(1), 1–12.

Hoegl, M., Parboteeah, K. & Gemuenden, H. (2003). When teamwork really matters: Task innovativeness as a moderator of the teamwork-performance relationship in software development projects, *Journal of Engineering and Technology Management*, *20*(4), 281–302.

Holtz-Bacha, C. (1997). Development of the German media market: Opportunities and challenges for US media firms. *Journal of Media Economics*, *13*(2), 81–101.

Lacy, S. & Simon, T. F. (1993). *The economics and regulation of United States newspapers*. Norwood, NJ: Ablex Publishing.

Leong, S. & Lim, K. (1991). Extending financial portfolio theory for product management, *Decision Sciences*, *22*(1), 181–193.

Hill, C. W. L. & Hoskisson, R. E. (1987). Strategy and structure in the multiproduct firm. *Academy of Management Review*, *12*, 331–341.

Hill, C. W. L., Hitt, M. A., & Hoskisson, R. E. (1992). Cooperative versus competitive structures in related and unrelated diversified firms. *Organizational Science*, *3*(4), 501–521.

Hitt, M. A. (1997). International diversification: Effects on innovation and firm performance in product-diversified firms. *Academy of Management Journal*, *40*(4), 767-799.

Jung, J. (2003). The bigger, the better? Measuring the financial health of media firms, *JMM—International Journal on Media Management*, *5*(4), 237–250.

Kolo, C. & Vogt, P. (2003). Strategies for growth in the media and communications industry: Does size matter? *JMM—International Journal on Media Management*, *5*(4), 251–261.

Litman, B., Shrikhande, S. & Ahn, H. (2000). A portfolio theory approach to network program selection, *Journal of Media Economics 13*(2), 57–79.

Maloney, T. (2003). Delivering on a clear strategy. Emap Annual Report.

Markides, C. C. & Williamson, P. J. (1994). Related diversification, core competencies and corporate performance. *Strategic Management Journal, 14,* 149–165.

Markides, C. C. & Williamson, P. J. (1996). Corporate diversification and organisational structure: A resource-based view. *Academy of Management Journal, 39*(2), 340–368.

Nevaer, L.. & Deck, S. (1988). *The management of corporate business units: Portfolio strategies.* Quorum Books.

Picard, R. G. (2001a). Effects of recessions on advertising expenditures: An exploratory study of economic downturns in nine developed nations, *Journal of Media Economics, 14*(1), 1–14.

Picard, R. G. (2001b) Strategic responses to free distribution dailies, *JMM— International Journal on Media Management, 3*(3), 167–172.

Picard, R. G. (2003). Cash cows or entrecôte: publishing companies and new technologies. *Trends in Communication, 11*(2), 127–136.

Picard, R. G. & Rimmer, T. (1999) Weathering a recession: Effects of size and diversification on newspaper companies, *Journal of Media Economics, 12*(1), 1–18.

Porter, M. E. (1985) *Competitive advantage: Creating and sustaining superior performance.* New York: Free Press

Porter, M. E. (1990). *The competitive advantage of nations.* New York: Free Press

Price, C. (2003). *Threats and opportunities of free newspapers.* Dallas: International Newspaper Marketing Association.

Proctor, R. A. & Hassard, J. S. (1990) Towards a new model for product portfolio analysis. *Management Decision, 28*(3), 14–24.

Pruitt, G. (2003). *Address to shareholders.* Available at www.mcclatchy.com/investors/annualmeeting

Saksena, S. & Hollifield, C. A. (2002). U.S. newspapers and the development of online editions. *JMM-International Journal on Media Management*, 4(2), 75–84.

Samli, A. C. (1996). Developing futuristic product portfolios: A major panacea for the sluggish American industry, *Industrial Marketing Management*, 25(6), 589–601.

Scardino, M. (2003). Chief executive's review: The value of knowledge. *Pearson Annual report*. London: Pearson.

Sharpe, W. F. (2000). *Portfolio theory and capital markets*. New York: McGraw-Hill.

Sherer, F. M. & Ross, D. (1990). *Industrial market structure and economic performance* (Third edition). Boston: Houghton Mifflin.

South, J. B. & Oliver, J. E. (1998). What is a profitable product? *Industrial Marketing Management*, 27(3), 187–196.

Teece, D. J. (1980). Economics of scope and the scope of the enterprise. *Journal of Economic Behavior and Organization* 1(3), 223–247.

Teece, D. J. (1982). Towards an economic theory of the multiproduct firm. *Journal of Economic Behavior and Organization*, 3(1), 39–63.

Thomas, K. & Schmidt, W. A. (1976). A survey of managerial interests with respect for conflict. *Academy of Management Journal*, 10, 315–318.

Thorn, W. J. (1987). *Newspaper circulation: Marketing the news*. White Plains, NY: Longman Publishing.

Todreas, T. M. (1999). *Value creation and branding in television's digital age*. New York: Quorum Books.

Willis, J. (1988). *Surviving in the newspaper business: Newspaper management in turbulent times*. New York. Praeger.

van Kranenburg, H. L., Cloodt, M. & Hagedoorn, J. (2001). An exploratory study of recent trends in diversification of Dutch publishing companies in multimedia and information industries. *International Studies of Management and Organization,* 31(1), 64–86.

Varadarajan, P. R. & Ramanujam, B. (1987). Diversification and performance: A re-examination using a new two-dimensional conceptualization of diversity in firms. *Academy of Management Journal,* 30(2), 380–393.

Wilkinson, E. J. (1998) *Branding and the newspaper consumer.* Dallas: International Newspaper Marketing Association.

Wind, Y. & Mahajan, V. (1981). Designing product and business portfolios. *Harvard Business Review,* 59(1), 155 (January/February).

World Association of Newspapers (2000). *Free newspapers: A threat or opportunity? The case of the London Metro.* Paris: World Association of Newspapers.

2
Product Portfolios, Diversification, and Sustainability of Media Firms

H.L. (Hans) van Kranenburg
University of Maastricht

For the past 20 years, diversification in large media companies has proceeded at a rapid pace. Nowadays, many large media companies operate in various media and information markets. Technological developments, convergence of markets and changes in behavior of customers have increased the intra-market competition and made the inter-market competition for media companies greater. Due to these developments the importance of diversifying has increased. The media companies that wish to survive in the long run are challenged to choose the direction of their businesses. The company's direction can be to achieve growth and/or reduce overall risk by investing in businesses or activities directly supporting the competitiveness of existing businesses or in new products, services, or geographic markets. However, these markets have different structural characteristics, and these different structural characteristics result in different average and potential profits in each market. Given the developments and the characteristics of markets the company must decide which businesses and countries it will enter, the degree to which it will build on past strengths and competences or require the development of new ones, and the degree to which it will diversify. A well-defined diversification strategy may help the company to choose its direction and to create or sustain its competitive advantages.

This chapter discusses the importance of a well-defined corporate diversification strategy for media companies, in particular publishing companies, in their attempt to improve their long-term performance. It emphasizes that the development of the corporate diversification strategy of media companies has increased in importance due to increasing uncertainty in the media, information, and communications landscape. The company needs to decide whether it will implement a more focused, related, or unrelated diversification strategy to develop its capabilities for survival and future growth. One of the main determinants for a media company to choose a particular strategy is its success in performance. However, empirical studies of the effects of corporate diversification on performance are not conclusive. These studies have generally been too preoccupied with cross-industry research and placed too little emphasis on diversification strategy within one particular group, such as the publishing companies. Due to current developments in the media, information, and communications landscape, it may be possible that a particular diversification strategy outperforms the others. Therefore, this chapter presents a study that not only explores the corporate diversification strategy for media companies, but also investigates the relationship between their business and international diversity and performance.

CORPORATE AND BUSINESS STRATEGIES

The strategy of a company is a comprehensive plan stating how the company will achieve its mission and objectives. It maximizes competitive advantages and minimizes competitive disadvantages. A distinction can be made between two levels of strategy: corporate strategy and business strategy. The latter strategy usually occurs at the business unit or product level, and it emphasizes improvement of the competitive position of a company's products or services in the specific business or market segment served by that business unit. Business strategy asks how the company or its units should compete or cooperate in a given particular business, market segment, or country. A company's corporate strategy defines the company's overall mission, specifying achievable objectives, developing strategies, and stating policy guidelines. It deals with three key strategic issues facing the company as a whole (Hunger & Wheelen, 2003):

1. It provides direction to the company's overall orientation towards growth, stability, or divestment.

2. It defines the portfolio of the businesses, markets, and countries in which a company competes through its products and business units.

3. It views the company in terms of resources and capabilities that can be used to build business unit value as well as generate synergies.

The company VNU, for example, illustrates the importance of strategy to a firm's survival opportunities and success. After the information and multimedia company VNU realized that it could no longer achieve its objectives by continuing its strong competitive position as a publishing house in the Netherlands, it reconsidered its strategy and sold its newspaper activities to the

2. Portfolios, Diversification, and Sustainability 25

Dutch publishing companies Wegener N.V. and Holdingmaatschappij De Telegraaf and its consumer information group to the Finnish publishing company SanomaWSOY in the 1990s. VNU instead chose to concentrate on professional information services and to expand its businesses in the United States, an area that management felt had greater opportunities for growth. Guided by its new strategy and using resources obtained from divestments, VNU has transformed the company gradually into a multinational media conglomerate.

In firms, the corporate center is usually responsible for developing the corporate strategy. In some companies the corporate center plays an active role in the development of the business strategies, while in others, the development of business strategies is the sole responsibility of the business units. The corporate center can play an important role in the development of business strategies when internal and external forces require clever strategies that are difficult or impossible for individual business units to mastermind. These forces include regional or global economies of scale, brand benefits, flow of resources, the convergence of consumer tastes, and the applicability of technology and know-how across different product areas and regions.

The role of the corporate center has increased in the development of the strategies of media companies given the dynamics of their environment. Especially in the last decade the media, information, and communications landscape has changed decidedly. Technological and demographic developments, deregulation and the convergence of different media, information, and communications markets have left an important mark on the configuration of the traditional markets (Picard, 2003; Wirtz, 2001). Not only do these developments pose threats to companies operating in these markets, but they also create new opportunities for companies to engage in profitable new ventures and businesses both in home markets and abroad. The media company's reaction to these developments may have consequences for the organizational structure and performance of the company. The strategic decision of a media company to diversify internationally or diversify its product portfolio may alter the fundamental nature of the company and may also involve a substantial redeployment of resources and a redirection of human energy (Rumelt, 1974). The degree of diversification of the company includes both product diversification and (international) geographic area diversification. Corporate diversification strategy has become an integral part of the strategy of many media companies.

DIVERSIFICATION STRATEGIES

Corporate diversification is a phenomenon that has received considerable attention in the strategic management and industrial organization literature. There is a great variation in the way diversification is defined. The reason is that diversification strategy is a multidimensional phenomenon. It includes the goals of diversification, its direction, and the means by which it should be accomplished. Rumelt (1974) defined diversification strategy as a "firm's commitment to diversity per se, together with the strengths, skills or purposes that span this diversity, shown by the way in which business activities are related one to another" (p. 29). This definition does not have a decision focus insofar as it stresses the different types of investment decisions that qualify as diversification moves. The definition provided by Booz, Allen, and Hamilton (1985) attempts to capture all these aspects. Or as Ramanujam and Varadarajan (1989) pointed out:

> Booz, Allen and Hamilton ... defined diversification as a means of spreading the base of a business to achieve improved growth and/or reduce overall risk that (a) includes all investments except those aimed directly at supporting the competitiveness of existing businesses, (b) may take the form of investments that address new products, services, or geographic markets; and (c) may be accomplished by different methods including internal development, acquisitions, joint ventures, licensing agreements, etc. (p. 524).

A number of influences may be at work that induce a media company to diversify its product portfolio and geographical scope. The company's decision to diversify can be based on both proactive and reactive reasons. In general, the main influences on a company's diversification decisions are the general environment (i.e., the legal-political-economic-technological-social environment in which the company operates), the industry's competitive environment, specific characteristics of the companies themselves, and their performance (Ramanujam & Varadarajan, 1989; Reed & Luffman, 1986). Once the decision to diversify has been made by the management of the media company, the next issue they face is that of the direction of diversification. The company tries to maximize its set of performance objectives. The lines of business and activities into which a publishing company chooses to diversify involve modifications of its existing businesses and activities. The media company should mainly focus on those businesses and activities that represent the greatest strength or offer the greatest opportunity to improve the performance of the company and to create or sustain a competitive advantage. The fundamental elements in making the choice of diversification direction are customer functions that the company seeks to satisfy, what customer groups are being targeted, and which technologies are used or needed to satisfy the customer functions sought by the targeted customer groups.

The media company's diversification direction can range from being very closely related to totally unrelated to its existing activities and businesses. The degree of relatedness depends on the motives of the management. A media company can diversify because of the existence of synergy. The synergy—economies of scale and scope—can be achieved by sharing resources and transferring resources from one activity to another. Resource sharing refers to operative processes such as the sharing of production processes or distribution channels. The transfer of resources, on the other hand, involves resources that can be used in different businesses. For instance, the application of technological know-how in different businesses may be a source of value creation through the transfer of resources (Robins & Wiersema, 1995). Indeed, the diversification into new geographic and product markets or businesses may be related in several ways to a current activity but may still require the understanding of a different production technology, different marketing concepts and methods, or new approaches to investment decisions, planning, and control.

Diversification moves are not only connected to the synergy motives. Corporate diversification may be a desirable alternative to reduce a media company's business risk. A media company may control internal factors such as inventory and R&D policy, but it cannot reduce the environmental effects of a firm's exposure to economic fluctuations, threats of rivals, new technological developments, and uncertainty. The company may decide to operate businesses that sell their products in different product and geographical markets. The motive would be that the businesses and markets are not simultaneously affected by the developments. For instance, when one market begins to contract, another may just begin to peak, thereby smoothing the cyclical behavior of the company's sales and profit. Furthermore, in dynamic markets companies must adapt quickly to new technologies, products, production methods, regulations, and competitive strategies to create or sustain its competitive advantages. Due to the competitive environment, media companies do not know what combination of activities will give them a competitive advantage in the future. In their search for competitive advantages and higher profitability, companies could examine the opportunities to enter a new set of activities within new businesses. The risk reduction motive induces a strategy that is more based on the rationale for unrelated diversification (Amit & Livnat, 1988).

Another motive for risk reduction is related to the aspirations and goals of top management. This is a more intangible motive. Managers can also decide to diversify the media company to reduce the probability of bankruptcy in order to provide job security and increase their bonuses. Or as agency theory (Jensen, 1986) emphasizes, managers are not inclined to return free cash flows to shareholders, but rather spend them on diversification projects, because of motives like empire building and reduction of employment risk.

Diversification may be a successful strategy when the corporate mission is to grow, in particular when the company operates in a mature or declining industry. Diversification into less-related or unrelated businesses could trigger the growth of the media company.

PERFORMANCE AND DIVERSIFICATION

To formulate the right corporate diversification strategy, media companies need to know the success of the various strategies. As part of the understanding of the success of a diversification strategy, it is appealing to focus on the effect that the diversity of business (or product) and market portfolio has had on the performance of lowly and highly diversified companies. Since Rumelt's (1974) pioneering study, the relationship between corporate diversification and firm performance has attracted serious attention in the strategic management research area. Despite all the attention received in the literature, no consensus has emerged as to the impact of corporate diversification on performance. The literature is inconclusive in showing which diversification strategies should be used. Rumelt (1974) found a relationship between diversification strategy and performance. The related diversified firms were found to outperform the non-diversified and unrelated diversified firms. The unrelated diversification strategy was found to be one of the lowest performing on average. However, Bettis and Hall (1982) showed that the performance advantage findings by Rumelt were due largely to industry effects. Varadarajan and Ramanujam (1987) suggested that related diversification may be a necessary, but not sufficient, condition for superior performance, and that unrelated diversification serves a number of firms as well as, if not better, than more related or focused strategies. Markides (1995) showed that a curvilinear relationship appeared between diversification and performance. This implies that a limit exists as to how much a firm can grow and diversify. An explanation for this inverse U-shaped relationship is that as firms diversify away from their core businesses, their assets lose some of their efficiency and earn declining returns.

A study by Szeless, Wiersema, and Müller-Stewens (2003) found no significant relationship between product-market diversification and performance. However, their defined resource-relatedness diversification measure showed a positive linkage with performance. The resource-relatedness measure captured the aspects of potential synergy from the transfer of technological know-how between different businesses of a company, which the product-market measure did not do.

Another option available to companies confronting the decision as to how to deploy its resources for competitive advantage is to diversify internationally. For instance, a broad geographic scope of operations may allow a company to exploit interrelationships between different product markets, geographic areas, or related businesses. Increased geographic scope may increase a company's ability to achieve economies of scale, scope, and experience. Although international expansion has become a popular corporate diversification strategy among companies, it has received less attention in the diversification research. A minority of studies tried to analyze international diversification strategies and their effects on the performances of the companies. Research showed that internationalization was positively related to performance (Geringer, Beamish & daCosta, 1989; Hitt, Hoskisson & Ireland, 1994). However, the linkage between internationalization and performance is not monotonic but curvilinear. The positive effect of international diversification on performance has its optimum, and beyond that point the effect declines due to increased managerial complexity and cost of coordination. Grant, Jammine, and Thomas (1988) found that profitability in the home market encouraged firms to expand abroad that, in turn, increased profitability. Studies that combined product and international diversification seem to suggest that the combined effects of both diversification strategies on performance are positive. For instance, Hitt, Hoskisson, and Kim (1997) found in their study a negative effect of international diversification on corporate performance for single-business firms, whereas the performance of high-product diversified firms showed a positive effect from increasing international diversification.

Finally, the findings of the studies on the relationship between diversification and performance may also be influenced by the quality of the performance data. The major problem encountered by relying on accounting data is that they can be easily manipulated by the company. Furthermore, the accounting standards differ from country to country.

Research on the effects of product and international diversification on performance is complex. Many factors may influence the effects of diversification and performance. Most of the research referred to above has been done using companies from many different industries. These studies have generally not considered that the decisions to diversify may be industry related. Empirical strategy research is generally too preoccupied with cross-industry research and places too little emphasis on diversification strategy within one group of firms. Thus, an empirical study based on the publishing companies might provide an interesting and complementary perspective on former product and international diversification research.

INDUSTRY APPLICATION:
Portfolios and Diversification in Publishing

Publishing companies operate in an industry in which ownership is regulated by both competition law and media policy (Picard, 2002). A company's ability to diversify may be influenced by the antitrust authorities and the political and cultural policies in many countries. In some countries, companies are restricted in the cross-ownership of media and information companies. On the other hand, the publishing companies experience a convergence of media and information markets (Picard, 2003; Wirtz, 2001). Due to introduction of new technological innovations, such as the Internet and mobile telecommunication, many new firms could enter the media and information markets and incumbents could operate in related markets. These developments have led to the transformation of the media and communications markets. Furthermore, consumer preferences have also changed, and advertisers are responding to the new opportunities and changes to reach potential customers. For instance, the increasing choices for news, information, and entertainment products that are available to customers and advertisers reduce the demand for traditional products. This leads, on the one hand, to increased intra-market competition and, on the other hand, to greater inter-market competition. Traditional publishing companies may respond to these developments by diversifying into other markets.

Another interesting characteristic of the traditional publishing markets is the stage of the life cycle. The four stages of the life cycle are introduction, growth, maturity, and decline (Kranenburg, Palm, & Pfann, 1998). The three major publishing industries—newspaper, magazine, and books—are mature industries in which opportunities for natural growth are generally limited (Picard, 2003). Furthermore, the barriers to entry are relatively low in the magazine and book publishing industries, but higher in the newspaper industry. However, the newspaper industry has experienced a gradual decline in demand and penetration of their products in many industrialized countries.

The publishing companies also face challenges due to increased cost structures. Publishing is highly labor intensive and requires specific capabilities and resources, and the selling of products depends on an expensive distribution network. At the same time, the profitability of publishing companies may also be influenced by economic fluctuations. Revenues especially in the newspaper and magazine markets are highly affected by downturns (Picard & Rimmer, 1999). Diversification in other businesses or geographic markets may reduce the effects of recessions on company finances.

In the last decade, the majority of large publishing companies began to operate in more than one media and information market. In general, they have diversified into traditional media, information, and entertainment-related markets. Nowadays, they are active in at least one of the following markets: books, magazines, newspapers, television, broadcasting, marketing, education, and the Internet.

For this study I have chosen large-sized publishing companies with respect to their revenues from Europe and North America. According to the database Worldscope, the selected companies are among the highest revenue-generating companies in the publishing industry. Another argument for choosing the large-sized companies is the current level of competition between these companies and the likelihood that they are involved in international activities. The period under investigation is between 1997 and 1999. In total, 27 publishing companies were selected. The sample consists of 14 European and 13 American publishing companies.

In order to identify the product and the international diversification strategies among publishing companies and to carry out a comparison, I used the diversification identifications presented by Kranenburg, Hagedoorn, and Pennings (2004). For product diversification, they classified the publishing companies according to the guidelines proposed by Rumelt (1974). The level of product diversification of each publishing company is classified as follows:

1. A single business diversified publishing company (SBD) is defined as a publishing company whose primary commitment is to a single business. More specifically, the publishing company derives 95% or more of its revenues or sales from a single business.

2. A dominant business diversified publishing company (DBD) has a primary commitment to a single business but has diversified to a small degree. The revenue or sales of a single business contribute between 70% and 94% to the publishing company's total revenues or sales.

3. A related business diversified publishing company (RBD) derives less than 70% of its revenues or sales from one business. Furthermore, it has diversified into new areas related to the primary business.

4. An unrelated business diversified publishing company (UBD) also derives less than 70% of its revenues or sales from one business and has diversified into new business areas without regard to the primary business.

Kranenburg et al. (2004) also classified the publishing companies according to the standard industry code (SIC-code) instead of using sales and revenue data. The computation of the diversification level is based on two- and four-digit SIC codes. This classification provides insights into the degree of diversity—high versus low—and the direction of product diversification, that is, predominantly concentrated in one product group or predominantly in more product groups. A similar method is used to classify the publishing companies according to their international diversification. The computation of the international diversification is based on the modified Eurostat/ European Union classification of countries. The following four general diversification categories are identified: (A) publishing companies with very low product or international diversity; (B) product or international related-diversified publishing companies; (C) companies with very high product or international diversity; and (D) product or international unrelated-diversified publishing companies. Table 2.1 provides an overview of the level of diversification of the publishing companies.

In this study, I actually measured diversity, which measures the extent to which firms are simultaneously active in many distinct businesses at a point in time, and not diversification, which measures changes in diversity over time.

As already discussed above, the use of accounting measures as indicators of a firm's performance has been a subject of considerable debate. To take these considerations into account, we use four financial performance ratios as primary measures of firm performance. Furthermore, according to Grant, Jammine, and Thomas (1988), the impact of corporate diversification strategy on a company's performance is more directly reflected in accounting profit than in stock price, which measures investors' expectations about future profits. The financial performance ratios were obtained from Worldscope. One of the most important indicators is the return on equity (ROE). It shows how much profit has been generated using the stockholders' capital. Return on assets ratio (ROA) indicates how effectively the assets of the publishing company businesses were working to generate profit. Another key performance indicator is gross profit margin ratio (GPM) which gives an indication as to whether the average mark-up on goods and services was sufficient to cover expenses and make profit. The last performance measure

Company	Level of Diversification			Financial Performance Ratios in %			
	Rumelt categories	SIC-Product Diversity	International Diversity	Return on Equity	Return on Assets	Gross Profit Margin	Operating Profit Margin
Axel Springer Ver.	RBD	B	B	30.29	10.26	30.67	6.57
Banta Corp.	RBD	C	A	8.34	5.42	20.36	7.7
Belo (A.H.) Corporation	RBD	C	A	9.59	5.43	18.43	18.43
Bertelsmann	RBD	C	D	25.99	6.84	30.21	-0.2
Daily Mail & General Trust	DBD	C	C	96.3	15.08	31.39	13.73
Emap	DBD	C	C	17.03	8.07	39.72	12.56
Gannett Co.	DBD	D	C	26.41	14.95	44.19	28.96
Hollinger International	RBD	B	A	30.42	9.41	47.57	12.49
Independent News And Media	SBD	C	C	10.02	5.85	45.31	15.83
Knight-Ridder	SBD	C	A	21.61	9.68	39.42	17.83
Lee Enterprises	DBD	C	A	20.37	11.31	46.79	20.47
McGraw-Hill Companies	RBD	C	D	25.33	10.88	48.08	15.86
Meredith Corp.	RBD	C	A	25.04	10.77	55.19	15.81
Pearson	RBD	C	C	28.35	14.88	52.38	8.64
Primedia	RBD	B	A	n.a	1.13	63.41	6.92
Reader's Digest Assn	RBD	A	D	35.39	6.19	62.2	4.9
Reed Elsevier	RBD	B	C	23.45	8.54	55.05	13.6
Sanoma-Wsoy Oyj	RBD	C	D	19.61	10.75	3.98	3.72
Schibsted Asa	RBD	C	B	4.6	3.57	43.66	3.55
Scripps Co., (E.W.)	RBD	C	A	13.13	7.33	52.24	18.93
Thomson Corp.	RBD	D	C	25.1	10.65	14.28	13.48
Trinity Mirror	SBD	A	A	19.57	13.93	50.28	23.36
United News & Media	RBD	C	A	-12.39	10.85	27.58	27.58
VNU	RBD	C	B	52.43	16.56	34.59	17.79
Washington Post Co.	RBD	C	C	24.66	14.68	39.19	17.74
Wegener	RBD	D	B	37.3	12.56	21.69	8.3
Wolters Kluwer	RBD	C	D	36.47	10.27	39.62	22.06

Sources: *Worldscope*, 2001; Kranenburg, Hagedoorn, and Pennings (2004)
Note. n.a = not available; SBD = single business diversification; DBD = dominant business diversification; and RBD = related business diversification; A = firm with very low diversity; B = related-diversified firm; C = unrelated-diversified firm; and D = firm with very high diversity.

Table 2.1 Level of Product and International Diversification and Average Financial Performance Ratios 1998-1999 among Publishing Companies

is operating profit margin (OPM). This indicates how effective the publishing company is at controlling the costs and expenses associated with their normal business operations. Table 2.1 also provides an overview of the average financial performance ratios for the publishing companies for the years 1998 and 1999. Incidental fluctuations are partly eliminated by taking the average over this period.

The purpose of this study is not only to show the product and international diversity of publishing companies but also to compare the performance between the various diversified publishing companies. The basic statistical technique used for comparing the performances in the study is the two-sample t-test for equal means. Due to the small sample size, two groups were constructed to compare the groups' mean financial performance ratios. The first group consists of non-diversified and low diversified publishing companies, whereas the more diversified and unrelated diversified publishing companies are classified in the second group.

COMPARISON BETWEEN PUBLISHING COMPANIES

Table 2.2 reports the distribution of the degree of diversified publishing companies based on the Rumelt diversification classification. One-third of the selected firms are single or dominant product diversified publishing companies, whereas the majority of publishing companies followed a related diversification strategy. On average, the single or dominant product diversified publishing companies perform better that the related diversified ones on all four performance ratios. However, only the operating profit margin shows a statistically significant difference. In other words, the publishing companies with a more specialized focus outperformed the more related ones. This may suggest that the single and dominant diversified publishing companies operate more efficiently than the related diversified publishing companies.

	Single and dominant business diversified firms		Related diversified firms		Groups' means equal	
	No.	Mean	No.	Mean	t-value	
Return on Equity	7	30.1871	19	23.3211	0.59	Yes
Return on Assets	7	11.2671	20	9.3485	1.19	Yes
Gross Profit Margin	7	42.4429	20	38.019	1.00	Yes
Operating Profit Margin	7	18.9629	20	12.1935	2.50	No

Table 2.2 Rumelt Diversification Classification and the Associated Financial Performance Ratios

In an effort to understand better the relationship between product diversity and company performance, I also compared the group means across the product diversification categories based on the two and four digit SIC codes. It does confirm that no significant difference exists between the return on equity and return on assets of the low product diversified publishing companies and the highly diversified companies. It seems that both kinds of diversified companies are more or less even in effectively generating profit. Table 2.3 shows the performance differences of diversified publishing companies based on the SIC codes. The findings show that the companies differ in the gross profit margin and not in operating profit margin. This suggests that the average mark-up on goods and services of the selected low product- and related-diversified publishing companies is more sufficient for covering expenses and making profit in comparison to the selected high product- and unrelated diversified companies.

	Product low and related-diversified firms		Product high and unrelated diversified firms		Groups' means equal	
	No.	Mean	No.	Mean	t-value	
Return on Equity	5	27.824	21	24.5376	0.61	Yes
Return on Assets	6	8.2433	21	10.3038	-1.07	Yes
Gross Profit Margin	6	51.53	21	35.6333	2.77	No
Operating Profit Margin	6	11.3067	21	14.7033	-1.05	Yes

Table 2.3 SIC Product Diversification Classification and the Associated Financial Performance Ratios

As already discussed above, many publishing companies have also followed an international diversification strategy to create or sustain competitive advantages. An interesting question that arises is whether the international diversified publishing companies outperform the more geographically focused companies. Table 2.4 shows the groups' mean financial performance ratios of the international high and unrelated diversified publishing and of the international low and related diversified ones.

The selected publishing companies are equally distributed across the identified international diversification categories. Pairwise comparison of groups' means across the categories shows that the publishing companies do not differ significantly with respect to ratios of performance. However, it seems that the international highly diversified publishing companies may

	International low and related diversified firms		International high and unrelated diversified firms		Groups' means equal
	No.	Mean	No.	Mean	t-value	
Return on Equity	13	20.0231	13	30.3162	-1.40	Yes/ No
Return on Assets	14	9.1579	13	10.5869	-0.97	Yes
Gross Profit Margin	14	39.42	13	38.8923	0.09	Yes
Operating Profit Margin	14	14.695	13	13.1446	0.54	Yes

Table 2.4 International Diversification Classification and the Associated Financial Performance Ratios

have on average a better return on equity in comparison to the relatively low diversified companies.

Significant differences in the corporate governance and regulatory environment of European countries as compared to North American countries may indicate that performance may be affected by these contextual factors (Szeless, Wiersma & Müller-Sterns, 2003). Therefore, it is important to ascertain whether the performance ratios differ between companies from the two continents. Table 2.5 shows the groups' mean financial performance ratios of European and North American publishing companies. The number of European and North American companies is equally distributed in our sample. Despite the existence of institutional differences, the group means of the financial performance ratios do not show significant differences.

	North American Companies		European Companies		Groups' means equal
	No.	Mean	No.	Mean	t-value	
Return on Equity	12	22.1158	14	27.7871	-0.80	Yes
Return on Assets	13	9.0638	14	10.5721	-1.02	Yes
Gross Profit Margin	13	42.4115	14	36.1521	1.10	Yes
Operating Profit Margin	13	15.3477	14	12.6493	0.96	Yes

Table 2.5 North American and European Publishing Companies and the Associated Financial Performance Ratios

DISCUSSION AND CONCLUSION

This chapter discussed the importance of strategy, in particular corporate product and international diversification strategy for media companies. In addition, it has also investigated the relationship between corporate diversification strategy and the performance of 27 large publishing companies between 1998 and 1999. The findings suggest that focused publishing companies may outperform the more related diversified companies. This is somewhat surprising. The literature suggests that related diversification might be a necessary condition to survive in the industry, although it is definitely not a sufficient condition. These results temper the claims of the absolute performance advantages attributed to product diversified companies to more focused companies. This is similar for the findings for international diversification. It seems that the more focused publishing companies were able to achieve synergy within one or a few product groups or geographic areas. In this study, in particular the large newspaper companies were able to achieve the synergy. They could have achieved economies of scale and scope by sharing resources and transferring resources within one business such as the sharing of production processes and distribution channels. Furthermore, the advantages of international diversification may have disappeared due to currency fluctuations. With the degree of internationalization, profits of publishing companies become very dependent on currency fluctuations. Furthermore, costs may increase with internationalization due to increased managerial complexity and co-ordination.

These results might be biased due to the small sample size and the fact that we selected large European and North American publishing companies. Thus, these firms are not necessarily representative of all publishing companies from these continents. However, the companies in the sample are some of the most visible and well-known companies in the publishing industry. These companies may set examples for many other media companies, especially if they are regarded as successful.

As we have not investigated long-term performance and due to the small sample size, we cannot draw definite conclusions regarding the relationships between product diversification, international diversification, and performance. However, as the sample must be regarded as representative of the group of large publishing companies, it must reflect the relationship between both product and international diversity and performance in this group and perhaps also the larger group of large media companies from Europe and North America.

In conclusion, there is little doubt that corporate diversification is an important strategy of many media companies. Given the trends in globalization and convergence of media and communication industries, the competition between traditional media companies but also between companies from emerging media and information markets will increase. A well-defined diversification strategy may help these companies to create or sustain their competitive advantages. Only time will tell which corporate diversification strategies outperform the other strategies and best create competitive advantages.

REFERENCES

Amit, R. & Livnat, J. (1988). A concept of conglomerate diversification. *Journal of Management*, *14*(4), 593–604.

Bettis, R. A. & Hall, W. K. (1982). Diversification strategy, accounting determined risk, and accounting determined return. *Academy of Management Journal*, *25*(2), 254–264.

Booz, Allen, and Hamilton. (1985). *Diversification: A survey of european chief executives*. New York: Booz, Allen, and Hamilton, Inc.

Geringer, J. M., Beamish, P. W. & daCosta, R. C. (1989). Diversification strategy and internationalization: Implications for MNE performance. *Strategic Management Journal*, *10*, 109–119.

Grant, R. M., Jammine, A. P. & Thomas, H. (1988). diversity, diversification, and profitability among British manufacturing companies, 1972-1984. *Academy of Management Journal*, *31*(4), 771–801.

Hitt, M. A., Hoskisson, R. E., & Ireland, R. D. (1994). A mid-range theory of the interactive effects of international and product diversification on innovation and performance. *Journal of Management*, *20*(2), 297–326.

Hitt, M. A., Hoskisson, R. E. & Kim, H. (1997). International diversification: effects on innovation and firm performance in product-diversified firms. *Academy of Management Journal*, *40*, 767–798.

Hunger, J. D. & Wheelen, T. L. (2003). *Essentials of strategic management* (Third edition). Prentice Hall.

Jensen, M.C. (1986). Agency costs of free cash flow, corporate finance, and takeovers. *American Economic Review*, *76*, 323–329.

van Kranenburg, H. L., Hagedoorn, J. & Pennings, J. (2004). Measurement of international and product diversification in the publishing industry. *Journal of Media Economics*, *17*(2), 87–104.

van Kranenburg, H. L., Palm, F. C. & Pfann, G. A. (1998). The life cycle of daily newspapers in the Netherlands: 1848-1997. *De Economist, 146*, 475–494.

Markides, C. C. (1995). *Diversification, refocusing, and economic performance.* Cambridge: MIT Press.

Picard, R. G. (2002). *The economics and financing of media companies.* New York: Fordham University Press.

Picard, R. G. (2003). Cash cows or entrecôte: Publishing companies and new technologies. *Trends in Communication, 11*(2), 127–136.

Picard, R. G. & Rimmer, T. (1999). Weathering a recession: Effects of size and diversification on newspaper companies. *Journal of Media Economics, 12*(1), 1–18.

Ramanujam, V. & Varadarajam, P. (1989). Research on corporate diversification: A synthesis. *Strategic Management Journal, 10*, 523–551.

Reed, R. & Luffman, G. A.. (1986). Diversification: The growing confusion. *Strategic Management Journal, 7*, 29–35.

Robins, J. & Wiersema, M. F. (1995). A resource-based approach to the multibusiness firm: Empirical analysis of portfolio interrelationships and corporate financial performance. *Strategic Management Journal, 16*, 277–299.

Rumelt, R. P. (1974). *Strategy, structure, and economic performance.* Boston: Harvard Business School Press.

Szeless, G., Wiersema, M. F. & Müller-Stewens, G. (2003). Portfolio interrelation-ships and financial performance in the context of European firms'. *European Management Journal, 21*(2), 146–163.

Varadarajan, P. & Ramanujam, V. (1987). Diversification and performance: A reexamination using a new two-dimensional conceptualization of diversity in firms. *Academy of Management Journal, 30*(2), 380–393.

Vernon, R. (1966). International investment and international trade in the product life cycle. *Quarterly Journal of Economics, 80*, 190–207.

Wirtz, B. W. (2001). Reconfiguration of value chains in converging media and communications markets. *Long Range Planning, 34*, 489–506.

3
Media Portfolio Development: Strategic and Organizational Challenges

Leona Achtenhagen
Jönköping International Business School

For a long time, traditional media companies (print, television, and radio) faced rather comfortable market conditions without tough competition. However, many traditional media products such as newspapers, books, and radio have now reached a maturity or decline stage in their life cycles. Not only are such traditional media products facing the prospect of decline, but new media products are slowly but steadily undermining the existing media industry base. If traditional media companies want to survive, they need to face this challenge and change—searching for new growth opportunities and rejuvenating their businesses.

New growth opportunities may be hiding in diversification and portfolio development. Media companies might either expand their business beyond the traditional media areas into new media, or they might build up a portfolio of different media products to complement their current offerings. This chapter addresses some major strategic and organizational challenges of such changes and is especially relevant because the media industry has so far attracted rather little attention from strategy and organization scholars.

The first section of this chapter briefly outlines some characteristics of the media industry and media companies. Then, it discusses generic strategic options and directions for strategic development for media firms, before pointing out some major organizational and strategic challenges these firms face when attempting to develop their portfolio.

MEDIA INDUSTRIES AND MEDIA COMPANIES

Characteristics of the Media Industries

Media industries are unique, as unlike other industries the media deal in ideas, information, and culture. Thus, they inform and entertain, they influence how people understand themselves and their world, and they have a big impact on how people spend their leisure time (Croteau & Hoynes, 2001).

Media industries differ from other industries in at least three respects (Croteau & Hoynes, 2001). First, advertising plays a central role in some media, creating unique relationships and leading to media markets that are not entirely responsive to their audiences. These so-called dual-product markets are ones in which media companies sell two completely different types of products to two completely different sets of customers (Picard, 1989). They produce the media products sold to consumers, and they provide access to consumers that is then sold to advertisers. The balance between the two differs between different types of media. Advertisers can have a big impact on the strategic freedom of media companies, as they might be interested in specific segments of the public only, putting pressure on media companies to redirect their attention to those customers interesting for the advertisers. Picard (2002) argues that in non-profit and public media, the main intent is to produce information and programming useful and interesting to audiences, whereas in commercial media the prevalent aim is to create audiences for advertisers, due to the necessity to obtain revenues to finance continuing operation. Thus, content decision-making in commercial media includes the creation of certain audiences most desirable to their advertisers.

Second, media cannot be considered as merely a product to be used by consumers. Rather, media have informational, educational, and social integration functions. They provide the background to allow people to be informed citizens and active participants in social and political life.

Third, the unique role of media is reflected in the legal protection that media companies face. Media have power, as they can influence the opinions and actions of people. Because of this potential impact on the public opinion, many countries have special rules regarding these media, for example, to ensure undistorted public information or to ensure that the transmitted content is not harmful to the "public interest" media companies are expected to serve.

Trends in the Media Industries

A number of trends that currently influence the media industries are commonly cited. Mainly the commercialization of media as a result of deregulated radio and telecommunication, the increasing concentration in the industry, the globalization of media markets, and the convergence of media and ICT appear to be of importance. At least four developments are related to the strategy and organization of media companies (cf. Croteau & Hoynes, 2001): (1) *Growth* of some media firms, mainly through mergers and acquisitions; (2) *Integration of business activities*, horizontally by moving into multiple forms of media such as film or radio, or vertically by owning different stages of production and distribution; (3) *Globalization*, with the major media companies marketing their products worldwide as domestic markets are saturated; (4) *Concentration of ownership* due to merger and acquisition activities of media companies.

Challenges

The technological advances of recent years have a dramatic impact on media companies. By now, the Internet has gained a position of opinion-building capability and is now often considered a medium; similarly, content-providers are seen as media companies. Even entertainment companies as new media companies have become part of a definition of media industries, based on the argument of convergence of the different media (e.g., Rogers, 2002a; 2002b). New electronic media and digital media are challenging the long-grown structures of traditional media companies (Picard, 2003). As traditional media companies had long faced a low level of competition, many have become resistant to change. However, they will have to change if they want to survive. Picard (2003) formulates the challenge as follows: "Because of their industry cultures, because they have traditionally had little impetus to innovate, because they have tended not to offer portfolios of media products, and because their business models have been stable, managers of many print media firms are now struggling to determine how to respond to the disruptive information and communication technologies" (p. 129).

Another characteristic of the media industries also poses a major challenge to the companies—they have to perpetually reinvent their product offerings. A broadcaster, newspaper, or radio station cannot offer the same product two days in a row, and a publishing company needs to continuously update its offerings. A book club sends out new catalogues with offerings several times a year. Companies in other industries have a learning curve in their product offering that allows them to free resources as learning progresses. These resources can then be re-employed to expand the market presence, for example, by increasing marketing or R&D activities. Media companies, however, have to re-employ most of their resources to develop a new content version of their same product, which creates a—if not *the*—major challenge when trying to develop a portfolio beyond the products currently offered.

GENERIC STRATEGIES AND STRATEGIC DEVELOPMENT IN MEDIA FIRMS

Generic Strategies in Media Firms

Ansoff (1965) proposed a categorization of generic strategies regarding product/market combinations, which is applied to media companies in the following.

Market penetration: A media company could choose to focus on its existing products and markets. It could withdraw those activities from the market that are performing badly and for which no re-launch appears feasible, and consolidate the remaining activities in an attempt to further penetrate the existing market, for example, by renewed marketing efforts. Similarly, a media company could attempt to employ its existing staff and technical facilities more profitably. For example, a weekly newspaper could acquire other weeklies. Printing several newspapers in a central facility would allow for economies of scale.

A second generic strategy is *product development*. Here, new products are developed for the old markets; for example, a newspaper company offers selected book titles to its existing client base. Here, the major aim is to reduce reliance on single products. If the "product development" generic strategy cannot be based on existing competences and resources, additional competences/ resources have to be acquired or developed internally. Usually, the aim with product development is to achieve economies of scope.

A third generic strategy is *market development* with the aim of achieving geographic spread and protecting the company from relying on a single local or regional economy. For example, a regional newspaper might want to expand beyond that region to avoid a large impact of recession if the region depends mainly on one industry. A major aim of expanding the market of product sales is to achieve economies of scale.

The fourth generic strategy is *diversification*, namely moving into new markets with new products (Johnson & Scholes, 1999). This option provides the opportunity to reduce reliance on a single medium and exploit new markets, such as the diversification into broadcasting by newspapers. The German magazine *Stern* is attempting to leverage and reinforce its brand by offering its somewhat provocative "Stern TV."

In the field of strategic management, the normative assumption prevails that companies eventually have to diversify if they want to grow and survive in the longer run. Thus, the importance of diversification for portfolio development becomes clear. In the next section I briefly review the discussion around diversification, followed by an application of the discussion to the media industries.

Diversification

Outcome-Oriented Literature on Diversification: Risk Reduction. Much of the early discussion of diversification in the field of strategic management has been inspired by financial portfolio theory, which argued that the systematic risk[1] of companies could be reduced by investing into a portfolio of different businesses. However, this assumption has been challenged by a number of other researchers, starting with Montgomery and Singh (1984). Lubatkin and O'Neill (1987) stressed the role of related diversification in reducing systematic risk, based on its ability to achieve relative competitive advantage. Because unrelated diversification would contribute little to achieve competitive advantage, it may actually increase systematic risk. These findings would suggest that a newspaper company could reduce its systematic business risks by for example offering selected book titles, while it might increase its risks by diversifying into furniture retailing.

Still based on financial theory, Devinney and Stewart (1988) argue that the concept of a portfolio of products implies nothing more than the fact that products are investments and should be treated as such. Yet, their model does not take into consideration the derivation of product interactions (1988, p. 1093). They argue that risks *within* the firm, such as managerial actions, might be more important for the product portfolio than the systematic risk proposed by financial theory. Leong and Lim (1991) argue that the major differences between financial and product portfolios are the following: (1) Unlike financial portfolios, product portfolios undergo different phases (life cycles); (2) the decisions to restructure the portfolio are more difficult for products, and have more impact on performance; (3) product markets are not equally liquid—for the sales of a product line a company cannot just call a broker; (4) the synergies between different product lines may change over time, while in financial theory correlations between securities are treated as constant. What can we learn from this rather abstract discussion for the practice of media companies? First of all, it cannot be taken for granted that diversification into different media products necessarily reduces risks. The excursion of Bertelsmann AG into investing heavily into new information and communication technology (ICT) based start-ups is a case in point. Second, different products do not lead a static existence side-by-side; rather the different products have an impact on each other, which moreover changes over time. These relationships between products and their

---

[1] Systematic risk is the sensitivity of a firm's return to overall market risk.

embeddedness into an organization imply that adding and selling parts of the product portfolio is a difficult process.

Outcome-Oriented Literature on Diversification: Performance. The major focus of another group of studies no longer is on the effects of diversification on business risk, but on business performance. We can differentiate two types of studies on diversification in the field of strategic management that are mainly concerned with the impact of diversification on performance. The *industrial organization approach* to diversification concentrates on the external manifestation of diversity in terms of a firm's spread of business activities across SIC industries (cf. Grant & Jammine, 1988). Despite many attempts, little evidence of any relationship between these count measures of diversity and corporate performance could be found (cf. discussion in Capon et al., 1988). However, Capon et al. (1988) propose that this absence could stem from a lack of validity in the diversity measures. They argue that the count method does not incorporate how diversification decisions affect corporate functioning: "There is no explicit appreciation in the business count measures that skills, resources, knowledge, assets and so forth may be transferred across like businesses to improve performance" (Capon et al., 1988: 62). However, some researchers continue to argue in favor of the SIC code-based measures due to their "objectivity," as compared to, for example, Rumelt's "subjective" measure of diversification (cf. discussion in Hoskisson, et al., 1993).

A Management Perspective on Diversification. This approach was introduced in the seminal works of Wrigley (1970) and Rumelt (1974). Previously, Chandler (1962) had established the general nature of the diversified firm and the interaction of organizational structure with diversification. From a management perspective, the significance of diversification lies in the need to extend the skills of the firm and to adjust the organization to encompass a wider range of activities. Wrigley (1970) extended Chandler's work by investigating the different options open to a diversifying firm. Based on a random sample of 100 companies, he showed that different strategies were available for diversification. The measures of diversification introduced by Wrigley and Rumelt refer to the ratio of a firm's sales within its major activity to total sales, and the proportion of total sales that are related to each other.[2] Rumelt expanded on Wrigley's classification of diversification strategies and introduced different dimensions of relatedness. *Constrained diversification* refers to activities that are related to one

---

[2]More specifically, Wrigley's classification consists of single, dominant, related, and unrelated businesses; Rumelt's classification expands these to single business, dominant vertical, dominant constrained, dominant-linked, dominant-unrelated, related-constrained, related-linked, and unrelated business.

another. *Linked diversification* requires that each activity be related to at least one other activity, but not all other activities. Rumelt investigated the relationships between organizational structure, diversification strategy, and performance. He found that related diversification led to clearly higher performance than unrelated performance. This finding was challenged by Bettis and Hall (1982) who argued that the finding would be due only to the pharmaceutical companies represented in the sample. They showed that without the pharmaceutical companies no significant performance differences between related and unrelated diversification would exist. For a newspaper company, this finding would imply that it would not necessarily perform better if diversifying into books than if diversifying into selling groceries. Still, Rumelt's study had a major impact, as it had (finally) identified a relationship between corporate diversity and performance.

A large number of later studies also built on Rumelt's categories, and incorporated different issues such as market share, market growth, firm size, or measures of risk into the discussion. Montgomery (1985) found that highly diversified firms compete in less attractive markets, have lower market share, and are less profitable than less diversified firms. This early research on diversified firms usually used accounting data to assess performance, while in a next wave stock prices were employed as the market's perception of the firm's future performance (Dubofski & Varadarajan, 1987). An example of such a study is the one by Lubatkin and Rogers (1989), who combine Rumelt's classification scheme with security-market-based measures. They argue that previous studies had examined the performance effects of diversification, but not accounted for risk (see discussion above). They conclude that firms diversifying in a constrained manner (that is, the activities are related to one another) demonstrated significantly lower levels of systematic risk and significantly higher levels of shareholder returns than firms employing other strategies.

From a review of literature on diversification, Lubatkin and Rogers (1989) conclude that competitive advantage helps a firm defend its chosen market position—it lowers its systematic risk by forcing the burden of economic decline onto its weaker competitors. Also, they argue that competitive advantage would be best achieved when a firm combines distinct business units that are linked by certain core technologies (and thus, constrained diversified). Thus, constrained diversifiers manage to improve the competitiveness of their business positions. Constrained diversification was found to reduce systematic risk. Again, what can we learn from this for the context of media companies? Just as the effects of diversification on reducing risk are unclear, the performance implications of diversification are ambivalent. Even though the literature on diversification is extensive, it hardly takes into consideration a process perspective on individual firms (rather it regards populations or larger samples of firms), activities in them, or the managerial challenges deriving from the decision to diversity (cf. Ramanujam & Varadarajan, 1989). Namely, most of the contributions discussed above appear to assume that organizations could develop or expand by simply adding new businesses. Thus, only implicit attention is given to the strategic and organizational challenges faced when deciding whether to diversify or during the process of diversifying. These challenges will be addressed in more detail below.

Diversification Motives in the Media Industries

The discussion so far has introduced mainly the motives of achieving growth and risk reduction through diversification. Sjurts (2002) categorizes different "cross media" diversification strategies and motives for choosing them. *Intramediary diversification* refers to vertical diversification into prior or later value chain activities within the same media industry. As the underlying motive she suggests (in reference to Michael Porter's model of the five forces) the limiting of the bargaining power of suppliers or customers. *Intermediary diversification* can take place into related, unrelated, or converging media industries and might reduce the threat of substitutes in customer or advertising markets. In addition, diversification could take place into *extramediary industries* not related to media. Diversification triggered by convergence might derive from branded content as a bottleneck that is difficult to imitate or substitute. Different motives for diversification might prevail at different times. For example, Sjurts (2002) identifies different phases of media strategies in the development of the German media industries. Until 1984, intramediary diversification took place within print media, for example by acquiring the printers or the press distribution. Intermediary diversification took place into related markets, for example, from journals into newspapers, and from newspapers into ads. Between 1984 and 1990, intermediary diversification took place also in an unrelated fashion, namely journals into TV and radio, or newspapers into radio. After 1990, intermediary diversification took place mainly into Eastern Germany, as an expansion of the core business (newspapers expanded with newspapers, books with books, etc.). After 1995, aspects of convergence became more relevant, leading to online activities, as well as activities of telecommunications companies (such as digital TV).

STRATEGIC DEVELOPMENT

Once decided which of the generic strategies discussed above to follow, media companies have different options for their strategic development. They can attempt to increase the portfolio of products and services offered by founding new activities organically, in cooperation, or by mergers and acquisition (M&A). M&A activities have an impact on the level of integration of a company. *Horizontal integration* in media firms might fulfill different aims. A more diversified organization might allow the firm to better market and promote their different types of media products. For example, the success of Astrid Lindgren's children books (*Pippi Longstocking, Springtime in Noisy Village, Ronia, the Robber's Daughter*) has allowed for the promoting of a variety of products, such as films, audio books, soundtracks, computer games, and a theme park. "The profit whole for the global media giant can be vastly greater than the sum of the media parts. A film, for example, should also generate a soundtrack, a book, and merchandise, and possibly spin-off TV shows, CD-ROMs, video games, and amusement-park rides. Firms that do not have conglomerated media holdings simply cannot compete in this market" (McChesney, 2000: 59). The overarching aim is to exploit synergy potential (cf. Goold & Luchs, 1993). Thus, new releases of expected blockbuster movies are now often accompanied by an entire integrated campaign of different products. Integration also refers to the blurring of boundaries between formerly distinct media due to the advent of digital media.

   Vertical integration involves owning assets involved in the production, distribution, exhibition, and sale of a single type of media product, such as movie centers or book clubs. Alternatively, the companies could increase their portfolio by cooperation with other companies in alliances or networks. Cooperation might be quicker to realize, but also bears the risk of instability.

   The different options of strategic development will be discussed in more detail in this section.

Strategic Development: Internal Development

When a media company has complementary resources/competences, or can develop those, it can develop internally into new products and/or markets. For example, the development of content, or the selection and bundling of contents into specific offerings could open the possibility for internal development. Similarly, the brand name of a print product might be transferable to multimedia applications. An important question to consider in this decision is whether the development of these complementary resources adds value to the existing contents, and whether substitution of, for example, the print product will take place. However, the opportunity for internal development will be restricted to the extent to which the management of a company does not see opportunities for development and growth, is unwilling to act on them, or is unable to respond to them (Penrose, 1959).

Strategic Development: Cooperation and Strategic Alliances

Giant media companies have the advantage that they can afford to develop expensive projects due to their access to investment capital (Croteau & Hoynes, 2001). Still, alliances in the form of co-production with other large media firms or in the form of paying actors, directors, and writers shares of the profits instead of up-front have become more common. And even between the media giants and smaller media companies, more cooperation emerges. There are several important reasons for this. First, smaller media companies often turn to larger partners to receive infusions of capital. Large media firms are able to buy into projects that smaller companies cannot adequately capitalize. Second, smaller media companies must sometimes rely on the media giants for distribution agreements, such as in movies and recorded music. Due to their vertical integration, the major media companies have control over distribution networks. If smaller, independent media firms want to enter national and international markets, they often must sign distribution agreements with the large companies. And third, smaller media companies enter into joint ownership agreements for the defensive motive of avoiding being taken over (Croteau & Hoynes, 2001). Another type of alliances is the joint digitalization of contents for an online service, for example of different scientific publishers. A crucial challenge is to assess the potential customer demands in a first step and to then choose cooperation partners based on these in order to get access to complementary contents. However, many alliances fail. To enhance the chances for success of an alliance, it is important to provide clear organizational arrangements to avoid the risk of expropriation of knowledge and to limit ambiguities. Alliances should be characterized by a desire to learn, and not just to substitute the lack of a firm's own resources with external resources. This learning can be facilitated by displaying a proactive attitude of trust, cultural sensitivity, and by developing interpersonal relationships. Yet, it should be kept in mind that these attitudes take time to grow. Therefore the alliance should be allowed to evolve, rather than expecting results from the first day.

Strategic Development: Mergers and Acquisitions

The following quote underlines the importance of mergers and acquisitions for strategic development in the media industry: "The challenging conditions facing the media industry today—a brutal advertising environment, a radical change in existing channels or distribution, and the unlikelihood that organic market growth will create value—will test a new generation of executives. But one thing is common to the old guard and the new: the urge to merge" (Wolf, 2002). The urge to merge in the media industry is triggered by the size of global projects, and the company size needed to market blockbuster products. Companies focus resources and attention on a few titles that might become blockbusters or bestsellers. Other advantages of size are the opportunity to develop economies of scale as well as the ability to withstand short-term losses. With the advent of the Internet, it was believed that the importance of size would diminish. However, instead it turned out that media giants acquired many promising ventures, leading to a new wave of M&A activities in the media industries (Croteau & Hoynes, 2001). Yet, while the integration of smaller targets into the bidding firms is relatively unproblematic, full-fledged mergers or acquisitions of larger companies often fail. The merger of AOL and Time Warner is an example in point. The higher the level of attempted integration between the two companies, the higher the potential problems arising from it. Bertelsmann AG can look on a number of rather successful acquisitions, following the clear strategy to delimit integration problems by keeping acquired units largely autonomous.

ORGANIZATIONAL AND STRATEGIC CHALLENGES

As already stated above, surprisingly little has been written about the organizational and strategic challenges in diversification processes and portfolio expansion. In one of the few more process-oriented contributions, Kazanjian and Drazin (1987) depict an ideal-typical process of diversification as occurring over time and through four, more or less discrete, stages: In a first stage, the desired core or business domain strategy is conceptualized. The second stage consists of generating ideas and proposals to implement this strategy. In the third stage, diversification alternatives are selected, reviewed, and developed. The final fourth stage is the implementation stage. This proposed process corresponds nicely to the assumed linear, rational model of strategy-making following the stages of "analysis-choice-implementation," which is still propagated by many textbooks. As a result, it also shares the major point of criticism—strategy is hardly made in a rational, linear way, and there is no reason to believe that diversification processes should instead follow this predetermined path. In the following, a number of major strategic and organizational challenges in the process of diversifying the product portfolio of media firms are discussed: the allocation of resources to new products, establishing the linkages between products, an entrepreneurial orientation of the media firm's management, as well as meeting resistance to change.

The resource allocation process is of great importance not only in the diversification process itself, but also in managing a diversified firm. Since the 1970s, portfolio ideas have played a useful role in resource allocation. Portfolio approaches can be viewed as conceptual and analytical tools at the strategic level to determine the mix of product offerings and the resource allocated to them (Devinney & Stewart, 1988, p. 1080). Portfolio approaches became highly popular among large diversified firms in the United States and Europe during the 1970s and 1980s. Bettis and Hall (1981) claimed that at least 200 of the Fortune 500 companies were using a portfolio concept. Although a number of different portfolio concepts exist, the one developed by the Boston Consulting Group is probably the most well-known (cf. Henderson, 1970). The basic idea of this concept is that to be successful, companies should have a portfolio of products with different growth rates and different market shares. The portfolio composition is then a function of the balance between the cash flows. High-growth products require cash inputs to grow, whereas low-growth products generate excess cash. Every product should eventually be a cash generator. It is argued that only a diversified company with a balanced portfolio could use its strength to capitalize on its growth opportunities. Portfolio concepts view the corporate center as an active investor into a number of stand-alone business units. The role of the center is to select a promising portfolio of businesses and keep these under tight financial control. Resources are allocated according to the expected prospects. The task of each business unit is therefore also financial in nature, depending on the own position in the portfolio matrix (cf. de Wit & Meyer, 1998); even though the underlying idea is that the position a business unit occupies within the matrix should determine the strategic mission and general characteristics of the strategy for the business (Bettis & Hall, 1981).

In interviews with twelve large companies using the portfolio approach, Bettis and Hall (1981) found that companies applying the concept found it most useful for related diversified firms (to aggregate business for strategic analysis and repositioning) and for dominant vertical firms (to guide diversity away from low-growth sectors).[3] The triggers for the use of the concepts were stated by the firms as poor financial performance, too much growth, and strategic issues not surfacing. Even though many companies (and consultancies) still use different types of portfolio concepts, a range of criticism has been brought forward against them. Johnson and Scholes (1999) argue that in practice it would be very difficult to decide on the position of the portfolio products along the dimensions high and low in the matrix. They postulate that the portfolio regards strategic business units (SBUs) rather than markets and that the role of the headquarters

---

[3] Interestingly, they did not find the concept used in conglomerate firms (which would be closest to the idea of financial portfolio investment). Bettis and Hall (1981) explain this with the administrative problems of using the concept for strategic planning and administration, mainly due to the large number of SBUs that would have to be accommodated in the concept. In a related diversified firm, groups of related businesses can be aggregated to form aggregated SBUs, which reduces the complexity of applying the concept.

would be to add value by balancing the portfolio. The major focus of these approaches is on the cash generating function, which might neglect the innovative capacity or building on core competencies. The need to plan mainly the cash flow does not account for behavioral implications. Johnson and Scholes also argue that the position of dogs (as low-growth, low-market share products) might be misunderstood. The recommendation of the approach would be to leave these products and try to move into more cash generating "fields." However, dogs might be important; not only because they might be the brainchild of some people in the organization, but also because they might supplement the remaining product portfolio in a way underestimated by the portfolio approach. De Wit and Meyer (1998) argue that in the portfolio approach the business units do not need to be related in any other way than financially and criticize that it neglects synergies between units or the building on core competences. They argue that the portfolio idea is best suited for growth by acquisition, in which the acquired companies are not integrated but left as stand-alone units, only linked by reporting and control systems. As a matter of fact, the German Bertelsmann AG follows a portfolio approach. The underlying logic would be that excess cash could be invested into more attractive business opportunities than the company has internally.

De Wit and Meyer (1998) argue that the portfolio concept is at odds with the idea of core competences, as multi-business firms should be more than a loose federation of businesses held together by a common investor. Rather, according to Prahalad and Hamel's (1990) ideas of core competences, the different units should be in close cooperation, rather than being independent, and coordination between activities is considered important. The idea of gaining synergies and sharing core competencies is closely connected to the concept of relatedness introduced by Rumelt and the subsequent studies (see previous discussion). However, in view of the concepts of core competences and the resource-based view, it becomes clear that the concept of relatedness might have to be reconsidered to comprise not only product-relatedness, but opportunities for leveraging resources and for strategy alignment (Nayyar, 1993). Opportunities for leveraging resources means that businesses can be considered as related if (tangible or intangible) resources can be productively shared between them. Opportunities for strategy alignment refer to the creation of value through aligning market strategies.

Thus, portfolio development makes most sense when employed in a way that allows for linkages between the product offerings and strategy alignment. However, a major challenge in reaching a stage of portfolio development in media companies has been hinted at briefly above—the need to reinvent their business idea perpetually. This demand not only leads to considerable risk, as every new "launch" has to pass the market test, but it also requires a lot of resources. This process is an entrepreneurial process, in which media companies never leave the initial phases of market introduction to be able to generate enough resources for further growth (for a general discussion of the process of growth cf. Penrose, 1959). Rather, the companies go through some part of the initial stages over and over again. Newspapers, magazines, and broadcasters might face less risk than other media companies, as reading, viewing, and listening patterns tend to be relatively stable in the short-term. "Book publishers, audio recording companies, multimedia producers, and motion picture producers, however, have higher risks each time they introduce a new book, recording, production, or film. This is because the content is not stable from product to product, consumer consumption patterns vary, and it is difficult to determine how audiences will receive the combination of elements in each new product" (Picard, 2002, pp. 7–8). The fate of media companies with products that do not rely on advertising income depends on the success of the individual titles or productions offered at a certain point in time in the market. A major challenge here is to predict what the audience wants and how the taste of the audience might develop or change over time. Diversifying the product portfolio might here seem desirable, as it might reduce the risk that the audience might not react favorably to the market offering (cf. Picard, 2002, p. 10). However, diversifying a one-product media firm would be similar to a "portfolio entrepreneur" (cf. Wickham, 2000, p. 23; a well-known example of a portfolio entrepreneur is Virgin's founder Richard Branson), who instead of setting up one venture, have it running, and then set up the next venture, attempts to set up the second venture before the first one is established. This increases the risk of the diversification attempt in itself, especially if the company is facing scarce entrepreneurial and (strategic) management resources. The person in charge of the diversification attempt is often the CEO or another member of the top management team of the media company. This person faces the challenge of combining different roles (that of managing the media company and that of launching a new product as an entrepreneur).

An entrepreneurial process starts with opportunity recognition. This stage is crucial for the media company—for its existing product it has to redefine this opportunity on a regular basis, and for a new product a further opportunity needs to be recognized. This opportunity needs to fit strategically with the existing offering, to be able to leverage resources and competences. The diversification must make sense from a strategic perspective. Thus, the new product or service must be a better way of performing a task, must offer a customer advantage previously not offered, solve a problem, or provide better quality. Branding might be of importance to build on emotional aspects of the product. Attracting and managing resources is another crucial part of the entrepreneurial process. Media companies have traditionally had very little outside funding available

(Picard, 2002). Thus, the product launch of a one-product media firm might have to be financed by the company itself or, if part of a larger media house, by the mother company. However, if a company is following a rather defensive strategy of diversifying to reduce their risks, they might already be in a tight financial position. From such a position, it might be very difficult to finance the risky launch of a new product. In terms of organizing the media firm, coordination between the product offerings is needed, and resources need to be allocated differently than before.

Many entrepreneurial ventures do not have an explicit strategy, but rather follow emerging strategies. Likely, this will not be sufficient for the stage of diversifying. Here, it is important to assess what the company really wants to achieve with the new product, and the strategy can here be viewed as a call to action. Internal analysis (of resources and competences) and external analysis (of the competition and market) are just as important as the identification of new possibilities. The strategy also facilitates guiding decision-making and setting objectives. And last but not least, it provides a language to communicate with stakeholders, which in the case of media companies have a large influence.

Portfolio development might require quite substantial organizational changes, and might thus trigger resistance, not only from the side of the management, but also of staff. Managing a business portfolio requires the ability of the corporate management team to learn (Ginsberg, 1980). Ginsberg therefore argues for the need to understand the managers' belief systems in shaping diversification as a process of organizational learning. Engaging in new, and entrepreneurial, activities as response to the changing environmental demands might be in sharp contrast to the belief systems, values, and cultures that developed during the times of stability and low competition (cf. Grinyer & McKiernan, 1990). If the company is displaying poor performance, changes in leadership are often the result (Boeker, 1997); with the new leadership introducing a new set of beliefs about how business should be done. Also, the question of involving more people into the change processes needs to be addressed: "One management problem that continues to surface in media organizations is that of too little opportunity for subordinates to be involved in the decision-making process" (Lacy et al., 1993, p. 47).

Those affected by organizational changes often feel threatened. In this case, employees might resist change just because it is change (King & Anderson, 2002). Resistance can arise from "rational" or from "emotional" sources (Gray & Starke, 1984). Employees who rationally resist change decide, based on the information available to them at this point in time, that the change damages in some way their working conditions. Those who emotionally resist change are more influenced by anxiety, frustrations, and a loss of self-esteem. No matter whether an organizational change is threatening or not, resistance can be considered an "automatic reaction" (King & Anderson, 2002). Change might also be resisted by those who feel that the factors important to them at work will be affected. Moreover, change often brings an extra workload to employees affected by it (King & Anderson, 2002). Overcoming this resistance is an additional challenge for management in developing the organizational portfolio.

CONCLUSIONS

The long-term value of portfolio development by related diversification lies in allowing companies to more cost efficiently expand their stocks of strategic assets (Markides & Williamson, 1994). Strategic relatedness seems more important than market relatedness and related firms seem to outperform unrelated ones only in markets where accumulated assets are important. Markides and Williamson (1996) argue that diversification will only support long-run superior returns when it allows a firm to exploit resources or assets that are unavailable to its rivals at a competitive cost. "Diversification will enhance performance, therefore, if it allows a business to obtain preferential access to skills, resources, assets, or competences that cannot be purchased by nondiversifiers in a competitive market or replaced by some other asset that can be purchased competitively" (Markides & Williamson, 1996, p. 344). This leads to the assumption that no single source of diversification advantage can persist indefinitely, as nondiversified competitors will at some point eliminate the competitive advantage associated with any strategic asset by substituting or replicating it. The same authors (Markides & Williamson, 1996) also show that those companies benefit from related diversification that can share opportunities to exploit brand building and marketing as well as channel management skills. The German newspaper *Frankfurter Allgemeine Zeitung* (FAZ) is following this idea when successfully offering a series of specialized books under its FAZ brand, profiting from its reputation of credibility and of thoroughly researching and reporting on topics.

Finally, Markides (1997) suggests that in the decision on whether to diversify, managers should ask themselves the following questions: What can our company do better than any of its competitors in its current markets? What strategic assets do we need in order to succeed in the new market? Can we catch up or leapfrog competitors at their own game? Will diversification break up strategic assets that need to be kept together? Will we be simply a player in the new market or will we emerge a winner? What can our company learn by diversifying, and are we sufficiently organized to learn it? It seems that the decision to diversify only makes sense to media companies that have identified a competitive advantage they could leverage. In addition, as the diversification beyond the first product can be viewed as an entrepreneurial process, resources need to be acquired—of crucial importance here are entrepreneurial and strategic thinking skills as well as the financial resources needed to finance the product launch.

REFERENCES

Allen, T. (2002). Are your products profitable? *Strategic Finance*, *83*(9), 32–37.

Amit, R. & Livnat, J. (1988). Diversification and the risk-return trade-off. *Academy of Management Journal*, *31*(1), 154–166.

Barton, S. L. (1988). Diversification strategy and systematic risk: Another look. *Academy of Management Journal*, *31*(1), 166–175.

Bettis, R. A. & Hall, W. K. (1981). Strategic portfolio management in a multibusiness firm, *California Management Review*, *14*(1), 23-38.

Bettis, R. A. & Hall, W. K. (1982). Diversification strategy, accounting determined risk, and accounting determined return. *Academy of Management Journal*, *25*(2), 254–264.

Boeker, W. (1997). Strategic Change: The Influence of Managerial Characteristics and Organizational Growth. *Academy of Management Journal*, *40*(1), 152–170.

Capon, N., Hulbert, J. M., Farley, J. U. & Martin, L. E. (1988). Corporate diversity and economic performance: The impact of market specialization. *Strategic Management Journal*, *9*, 61–47.

Chatterjee, S. & Blocher, J. D. (1992). Measurement of firm diversification: Is it robust? *Academy of Management Journal*, *35*(4), 874–888.

Croteau, D. & Hoynes, W. (2001). *The business of media: Corporate media and the public interest*. Thousand Oaks: Pine Forge Press.

Devinny, T. M. & Stewart, D. W. (1988). Rethinking the product portfolio: A generalized investment model. *Management Science*, *34*(9), 1080–1095.

De Wit, B. & Meyer, R. (1998). *Strategy. process, content, context—An international perspective* (Second ed.), London: Thomson Learning.

Dubofsky, P. & Varadarajan, P. (1987). Diversification and measures of performance: Additional empirical evidence. *Academy of Management Journal, 30*(3), 597–608.

Fink, C. C. (1988). *Strategic newspaper management.* Carbondale/Edwardsville: Southern Illinois University Press.

Geringer, J. M., Beamish, P. W. & daCosta, R. C. (1989). Diversification strategy and internationalization Implications for MNE performance. *Strategic Management Journal, 10*, 109–119.

Gerwin, D. & Barrowman, N. J. (2002). An evaluation of research on integrated product development. *Management Science, 48*(7), 938–953.

Ginsberg, A. (1990). Connecting diversification to performance: A sociocognitive approach. *Academy of Management Review, 15*(3), 514–535.

Goold, M. & Luchs, K. (1993). Why diversify? Four decades of management thinking. *Academy of Management Executive, 7*(3), 7–25.

Grant, R. M. & Jammine, A. P. (1988). Performance differences between the Wrigley/Rumelt strategic categories. *Strategic Management Journal, 9*, 333–346.

Grinyer, P. & McKiernan, P. (1990). Generating major change in stagnating companies. *Strategic Management Journal, 11*, 131–146.

Henderson, B. (1970). The product portfolio. In Stern, C. W. & Stalk Jr., G. (Eds.) (1998), *Perspectives on strategy from the Boston Consulting Group* (pp. 35-37). New York: Wiley.

Hitt, M. A., Hoskisson, R. E. & Kim, H. (1997). International diversification: Effects on innovation and firm performance in product-diversified firms. *Academy of Management Journal, 40*(4), 767–798.

Hoskisson, R. E., Hitt, M. A., Johnson, R. A. & Moesel, D. D. (1993). Construct validity of an objective (entropy) categorical measure of diversification strategy. *Strategic Management Journal, 14*, 215–235.

Johnson, G. & Scholes, K. (1999). *Exploring corporate strategy* (Fifth ed.). London: Prentice Hall.

King, N. & Anderson, N. (2002). *Managing Innovation and change. A critical guide for organizations* (Second ed.). London: Thomson Learning.

Küng, L. (2003). *When old dogs learn new tricks: the launch of BBC News Online.* ECCH Collection, Case 303–119–1.

Lacy, S., Sohn, A. B., & Wicks, J. L. (1993). *Media management: A casebook approach.* Hillsdale, NJ: Lawrence Erlbaum Associates.

Lacy, S. (2001). Newspapers confront a barrage of problems: Societal trends make business decisions more difficult. *Nieman Reports*, Fall, 77–79.

Leong, S. M. & Lim, K. G. (1991). Extending financial portfolio theory for product management. *Decision Sciences*, 181–193.

Lubatkin, M. & O'Neill, H. (1987). Merger strategies and capital market risk. *Academy of Management Journal, 30*, 665–684.

Lubatkin, M., Merchant, H., & Srinivasan, N. (1993). Construct validity of some unweighted product-count diversification measures. *Strategic Management Journal, 14*, 433–449.

Lubatkin, M. & Rogers, R.C. (1989). Diversification, systematic risk, and shareholder return: A capital market extension of Rumelt's 1974 study. *Academy of Management Journal, 32*(2), 454–465.

Markides, C. C. (1997). To diversify or not to diversify. *Harvard Business Review*, November–December.

Markides, C. C. & Markides and Williamson, P. J. (1994). Related diversification, core competences and corporate performance. *Strategic Management Journal, 15*, 149–165.

Markides, C. C. & Williamson, P. J. (1996). Corporate diversification and organizational structure: A resource-based view. *Academy of Management Journal, 39*(2), 340–367.

McChesney, R.W. (2000). The global media giants. In Andersen, R. & Strate, L. (Eds.), *Critical studies in media commercialism* (pp.59–70). New York: Oxford University Press.

Meyer, M. H. & Zack, M. H. (1996). The design and development of information products. *MIT Sloan Management Review, 37*(3), 43–59.

Montgomery, C. A. (1985). Product-market diversification and market power. *Academy of Management Journal, 28,* 789–797.

Montgomery, C. A. & Singh, H. (1984). Diversification strategy and systematic risk. *Strategic Management Journal, 5,* 181–191.

Nayyar, P. R. (1993). On the measurement of competitive strategy: Evidence from a large multiproduct US firm. *Academy of Management Journal, 36*(6), 1652–1669.

Penrose, E. (1959/1995). *The Theory of the Growth of the Firm* (rev. ed.). Oxford, UK: Oxford University Press.

Picard, R. G. (1989). *Media economics: Concepts and issues.* London: Sage.

Picard, R. G. (2002). *The economics and financing of media companies.* New York: Fordham University Press.

Picard, R. G. (2003). Cash cows or entrecôte? Publishing companies and new technologies. *Trends in Communication, 11*(2), 127–136.

Prahalad, C. K. & Hamel, G. (1990). The core competence of the corporation. *Harvard Business Review 68*(3), 79–91.

Radhika, A. N. (2003). *Bertelsmann: Before, during and after Middelhoff.* ECCH Collection, 303–151–1.

Ramanujam, V. & Varadarajan, P. (1989). Research on corporate diversification: A synthesis. *Strategic Management Journal, 10*(6), 523–551.

Rogers, B. (2000a). *Uncertainty in the media industry (A): Emerging battlefronts.* ECCH 300–055–6.

Rogers, B. (2000b). *Uncertainty in the media industry (B): The threat from non-traditional players.* ECCH 300–056–6.

Rumelt, R. P. (1974). *Strategy, structure, and economic performance.* Cambridge, MA: Harvard University Press.

Salter, M. S. & Weinhold, W. A. (1979). *Diversification through acquisition.* New York: The Free Press.

Sjurts, I. (2002). *Strategien in der Medienbranche—Grundlagen und Fallbeispiele* (2nd ed.). Wiesbaden: Gabler.

Varadarajan, P. & Ramanujam, V. (1987). Diversification and performance: A reexamination using a new two-dimensional conceptualization of diversity in firms. *Academy of Management Journal, 30*(2), 380–393.

Wickham, P. A. (2000). *Strategic entrepreneurship: A decision-making approach to new venture creation and management.* Essex, UK: Pearson Education.

Wolf, M. J. (2002). *Wall Street Journal*, February 21, 2002.

Wrigley, L. (1970). *Divisional autonomy and diversification.* Unpublished PhD dissertation, Harvard Business School.

4
Strategic Leadership and Media Portfolio Development: Leaders and Impression Management

Ethel Brundin
Leif Melin
Jönköping International Business School

A variety of influences affect media companies worldwide and the sector is subject to dramatic changes (Küng, 2003; Picard, 2003). External influences, some of which are media-specific, and internal, firm-specific issues are broad factors that drive change (Picard, 2003). As a consequence, the media sector has seen a set of mergers and acquisitions and a diversification of media products and units. Within the sector we find a diversification of media, entertainment, Internet services, and telecommunications, and the diversification stretches into cosmetics and water utilities. Pursuing this overall global trend, new issues will come into focus in more detail. Strategic leadership is considered such an issue that needs to be analyzed and brought into the open (Küng, 2003, Picard, 2003; Sánchez-Tabernero, 2003). The development of portfolio-based media companies has been driven, in many cases, by the strategies of dominant leaders. The many failures in the international arena regarding media mergers and acquisitions within a relatively short period of time stress the strategic leadership issue. So for instance, the mergers that created AOL Time Warner; Vivendi Universal, and Bertelsmann call for a more detailed analysis of strategic leadership. Was the 75% decline of AOL Time Warner's stock value and the decrease of Vivendi Universal's market value of 80% over the past few years to be blamed on the strategic leaders of the conglomerates? The domino effect, in which a series of resigning CEOs within the industry were replaced, was sometimes comical and even bizarre. Strategic leadership—or lack thereof—and perceptions of that leadership are one of the explanatory factors involved in some of the media merger or portfolio development failures in which the strategic leader has been forced to leave the scene.

A broad and complex picture of global trends has emerged where different strategic interests within the media industry at times appear to be contradictory, paradoxical, or clashing. Ever since the merger between AOL and Time Warner, team rivalries between strategic key actors have been reported on the daily agenda. They are often fueled by stakeholders' and business analysts' comments and strong emotions in the boardroom and in combination with clashes between cultures. In the midst of this, the strategic leader is at the very heart of the organization. Strategic leaders at top levels are in possession of the most crucial—and scarce—resources when it comes to strategy formation, and their strategic choices have a bearing on the organization's long-term survival (Sjöstrand, 1997). Risberg et al. (2003) argue in a similar way that the choice of top management teams and the division of roles and responsibilities are some of the crucial factors in mergers in order to meet with stakeholders' demands.

Because the very essence of leadership is to influence, it can also be assumed that strategic leaders want to convey an image of being in control and to appear to know what they are doing. Under the circumstances of great uncertainty due to a range of situational and unpredictable factors this is at times a mission impossible. Strategic leaders simply do not always succeed in their attempts to stand out in a favorable light. For instance, Steve Case, CEO of AOL Time Warner, was criticized for his leadership style: "He thinks he is challenging people to do their best, to think creatively. But it does not motivate people—it pisses them off" (an employee's voice; Radhika, 2003b, p. 10). A shareholder declared that probably no shareholder of the company wanted Steve Case around anymore, and neither did the board (Radhika, 2003b). The same fate met Jean Marie Messier of Vivendi when the board started to lose confidence in him and he was accused of being "arrogant and cagey" (Sarvani, 2003b, p. 2) by his critics. Thomas Middelhoff of Bertelsmann was accused of stepping "on a lot of backs in the company to get where he is" (Radhika, 2003c: 2). These are examples of strategic leaders within the media industry that obviously did not succeed in their ambitions to create positive images of themselves or their expansions of their firms' portfolios, nor to create the success for the companies that they hoped for. When strategic leaders such as the above embark on complex missions in order to increase company values, the expectations from shareholders and board members are high and the leaders' strategic choices are of great importance for the future course of events. Behind strategic choices there are presumably well thought out strategies, derived from leaders' strategic thinking. The strategic thinking skill has an impact on the strategic development. As far as we know today, media strategic leaders' ways of thinking are not always successful and there is no single way to play the cards well.

The ambition of this chapter is to explore the role of strategic leadership in media and communications companies. To fulfill our purpose the following main questions will be addressed:

- What characterizes the strategic ways of thinking of strategic leaders in the media industry?
- What impression do strategic leaders of the media try to impose through media?
- How are strategic leaders and their strategies pictured by media?

The chapter is structured as follows: After the initial introduction we will address the concept of strategic leadership. In the third section we will elaborate on media strategists' ways of thinking. This will lead us to the fact that strategic leaders appear to give voice to their strategic thinking in public in order to influence the course of events. We have chosen to rely on impression management in order to analyze this phenomenon and the fourth section will give a framework of impression management. This is followed by illustrations of how strategic leadership can be executed in the media through impression management. Methodologically we have relied on available academic articles, journals, Internet sources, educational materials, magazines and newspapers about the three major global players AOL Time Warner, Bertelsmann, and Vivendi Universal, focusing mainly on their CEOs and/or chairmen. In the fifth section we will illustrate how impression management might affect strategic leadership in a way that is not intended by the strategic leader by turning to archetypes of strategic leaders. Finally, we discuss some practical as well as theoretical implications of impression management and propose an agenda for future research.

In addition to our attention to AOL Time Warner, Bertelsmann, and Vivendi Universal we will add an illustration from the Swedish media industry that gives an explanation of the emergence of portfolio expansions through diversification in this industry. A brief background on each group of AOL Time Warner, Bertelsmann, and Vivendi Universal is in order before we proceed.

AOL was founded in 1985 by Steve Case, Jim Kimsey, and Marc Seriff under the name of Quantum Computer Service. Steve Case was appointed CEO. Time Warner, established in 1989 was in turn a merger of Warner Communication, founded in 1927, and Time Inc., founded in 1918. In 1995, Turner Broadcasting Company was incorporated with Time Warner. In January 2000 AOL and Time Warner merged into AOL Time Warner and became the largest merger within the media industry as well as within the corporate world with an estimated value of $112 billion. Within the group are filmed entertainment, interactive services, television networks, cable systems, and publishing. Well-known brands are Netscape, MapQuest, MovieFone, Spinner Networks Inc., Digital-City, Nullsoft Inc., *Time, Fortune, Money, Sports Illustrated*; CNN, HBO, TNT, and Warner Brothers Studios. Gerald Levin became the CEO and Steve Case, the chairman of the board. However, senior executives were to report to Case rather than to the CEO. Levin retired in December 2001, Case stepped down from his position in May 2003, and Bob Parsons became his successor as CEO as well as chairman.

Bertelsmann dates back to 1835 and is one of Germany's oldest companies. The founder was Carl Bertelsmann. Initially the company published mainly within the fields of theology and education and issued two newspapers. Things changed radically during the third generation when the son-in-law Johannes Mohn took over. All sorts of literature were published and the company flourished. After the Second World War, the company had to be rebuilt and was in the 1950s one of the leading printing and publishing companies worldwide. The company was restructured in late 1950 and decentralized by Reinhard Mohn. During the sixties it became international and entered into film production. During the seventies and eighties Reinhard Mohn made a range of acquisitions worldwide including Doubleday publishers in the U.S.. In order to meet the harsh competition within the industry in the nineties when digital media were emerging, Thomas Middelhoff was appointed head of the strategy and corporate development division in 1994. He had been with the company since 1986 as an executive management assistant within one of the main printing companies. Middelhoff steered Bertelsmann into online services and made it into a global Internet group through acquisitions (e.g., Springer Verlag) and joint ventures (e.g., Vivendi Universal). In 2000, Bertelsmann was the third largest media group in the world with a range of media companies including TV and radio companies, book and magazine companies, entertainment companies, and on-line businesses. The main owners are the Bertelsmann Foundation and the Mohn family. In July 2002 Middelhoff resigned as chairman and CEO and Günter Thielen, who is close to the Mohn family, was appointed his successor as CEO of Bertelsmann.

Compagnie Générale des Eaux was the original name of Vivendi Universal. It was established in 1853 by the French government as a civil engineering and utilities company. During the later part of the nineteenth century it went international by providing water to Venice, Istanbul, and Porto. One hundred years later the company formed the first pay-TV channel together with Agence Havas. This was a news and advertising agency with a history longer than Compagnie Générale des Eaux. When Jean Marie Messier was appointed the CEO in 1994 the company was a global player with a diversified portfolio. Messier changed the company name to Vivendi, Latin for "to live." When Messier was forced to leave Vivendi in June 2002 the company was the second largest media group in the world and had a wide portfolio of businesses in publishing, television production and distribution, recreational and theme parks, retail, and music—and a reported loss of €13.6 billion. Jean-Rene Fourtou became the new chairman and together with a few new board members he began to restructure Vivendi.

STRATEGIC LEADERSHIP

All companies are constantly involved in strategic change processes. Sometimes these are more thorough and radical in character and sometimes they are more incremental with a continuously ongoing strategy formation. The term *strategic leadership* is usually connected to the person or persons who manage and lead these change activities, that is, people at top management levels, even if strategic leaders may be found on different levels (Johnson, Melin & Whittington, 2003). Most people also agree that the CEO is the predominant strategic leader, with responsibility for strategic change (Kotter, 1996; Mintzberg, 1988; Sjöstrand, 1997).

Strategic leaders face many challenges. Coping with the speed and complexity of the changes within the media sector is one of them. To merge one media company with another media firm; to diversify the product portfolio into a range of new offers to the media public; to create "tangible" visions that need to be communicated in an understandable way; to make sure that two (or more) cultures can work together; and to make organizational members able to identify with a new brand and a new organization and to act as a representative for owners as well as employees are just a few of the challenges that need to be addressed—often by a strategic leader. Overall developments in society have turned the focus toward visions, values, and communication (Yukl, 2002). Combined with structural and demographic changes these have become primary factors behind all challenges facing companies. The nature of the uncertainty that this brings into an organization justifies strategic leadership (Sjöstrand, 1997; Sjöstrand, et al., 2000) and is decisive for the outcome of the strategic change (Westerberg, 1998). Doz and Prahalad (1987) conclude in their study that lack of distinct strategic leadership was the reason for failure in two out of six "failure" cases and Grinyer, et al. (1988) found that a new strategic leader is the crucial factor for successful turnarounds. Strategic leadership is also considered a crucial factor in stimulating and trying to bring out ideas from organizational members (McCarthy, 2000). In conclusion, strategic leadership matters for a range of reasons to all of which we agree in this chapter.

The term strategic leadership is often used implicitly or explicitly for a specific purpose. Here, the strategic leader is seen as a key actor in change processes. We will denote the term strategic leader to the person, or persons, who work with conscious and planned strategic change with reference to the top management level in the media sector. Furthermore, strategic leadership is used to separate it distinctly from leadership or management in general. The word "strategic" implies the upper echelons and that the responsibility to be visionary and dedicated to change is included. In this chapter, strategic leadership is an executive process with a series of activities beyond exact description (Barnard, 1938). Strategic leadership refers to conscious as well as unconscious activities regarding change and transformation of media companies to fit with external and internal demands, in order to meet financial requirements. The person who fulfills this role is in this chapter called the strategic leader.

Ericson, Melander, and Melin (2001) present a typology of different roles of strategic leaders: the missing strategic leader who does not play any role; the great strategic leader who is recognized as the important, heroic strategic leader; the coalition view of the strategic leader includes the whole top management team or other dominant coalitions as taking an influential role; the elusive strategic leader is the strategic leader where cultural values and norms dominate the thinking and acting of individual leaders. The strategic leader should be defined from the actual participation in different relevant arenas where strategic dialogues take place. In our explorative study, we will see obvious signs of the great strategic leader and not much evidence of the missing strategic leader. However, in order to understand the emerging strategic patterns we need to consider the forces behind both the strategic leader coalition and the elusive strategic leader (e.g., the institutional forces of isomorphism). We also believe that the dialogue type of strategic leaders is important, even if our empirical observations do not capture this dimension.

We will now turn to the question of what are the strategic ways of thinking of strategic leaders in media firms?

STRATEGIC WAYS OF THINKING IN MEDIA FIRMS

In the concept of strategists' ways of thinking, Hellgren and Melin (1993) include values, assumptions and thoughts about leadership and strategic development and argue that strategic leaders tend to build up a strategic way-of-thinking that stabilizes over time and that they apply no matter what organization they operate in. This is not assumed to be a problem per se, because a strategic leader with a way of thinking that is new for the industry he or she is entering, may imply radical change even if the strategic way of thinking is stable for the leader him or herself. However, in other cases a stable way of thinking is the same as a resistance to be radical (Hellgren & Melin, 1993) when totally new approaches and strategic actions are needed (Virany, et al., 1992). A range of studies (Grinyer, et al., 1988; Samuelson, et al., 1985; Tushman, et al., 1986; Virany, et al., 1992) have found that new leadership is required to make a notable difference in turnarounds or in critical processes such as mergers and acquisitions.

From available sources on AOL Time Warner, Bertelsmann, and Vivendi Universal it is obvious that their strategic leaders are of various backgrounds. The AOL Time Warner organization chose at the point of the merger to appoint the former directors of the two respective companies of AOL and Time Warner as CEO and chairman of the board. The CEO and the chairman of AOL Time Warner were both "raised" within AOL and Time Warner respectively, which may indicate that their strategic ways of thinking remained the same within the new conglomerate. According to different stories, Steve Case was an entrepreneur all his life, starting in early childhood being involved in a set of start-ups. From various work experience he early adopted a strategy that followed him over the years, namely the KISS strategy (Keep It Simple, Stupid). This was also his strategy throughout the build-up of AOL, of which he was also one of the founders. In providing online services, the KISS strategy was no doubt a success. However, in his own words, one of his entrepreneurial driving forces was to meet challenges and constantly be in "pursuit of the idea" which in the AOL case was to build a global medium (Radhika, 2003b). Reportedly, Case also admits that managing a mature business is not "his thing." In the case of AOL Time Warner and Steve Case, we can sense a life-long built-in strategic thinking that for each particular acquisition in the past seemed to function but not so in the new merger with Time Warner. His ongoing commitment to make AOL Time Warner number one was probably not only a benefit for the group; rather, some strategic reorientation, reflection, and consolidation might have been a better and more profitable solution in the long run. In contrast to Case, Levin's long background in Time Warner was more colored by a culture of traditions. The strategic clashes between them seem to have been the rule rather than the exception and it did not take long until one of them had to leave the scene, which happened with the exodus of Levin in late 2001.

Middelhoff of Bertelsmann was made CEO after over a decade within the firm. Bertelsmann, which was a family-owned business from the very start in 1835, is today governed mainly by family interests, which implies "inherited" strategic values (Hall, 2003). When Middelhoff entered the company he embarked on a series of steps to make Bertelsmann one of the leading media players in the areas of digital media and Internet services and prepared to list the company on the stock exchange. Strategic choice clashes appear to have been the reason for Middelhoff's forced resignation in July 2002. The comments in media were that Middelhoff was too visionary (Radhika, 2003c). His successor was close to the family and dismissed the idea of a stock market issue to make Bertelsmann public and took action to get Bertelsmann back to the core publishing business. Being an external CEO, without family ties, in a family-owned business probably made it difficult for Middelhoff to adjust to family business rules and values. So in his particular case we see that novel strategic thinking was not a success factor in a family-controlled business.

Messier of Vivendi Universal and the successor of Steve Case at AOL Time Warner—Bob Parsons—were both relatively new to the companies on their appointments as CEOs.

The strategic leader of Vivendi Universal came with an elite background. He graduated from top business schools and his first posts were at the French Ministry of Economy and Finance and later he became chief advisor to the Minister of Economy, Finance and Privatization. He soon got a reputation as a successful "turn-around-manager." He then became an investment banker before he was appointed the CEO of Vivendi in 1994. In 2 years time, he had managed to financially reengineer the company and 2 years later he was declared chairman of Vivendi in addition to being CEO. After having sold out a lot of noncore businesses, Messier started to expand the firm's portfolio by acquiring companies within water and waste management services and communications. His strategic thinking within Vivendi was influenced by the American style, as it seems, with extensive plans to build up a "mega Franco-American business empire" that could compete with AOL Time Warner. He seemed successful and was regarded very talented and brave. The terrorist attacks of Sept. 11, 2001, had a negative impact on Vivendi's finances but Messier continued in the acquisition business. Analysts commented that he was good at making deals but lacked abilities to manage a company. Mightit be that he used his banking experience in his strategic way of thinking but was not able to see the consequences in practice at an operational level?

Bob Parsons is of African-American origin and is one of the three first CEOs with such a background in charge of a company of the size of AOL Time Warner. Bob Parsons had governmental experience at the White House, and he had received the best of references from the President himself. George W. Bush stated that Parsons represented "the spirit of business statesmanship at its highest" (Dingle & Hughes, 2002, p. 78). With such a background, he was held in high esteem straight from the beginning and his predecessor Gerald Levin expressed his total confidence in Parsons to accomplish far-reached goals. In Parsons' case, he was presumably a man with strategic skills that were out of the ordinary because he had contacts in Washington and was a previous White House employee. It might also have rendered him diplomatic skills that proved useful facing the turbulence after the Steve Case era.

From a factual dimension point of view (Hellgren, Melin & Pettersson, 1993), the competitive advantages within merged industries must come through combining them in a rational way. From earlier studies we learn that adapting and integrating the core competences are the decisive factors in order to be successful (Markides & Williamson, 1996; Pralahad & Hamel, 1990). To Markides and Williamson, new competitive strategies come as a result of experience and can serve as catalysts to other parts of a company or to new acquisitions and alliances. The strategic leaders' ways of thinking regarding the rapid portfolio growth through mergers and acquisitions in the world's leading media conglomerates point in an opposite direction. Diversification was prioritized without a real core competence strategy. Not until Parsons, with only a few years within AOL Time Warner and with a different background, entered the scene in 2003 as the new CEO did the strategic way of thinking seems to shift. He indicated that he wanted to consolidate the existing assets and explicitly stated that no more acquisitions or mergers were of interest at that time (Broadcasting & Cable Yearbook, 2003). Following Hellgren and Melin's (1993) findings that the strategic way of thinking is rather stable over time, it can be speculated whether Parsons transferred "political" strategies into business. Likewise, after Middelhoff's resignation as CEO the message from headquarters is that "Bertelsmann has focused its energy on the core businesses, cut its losses, and markedly increased its profitability" (Radhika, 2003c, p. 13). New—or revised—strategies eventually emerged as a result of turbulent years after the marriage between "new" and "old" media was robbed of its honeymoon.

However, the strategic leader's ways of thinking also include relational and ideological aspects (Hellgren, Melin & Pettersson, 1993) as well. The former includes power relationships and exchange relationships and the latter cognitive and cultural processes. With regard to the ideological level, Risberg's (1999) argument that "pre-acquisition ambiguities" need to be taken into account is appropriate. The term refers to the role of communication during an acquisition process and the strategic leader needs to allow for different ambiguities and be observant of these issues before the merger, not only afterwards. This is also in line with Brundin's (2002) findings that emotions need to play a major role in radical change processes, to which a cultural merger can apply. If the strategist allows for emotional processes including all organizational levels and members, resistance to change is not a decisive issue, rather a quite natural process whereby emotions can serve as driving forces within the merger process.

Published accounts about AOL Time Warner indicate that a lot of considerations regarding relational and ideological dimensions of the merger were left aside and that ignorance about them or their neglect seems to have been fatal. AOL policies and rules were imposed on Time Warner employees and AOL executives were accused of applying some sort of savior attitude, which made former Time Warner people furious and led to a range of disputes and also a high number of resignations among executives.

Taylor and Wheatley-Lovoy (1998) suggest that "the actions of one leader, multiplied by thousands of leaders, can reshape a culture" (p. 25). From this it can be concluded that where an old and ingrained culture exists it is impossible for a new strategic leader to change the matter of facts single-handedly in the merger process. This was probably the challenge that faced Middelhoff of Bertelsmann, when he had to operate within a family culture, where the management was aware of and treasured its traditions. Likewise, the top management in the merger of AOL and Time Warner combined one culture with its roots from the beginning of the last century with one formed during the latter

---

CASE STUDY
New Strategic Leaders, New Strategies
in Swedish Newspaper Companies

In the late 1960's and early 1970s three major Swedish newspapers, *Dagens Nyheter, Svenska Dagbladet,* and *Sydsvenska Dagbladet*, all got new CEOs, recruited externally. These recruitments were a break with earlier internal recruitment patterns and certainly with requirements of newspaper/publishing experience. For the first time, professional strategic leaders were recruited to these three newspaper companies and all new leaders had an academic degree in business administration.

The strategic consequence was that these strategic leaders soon questioned the taken-for-granted idea that these three newspaper companies would have their daily newspaper as their only product. At this time *Dagens Nyheter, Svenska Dagbladet,* and *Sydsvenska Dagbladet* all started product diversification, mainly through acquisitions. As a direct consequence of and parallel to the diversification the three companies also divisionalized their organizations.

Since then, and due to the changing character of this industry involved in major changes, strategic leaders have in most cases been recruited from outside the firms. The reasoning behind this is probably due to the inertia that is attributed to candidates who came from within the organizations whose strategies and structures are seen to require change.

Continued on next page

part of the century. Without taking these considerations into account even the best of intentions can be thwarted.

Due to limitations of empirical material, we have not been able to make further analyses with regard to the strategic leaders' ways of thinking. However, we have allowed for some speculative thoughts and the relational dimension of strategic leaders' ways of thinking will be elaborated upon a bit further. We can sense both power relations and exchange relationships being brought into the open by the strategic leaders themselves in the media as well as by writers such as editors-in-chiefs and business analysts among others. Let us therefore turn to impression management.

Continued from previous page

Before the 1970s, the predominant norms and knowledge expressed by the dominant leaders ways of thinking were focused around editing and publishing of the daily newspapers in these Swedish newspaper companies. Editing had a higher value, beyond matters of administration. Editing was surely the identity of the company. Up to the 1960s, no real conditions for activities other than those connected to editing and publishing existed (Sveningsson, 1999). But with the new CEOs entering around 1970, a new way of thinking came into the companies, a way of thinking representing a modern, more managerial and strategic view as to the role of a top leader. These externally recruited CEOs redefined both their companies and the industry, and they started to exercise power through their superior knowledge of strategy (Foucault, 1975). The strategic development that followed can be seen as a struggle with the old editorial norms. These included a strong belief in social-liberal rules of the press, with the critical task of newspapers as important, and the trustworthiness of the editors as a crucial part of the newspapers. The business-oriented type of strategic leader entering the arena was in strong contrast with the institutional norms of a classic newspaper company. Resistance towards these changes in the newspaper companies came from people that thought it violated editorial norms. Interestingly, both the new CEOs and the resisting editors were reproducing different sets of norms and values. The strategic patterns that followed can be interpreted as driven partly by the way of thinking of these new CEOs, disciplined by their business administration education, and partly by an industrial isomorphism, i.e., mimicking behavior where this industry was forced to act according to the main trends of management, which in the 1970s were strategic planning and portfolio diversification.

IMPRESSION MANAGEMENT

The interest in image and identity building has been in focus before within the media sector (Alvesson & Kärreman, 2001; Holmberg & Åkerblom, 2001; Risberg, et al., 2003; Sallot, 2002). However, and so far, little empirical evidence exists and we do not know much about how strategic leaders impose an image of themselves within this particular sector.

According to Rosenfeld et al. (1995) people can be involved in producing a notion in order "to seek to control the image others have of them" (p. 4). Through a specific rhetoric, well-thought out verbal as well as written statements, and body language, the strategist is able to convey his or her intended message. The phenomenon is called impression management. Definitions of impression management primarily stress that it is a process of controlling how other people perceive you (Cady & Fandt, 2001; Leary & Kowalski, 1990; Palmer, et al., 2001; Rosenfeld, et al., 1995; Sallot, 2002). By controlling the information that others get, the strategic leader can influence the perceptions that others have about him/her. However, as much as it is a conscious way of achieving certain goals, the process of impression management is in many cases created unconsciously or even through automatic behaviors. Moreover, such processes are probably at work at all times and at all occasions in organizational life.

Impression management has its root in James' (1890/1998) "multiple social selves" concept which implies that a person shows different sides of him/herself in order to meet his/her interests depending on the situation. James writes that a person "has as many social selves as there are distinct groups of people about whose opinions he [she] cares" (James, 1890/1998, p. 294). Goffman (1959) stresses that impression management is a natural ingredient in day-to-day activities. The phenomenon can be downsized to two main directions; the acquisitive and the protective directions as suggested by Palmer, et al. (2001). The former is a way to actively seek approval and is directed towards future events whereas the latter is occupied with a concern to meet already existing disapproval. A slightly other distinction is made by Cady and Fandt (2001) whose findings suggest that a set of tactics lead to three main impression management strategies: self-protection, self-promotion, and hedging. Self-protection is about defending one's own ego, motives, or image; self-promotion is about enhancing one's ego, motives, or image; and hedging is about taking credit for the outcome, avoiding critique (see Gardner & Avolio, 1998, for a review on impression management.)

We argue here that the strategic leader sees impression management as a tool to obtain certain goals, may it be consciously used or not. By making official comments, lobbying for certain actions, and behaving and dressing in a certain way, the strategic leader tries to influence his or her audience and thereby legitimatize his or her actions. Here the strategic leader often makes use of the tools closest at hand—the media. This can be a subtle process, because the audience is not only the "ordinary" readers of news magazines, watchers of TV, and users of the Internet. In this circle, we will also find business analysts, board members, persons from other key positions within the firms, shareholders/ owners, representatives of pressure groups, and the public at large, i.e., both real and imaginative audiences.

Possible reasons why it is worth the effort to engage in impression management can be interests such as obtaining or protecting certain personal or organizational goals or to gain more legitimacy. In a three-factor model, Leary and Kowalski (1990; in Rosenfeld, et al., 1995) label the process of impression management impression monitoring, impression motivation, and impression construction. Monitoring implies that the strategic leaders in media firms become aware of the influence they might have on other people and that it can be possible to influence them in one way or other. Motivation is a desire to use this influence, whereas construction refers to the manner in which they actually influence, depending on the context and the assumed values of the audience in combination with the strategic leader's own desired identity and goals. The process of influencing the audience can thus be a clearly thought-out strategy, used in a political way by the strategic leader to achieve an impression that serves his or her organizational goals (Giacalone & Rosenfeld, 1989; Pettigrew, 1973). Rhetorical devices, for example, are well-known and acceptable tools of impression management in strategic change processes (Müllern & Stein, 1999). However, as pointed out earlier, the grade of consciousness of impression management is debatable, and can also vary over time (Baumeister & Hutton, 1987; Tetlock & Manstead, 1985).

Impression management can include situations in which the strategist is put in a predicament (Rosenfeld, et al., 1995) such as a lapse or miscalculation, i.e., an "event that casts aspersions on the lineage, character, conduct, skills or motives of an actor" (Schlenker, 1980, p. 125). The predicament is a threat not only to the identity of the strategic leader but often has financial consequences (Crant & Bateman, 1993). In order to minimize the damage, the strategic leader can make use of remedial tactics. So-called accounts are a common way to reestablish confidence and credibility (Giacalone & Rosenfeld, 1984; Rosenfeld, et al., 1995) in order to regain as much as possible of the emerging distance between what has been done and what was expected (Scott & Lyman, 1968: 46; in Rosenfeld, et al., 1995). Accounts, in turn, can be offered as excuses about the predicament where the strategic leader admits what has happened but does not take responsibility for it. It can also include explanations/justifications in which the responsibility is acknowledged, but in which the incident and/or behavior are justified. The last resort among accounts is the apology where not only the responsibility is acknowledged but often expressions of remorse and/or a request for forgiveness are made (Rosenfeld, et al., 1995).

Illustrations of Impression Management

Turning to strategic leadership within the media sector it is quite possible that Middelhoff, CEO of Bertelsmann, tried to make use of impression management as a power tool when he tried to increase the speed of the decision-making process by saying: "We are changing the organization. We are changing the corporate governance. We are changing the culture" (Radhika, 2003c, p. 7). The statement has clear rhetorical ingredients and a strategic purpose. By repeating "we are changing" three times in a row, Middelhoff obviously has an intention of urging the importance of changes and to make the audience understand that he is in charge. Furthermore, one of his strategic purposes is probably that of impressing on the stakeholders his competence as a way of promoting himself (Rosenfeld, et al., 1995).

At the time of the merger, Steve Case, AOL Time Warner chairman, made the following comment:

> Together we can change the future for the better. The world is just scratching the surface of the Internet's potential, which new technology will soon make available to consumers anywhere they are and everywhere they go (Radhika, 2003a, p. 5).

At the same time, Levin, the CEO, made the following statement:

> This strategic combination with AOL accelerates the digital transformation of Time Warner by giving our creative and content businesses the widest possible canvas (Radhika, 2003a, p. 5).

The strategic rhetoric is obvious when both strategic leaders appear to be very well aware of the impression they need to make at this stage; they both show confidence in the merger and legitimize it by emphasizing future benefits of the broadened portfolio that would seemingly not exist without the merger.

Steve Case of AOL Time Warner was very conscious of making the right impression. In a statement he indicated that he was a great visionary and the right strategic leader of the merger:

I really do plan myself five to ten years into future. I spend almost none of my time focused on challenges of executing our plans, today, tomorrow, this week, this month, this quarter, this year (Radhika, 2003b, p. 9).

This was confirmed by a chairman within the group who claimed that Case was a survivor who always seems to be able to make the right moves (Radhika, 2003b). The step to manipulation and making use of impressions at all costs is not far. Steve Case was obviously accused of this by one of his colleague executives, who saw his impression management as seemingly exercised at the expense of the closest environment: "Thank God, it was as if it was the middle ages and we had been leeched for three years. There was almost no blood left" (Radhika, 2003a, p. 2). From this statement it appears that the strategic leader has made use of his position to even dupe his audience (Rosenfeld et al. 1995) in an almost Machiavellian way, ruthlessly prioritizing the device "the end justifies the means" (Machiavelli, 1958).

When the merger of AOL and Time Warner did not render the profits that have been predicted, Steve Case made the following statement:

Perhaps it is a lesson learned—even though you think you may be right; if the environment is such and the facts are such, it requires you to take a more pragmatic way and perhaps a more selfless view. That is what you have to do. My case, it is about putting the company's interest first. This company cannot afford any distractions. There are a lot of challenges we face. We need to focus on those, not some debate around Steve Case (Radhika, 2003a, p. 3).

Here Steve Case tried to give an excuse for the declining figures after the merger, blaming on circumstances out of his control. At the same time he tried to redirect the focus on himself as the CEO to other, non-named circumstances— perhaps media journalists. He continued:

It is never over till it is over. There is no question that this merger so far has been a disappointment. But if you look out 10 to 15 years, I think people will look back and have a different view on this merger (Radhika, 2003b, p. 11).

Case did not want to let go, and he insisted that he had made the right strategic moves.

After his resignation, Messier, former CEO of Vivendi Universal told his audience through *The Guardian*: "I tried to do too much too quickly" (Sarvani, 2003a, p. 2). This statement can be interpreted as Messier's justification of his resignation and his taking responsibility for it. On the other hand, it might as well have been an excuse by which he admitted facts but did not take responsibility for the resignation and/or its consequences. In both cases, Messier appeared to convey his innocent self to his audience of shareholders, indicating that his competence was not at fault.

Middelhoff of Bertelsmann claimed after his resignation to his audience via the web: "Shareholders had mid and long-term development prospects that were different from mine. In this context, I had no choice but to resign" (Radhika, 2003c, p. 2). Here Middelhoff excused his resignation, indicating he was not at fault, rather that the Mohn family did not go along with Middelhoff's intentions to make Bertelsmann publicly owned. The statement at the same time worked as a justification clearly showing his loyalties to Bertelsmann by the self-sacrifice he suffered in order to ease the new strategic intent.

Middelhoff's successor, Günter Thielen, was urgent to make an impression and announced that Bertelsmann needed to consolidate the group. He also wanted to make clear that it was important to cooperate with him/the family and that the Middelhoff era of centralization efforts were at an end:

> Bertelsmann is proud of the entrepreneurs in its enterprises. Strong senior executives who cooperate with one another make the best entrepreneurs. Synergies and cooperation must become part of our daily business. This includes further improving profitability and extending our financial scope to enable greater growth under our own steam (Radhika, 2003c, p. 12).

The new CEO of AOL Time Warner, Bob Parsons, with a political background from the White House, made use of impression management before more difficulties arose: "You have got to get over that [the present bad financial situation]. You cannot go back and undo the past. We are where we are and the question is how do we build value back, going forward?" (Radhika, 2003a, p. 2). The strategic leader here was preparing audiences for the potential lack of success in his new role by relying on a so-called disclaimer—an anticipatory excuse before a predicament (Hewitt & Stokes, 1975; in Rosenfeld, et al., 1995). Should something in his future strategy formation go awry, he has already dampened the possible damage. His political training might have taught him this.

During his tenure, Messier of Vivendi Universal had to handle a range of predicaments when the group faced severe financial problems. Messier tried to conceal them when he repeatedly said that Vivendi did not have any "immediate and severe cash shortage" (Sarvani, 2003a, p. 6). In addition, Messier made some moves and statements that were doomed from the beginning. For example, he claimed that the "French Cultural Exception was dead"[4] (Sarvani, 2003a, p. 6) and got rid of executives who had different opinions from himself. Eventually, because his impression management did not work, he had no other option but to resign in July 2002. However, he tried to the very end, but lost a vote of confidence among board members. A set of accusations and legal actions toward Vivendi Universal followed the resignation of Messier. He tried to excuse himself:

> I am leaving so that Vivendi stays. I built this company with my team. I love it passionately. But there is an undeniable truth—you cannot lead a company if the board is divided (Sarvani, 2003b, p. 8).

His successor Jean-Rene Fourtou continued with remedial tactics as a consequence of his predecessor's strategic leadership when he offered the following account: "I want to reassure you: the company's situation is certainly tense, but I have identified the way out of this crisis and the way to be back on track" (Sarvani, 2003a, p. 8). Fourtou stated "Vivendi considers it has a duty to take legal action in the interests of shareholders and employees, who should not be victims of biased information" (Sarvani, 2003a, p. 8). In order to work on his own impression, Fortou declared that "2002 was a difficult year, 2003 would not be calmer waters … it will be a transition year … our real focus is on 2004, not on the next six months" (Sarvani, 2003a, p. 10).

In addition to behavior and verbal statements of different kinds, written accounts play a major role in impression management. One of the most persuasive means is the annual report. Here the strategic leaders of a company are able to analyze the past year rather freely and without interference and take credit for and/or blame bad results on whatever factors they see fit. A deeper analysis of the accounts for AOL Time Warner, Bertelsmann, and Vivendi Universal will probably show a whole set of impression management attempts where acquisitive (the urge to be favorably seen) as well as protective (the avoidance of looking bad) strategies are in practical use.

An intriguing question at this point is: how successful are the strategic leaders in obtaining the "desired impression"? Impression management is a process with many co-producers in the audience and therefore there is a need to consider whether it always works as intended. As we see it, the creation of images goes the other way around as well—and sometimes even backfire on the intentions of the strategic leader. Risberg, et al., (2003) argue in their paper on national identification in mergers and acquisitions that the media discourse plays

---

[4] This refers to the future of the exception in the WTO agreement that permitted the French film industry to be financed through government subsidies and taxies. Its removal would force significant change on media company audio-visual activities in France.

a vital role and may construct power relations of superiority and inferiority within the merger by using a specific rhetoric.

Let us turn to the very tool that strategic leaders most often use themselves and that at the same time is their own "baby": the media. In many cases the media channel is the underlying reason from the start to make use of impression management. Because impression management obviously does not work in a one-way direction, we will now focus on the images of the strategic leaders that the press offers its public. According to the prevailing discourse about media people, they are supposed to report on events in an "objective" way. However, this is not always the case and—in their ambitions to meet political expectations—they make use of impression management themselves as a means of constructing and fostering images of the strategic leader and developments within their own industry. Leaning on the interests of other people in the media audience, such as board members, executives, shareholders, and the like, journalists have a major impact on readers, viewers, and/or listeners' perceptions of the strategic leader. It is not so much what the strategic leader does or does not do; it is rather the perception, created and reproduced by the media people— and indirectly the audience—about the strategic leader that directs what strategic leadership becomes. As we shall see, by investigating the picture that emerges in media, it is a matter of delicacy whether impression management is a successful strategic route or not.

We will therefore claim that the media helps in creating stereotypes, or archetypes of strategic leaders.

ARCHETYPES OF STRATEGIC LEADERS

One of the first to introduce the concept of archetypes was Carl Jung, who referred to the three stages of human psychological development within the individuation process: the Ego, the Soul, and the Self (Pearson, 1991). Jung referred to a set of themes of the collective unconsciousness (Carr, 2002; Tallman, 2003). Archetypes affect "the way we perceive, imagine and think and by structuring psychic apprehension, influencing behavior profoundly" (Matthews, 2002, p. 461). Northouse (2004) defines an archetype as a strong pattern in the human psyche which is consistent over time; or as an original pattern consisting of many reproductions in time and space; or just a pattern of human behavior. When we refer to archetypes in relation to strategic leaders within the media sector we understand all three of these. Archetypes are patterns created and co-produced about strategic leaders regarding their behavior that tend to build up our perceptions about them. These also influence what we tend to think about the strategic leaders and their strategies and how we tend to talk about them. Archetypes thereby create a taken-for-granted notion about the strategic leader and his or her future behavior. Journalists, analysts, investors, board member colleagues, and the like can facilitate the creation of this image or contradict it by their choices what to write or say. Through statements, following certain logic, it therefore seems possible to "write" a strategic leader's destiny.

Archetypes are said to embark on a journey that has three different stages: the preparation (cf. developing an Ego), the journey itself (cf. to encounter the Soul), and the return (cf. to give birth to a unique Self). All are on "the hero's journey" as labeled by Campbell (1968; in Northouse, 2004) and as characterized, among others, by Odysseus' adventure in which he set out in the world to meet trials and temptations from which he eventually returns as a hero. Archetypes come in twelve different shapes: the innocent, the orphan, the warrior, the martyr (the caregiver), the seeker, the destroyer, the lover, the creator, the ruler, the magician, the sage, and the fool (Pearson, 1991).

The first four prepare for the journey; the middle four help during the journey, and the last four mediate the return. We will not go into detail for all those but highlight a few. The innocent has not yet been tempted by the adventure; the orphan is leaving the security that a home offers in order to seek the adventure; the warrior fights the battle; and the martyr puts others' interests before his or her own. The seeker shows counter dependency in the battle and dwells toward the unknown in order to reach improvement. The creator has a sense for newness and creativity in the battle. The magician is able to make wonders and make a transformation that seems impossible, and the fool allows the different selves to express themselves without too much lecturing. It is also emphasized by Pearson (1991) that the archetypes do not necessarily come in a specific order, neither is the archetypical role a static one.

Other researchers have made a division into slightly different and smaller numbers of archetypes such as the king, the warrior, the magician, and the lover (Tallman, 2003), which Tallman labels the "four foundational masculine archetypes." Maccoby (1976; 1981) characterized four archetypes; the craftsman, the jungle fighter, the company man, and the gamesman. The craftsman as a leader is the good administrator, independent and demanding; the jungle fighter is brave and driven by power and a struggle; the company man is loyal and cautious and lacks in courage and risk taking; and the gamesman is daring and likes to take risks. In a speculative comparison we see parallels between the warrior and the jungle fighter as well as between the gamesman and the magician.

Maccoby (1976) and Carr (2002) claim that depending on what the organization wants, the organizational leaders more or less consciously try to mirror these expectations. They want to be recognized as good organizational citizens of their organizations. From this we can interpret that the different types become "sedimented" in the culture and that managerial behavior—and strategic thinking—to a certain extent is formed and reproduced by the organizational context. This is also something that we can sense in the illustrations that are to follow next.

Illustrations of Archetypes

When things were still going the right way, the *Wall Street Journal* described Steve Case in the following way, very much like the warrior:

> He woke up one day and decided his business was not about rationing access to a scarce resource; his business was about attracting as many eyeballs as possible to his bill-board-lined shopping mall, cum singles bar cum newsstand cum mailbox cum anything else the AOL universe wants it to be. Mr. Case's plan has always been to capture the biggest online audience any way he can (Radhika, 2003b, pp. 5-6).

The warrior is considered courageous, disciplined, and an expert of strategic moves. S/he takes risks but they are calculated. S/he is said to be devoted to a cause or a vision (Tallman, 2003). This can be sensed in the above statement, not without some irony.

In his announcement to resign, toward the end of the journey, the media chose to refer to the following statement by Steve Case of AOL Time Warner:

> Although I prefer being Chairman and I will miss not being Chairman and I am obviously disappointed by it, I still will continue to play a role (Radhika, 2003a, p. 2).

We interpret this as a martyr role; for the sake of the best for AOL Time Warner, Steve Case resigned, but the audience was to know that he was disappointed and that he could have weathered the storm, had he only been given the chance. He would still help out the best he could by remaining in another position.

In the following statements made by two employees, we can sense that Middelhoff of Bertelsmann was pictured as someone who entered the journey but did not "come home" as a hero—and really had no fair chance to do so:

> He [Middelhoff] stepped on a lot of backs in the company to get where he is, and he is trying to change a culture that has more than 100 years of history to it (Radhika, 2003c, p. 2)

The Bertelsmann businesses are very autonomous but Middelhoff ran into opposition as he tried to force them together. A lot of empires had been built up and their masters did not want to be shifted Radhika, 2003c, p. 2).

Next, consider the following statement about Messier of Vivendi Universal. A Paris stock market analyst wrote that:

Messier [of Universal Vivendi] may have unloaded a lot of excess business, but he's still got ways to go. The strategy with the water business is to reinvest part of the expected profit into the communications side. At some point, however, you have to wonder if it's a good idea to be world leader, on one hand, and the key European player, on the other, in two very different sectors that have nothing to do with one another at the end of the day (Sarvani, 2003b, p. 5).

Here we see signs the portrayal of Messier as an orphan seeking adventures, entering upon risky undertakings. However, in a few sentences an image is also created of someone who wants to be a warrior using a doubtful strategy. The underlying message here is that Messier might not cope with the situation and lose the battle. This was confirmed when a journalist of *The Telegraph* noted that

Messier's stellar rise and catastrophic fall has grabbed headlines all over France and attracted other authors, most of whom agree he became a victim of his own arrogance and addiction to deal-making without thinking fully of the consequences (Sarvani, 2003b, p. 2).

The warrior was defeated and did not return as the hero. In fact, this goes for the whole executive team as well. An investor in Vivendi Universal confirmed the *fait à complit* and thereby the lost battle: "We have been wronged by Vivendi's former management; its board and its auditors and we now trust that the investigation will get to the bottom of the matter" (Sarvani, 2003a, p. 8).

By creating archetypes, the audience usually think of these archetypes as representing the "good" or the "bad" (Carr, 2002).

In order to stress his selflessness and martyrdom, Messier added to the conversation: "I hope the market will give my successor what it withheld from me, time to act in calm fashion" (Sarvani, 2003b, p. 8). The consequences of impression management in combination with the construction of archetypes were even more strongly reinforced in the following report:

While many critics believed that Messier was the victim of his own excessively ambitious plans, there were many who said that his fall was a simple case of ignoring the risk of overexposure. Some analysts claimed that his inclination towards the American style of management coupled with his views regarding the French way of running businesses had made the French media and political establishment turn against him, precipitating his downfall (Sarvani, 2003b, p. 2).

The magician is sometimes said to think of him or herself as the higher power (Tallman, 2003) and this was perhaps what Messier did think of himself, but if so, the above statement would definitely imply that he failed in his efforts.

Indeed, at times, a whole nation can be made into an archetype and a strategic leader cast as its representative:

> We have lately been seeing signs of the French becoming red-blooded, enthusiastic capitalists—creating their own opportunities rather than waiting for help from friends in government as in the past. Messier has been representative of that change (Paul Horen, European economist; Sarvani, 2003b, p. 4).

Whether present strategic leaders will be able to fulfill the role of the magicians of the media firms in focus here remains to be seen. However, in recent years there has been an increased acceptance of the view that visionary creation of extensive media product portfolios is necessary for the future of media firms and that astute, forward-looking leaders are needed for that task.

It needs to be understood that sometimes the impression that the strategic leader wants to convey to his or her public is designed to be congruent with the archetypes that are produced by that very same public. However, a usual course of event seems to be that the public first creates archetypes of future magicians and at the very first mistakes is tempted to turn this image into less appealing archetypes.

Implications of Impression Management

Why is impression management of interest and why do strategic leaders more or less consciously exhibit their own strategies in the open? For one, this chapter has illustrated that impression management, used as a behavioral and rhetorical device, seems to have a great impact on the course of events, especially in a strategic sense. Strategic leaders in top-level positions in companies with a broad and diverse public need strategies to build up the images of their companies. Moreover, it seems more or less impossible to avoid situations where strategies for acquisitive as well as protective impression management are needed. Strategic leaders therefore would benefit by becoming aware of the mechanisms of the phenomenon and processes involved in impression management.

Second, Sallot (2002) brings up impression management within public relations. She argues that when the audience perceives impression management as a conscious strategic move, the audience tends to regard this as manipulation and deceitful behavior, however altruistic or pro social the purpose may be. In her study she shows that those who are able to make use of good communication skills and professionalism can enhance trustworthiness. Therefore the strategic leader's PR team or lack of such a team is a crucial or missing link in how the public perceives the impression management efforts by the strategic leader.

Third, to be engaged in impression management is to be engaged in social interaction, and as illustrated in our case, this is sometimes a paradoxical interaction. This paradox makes the process even more dynamic and creates political tensions with uncertain strategic outcomes. Therefore, it is not only important to be aware of the general process of impression management but also of political factors that are working in such a process.

Fourth, impression management is also a process the individual level at which the strategic leader's ego is at stake, thus not only the company's reputation, image, and future development. Making impression management into an intrapersonal process opens up for analyses of psychodynamic processes where both verbal and nonverbal impression management is involved. Emotional processes are certainly part of these. Hidden agendas, known or unknown to the strategic leaders may also contribute to unpredictable strategic events and thereby strategic outcomes. Bringing in social-role theory might be one way forward, where it is of interest to examine how top executives' behavior is consistent with their roles as strategic leaders of huge media conglomerates (cf. Bolino & Turnley's (2003) discussion on how intimidation implications differ between the sexes).

Fifth, strategic leaders may have high self-esteem and a good deal of self-efficacy (Palmer, et al., 2001). The strategic leaders in the media sector that have been in focus here are all part of the upper echelons and it is reasonable to assume that they at the same time think positively of themselves as well as they attributing high competence to themselves. Therefore they are probably willing to take risks and work hard on their impression management tactics, not pursuing a play-it-safe-strategy, rather a high-risk-strategy (cf. Palmer, et al., 2001) where failure is one possible outcome. Viewing it this way, an intriguing question is whether the strategic leaders only play a role, and if so, whether they really want to pursue this role or are they only trying to meet with the expectations that top managers are assumed to create ways for change and to consolidate the organization (Mantere, 2003). Mantere argues that strategic leaders are expected to be champions and that the audience expects them all to have the same personality traits such as being prone to being innovative, persistent, and inclined to take risks, and to use various tactics to influence their audiences. In doing so, we argue that the strategic leaders are actively involved in a power as well as relational exchange play. And, as has been illustrated here, it is not always for the strategist to be capable of fulfilling his or her role in this sense—and not even "allowed" to do so. If so, then we are perhaps moving away from strategic outcomes that are considered to be optimal for the sake of the organization, rather in the best of one's own self interests.

Sixth, and finally, impression management is not an individual or inter-individual phenomenon alone. From the illustrations we can sense a paradoxical clash between the individual and organizational level. At the individual level we can see how strategic leaders' individual ways of thinking seem to stabilize over time and influence the strategic leaders through their careers. At the same time, when the strategic leader moves from one organization to the next, s/he is supposed to assimilate to the new culture and mirror the expectations of the new organization. The individual and organizational levels have to meet in order to avoid a clash between a new way of thinking for the organization and an established organizational culture with strong historical sediments (cf. Hellgren & Melin, 1993). Because this meeting is a conscious as well as unconscious process it can be a hurtful process and—as we have witnessed here—not always a successful one. By being more aware of such consequences of recruiting a new strategic leader, both the individual strategic leader and the organizational members can be more prepared for the possible course of strategic events.

CONCLUSIONS

In this chapter we have elaborated upon the role of strategic leadership within media firms with a focus on strategic leaders' ways of thinking as well as the official picture of strategic leadership in media itself. Furthermore, attempts have been made to point out some implications that strategic leadership may thrust upon top management as they guide the development of the companies, and their activities of guiding the development of the companies, creating visions, and assembling and improving portfolios.

Strategic leadership is a complex phenomenon including a set of activities that are consciously outlined by the strategist at the same time as it involves contextual conditions, organizational, socio-cognitive, and psychodynamic processes that cannot be mastered and/or foreseen. They all go hand in hand when strategy formation takes place. To make sense of what is happening and what is about to happen is sometimes a task out of hand for the strategic leader. The way from being a role-seeker to a possible role-player (see Mantere, 2003) is a thorny route and the sense-making gap might lie in the heart of the ambiguities we witness in the failures of top strategic leaders in the international media arena.

A main characteristic of the present situation in the media industry seems to be uncertainty. There are many driving forces (representing both threats and opportunities) that are intertwined and create complexity that makes it difficult for any strategic leader to cope in a rational and predetermined way. According to Sjöstrand (1997), strategic leaders at the upper echelons have a unique position because the position comes with access to networks, economic as well as human resources. This creates the ability to influence strategic choices. In this chapter we have seen that this can be both advantageous and an impediment to the strategic leader. Furthermore, as stressed in this chapter, the strategic leaders' background and personality (which would not change over time) are important when it comes to strategy formation (Melin, 1991).

This chapter has illustrated that not only impersonal calculations and rational long-term planning are parts of strategy formation and determinations about firms' product portfolios. Indeed, a range of personal and psychological intrinsic factors play a major role as well. Therefore, strategy formation is about multi-rationalities and being a strategic leader has two sides to it: the rational and the irrational approach (Sjöstrand, 1997). The traditionally labeled irrational side of strategic leadership is not always just that, however. Emotions, for example, can work as driving forces in strategic processes (Brundin, 2002). We may believe that we can foresee the course of events by identifying strategic leaders' ways of thinking and strategic patterns. At the end of the day, however, we can only make predictions regarding strategic actions that are about to happen but not about the eventual strategic outcome themselves.

REFERENCES

Alvesson, M. & Kärreman, D. (2001). Making newsmakers: Conversational identity at work. *Organization Studies*, 22(1), 59–89.

Avolio, B. J. (1999). *Full leadership development: Building the vital forces in organizations*. Thousand Oaks, CA: Sage.

Barnard, C. (1938). *The functions of the executive*. Boston: Harvard University Press.

Bass, B. M. & Avolio, B. J. (1994). *Improving organizational effectiveness through transformational leadership.* Thousand Oaks, CA: Sage.

Baumeister, R. F. & Hutton, R. F. (1987). Self-presentation theory: Self-construction and audience pleasing. In B. Mullen. and G. R. Goethals (Eds.), *Theories of Group Behavior* (pp. 71-87). New York: Springer Verlag.

Bolino, M. & Turnley, W. H. (2003). Counternormative impression management, likeability, and performance ratings: the use of intimidation in an organizational setting. In *Wiley InterScience* (www.interscience.wiley.com) DOI:10.1002/job.185.

Broadcasting & Cable Yearbook, 2002-2003 (2003). New Providence, NJ: R.R. Bowker.

Brundin, E. (2002). *Emotions in motion. The strategic leader in a radical change process.* JIBS Dissertation Series No. 12. Jönköping: Jönköping University, Sweden.

Cady, S.H. & Fandt, P.M. (2001). Managing impressions with information. A field study of organizational realities. *The Journal of Applied Behavioral Science, 37*(2), 180–204.

Campbell, J. (1968). *The hero with a thousand faces* (Second edition). Princeton, NJ: Princeton University Press.

Carr, A. (2002). Jung, archetypes and mirroring in organizational change management: Lessons from a longitudinal case study. *Journal of Organizational Change Management, 15*(5), 477–489.

Crant, J. M. & Bateman, T. S. (1993). Assignment of credit and blame for performance outcomes. *Academy of Management Journal, 36*, 7–27.

Dingle, D. T. & Hughes, A. (2002). A time for bold leadership. *Black Enterprise, 32*(7), 76–81.

Doz, Y. & Prahalad, C. K. (1987). A process model of strategic redirection in large complex firms: The case of multinational corporations. In A. Pettigrew (Ed.), *The management of strategic change* (pp. 63-83). Oxford, UK: Basil Blackwell.

Ericson, T., Melander, A. & Melin, L. (2001). The role of the strategist. In H. Volberda and T. Elfring (Eds.), *Rethinking strategy* (pp. 57-68). London: Sage Publications.

Gardner, W. L. & Avolio, B. J. (1998). The charismatic relationship: A dramaturgical perspective. *Academy of Management Review, 23*, 32–58.

Giacalone,, R. A. & Rosenfeld P. (1984). The effect of perceived planning and propriety on the effectiveness of leadership accounts. *Social Behavior and Personality*, 12, 217–224.

Giacalone, R. A. & Rosenfeld, P. (Eds.). (1989). *Impression management in the organization.* Hillsdale, NJ: Lawrence Erlbaum Associates.

Goffman, E. (1959). *The presentation of self in everyday life.* Garden City, NY: Doubleday Anchor.

Grinyer, P., Mayes, D. & McKiernan, P. (1988). *Sharpbenders: The secret of unleashing corporate potential.* Oxford: Blackwell.

Hall, A. (2003). *Strategizing in the context of genuine relations: An interpretative study of strategy formation in the family business.* JIBS dissertation series No. 18. Jönköping, Sweden: Jönköping International Business School.

Hellgren, B. & Melin, L. (1993). The role of strategists ways-of-thinking in strategic change processes. In J. Hendry and G. Johnson. (Eds.), *Strategic thinking, leadership and the management of change* (pp. 47-68). Chichester, UK: John Wiley and Sons Ltd.

Hellgren, B., Melin, L. & Pettersson, A. (1993). Structure and change: The industrial field approach. *Advances in International Marketing*, 5, 87–106.

Hewitt, J. & Stokes, R. (1975). Disclaimers. *American Sociological Review*, 40, 1–11.

Holmberg, I. & Åkerblom, S. (2001). The production of outstanding leadership– an analysis of leadership images in the Swedish media. *Scandinavian Journal of Management, 17*, 67–85.

James, W. (1890/1998). *The principles of psychology*. New York: Henry Holt and Co.

Johnson, G., Melin, L. & Whittington, R. (Eds.). (2003). Micro strategy and strategising: Towards an activity-based view. *Journal of Management Studies, 40*(1), 3-22.

Kotter, J.P. (1990). *A force for change. Why transformation efforts fail*. New York: The Free Press.

Kotter, J.P. (1996). *Leading change*. Boston: Harvard Business School Press.

Küng, L. (2003). What makes media firms tick? Exploring the underlying drivers for firm performance. In Picard, R.G. (ed.), *Strategic responses to media market changes*. Jönköping: JIBS Research Reports No. 2004–2. Media Management and Transformation Centre, Jönköping International Business School.

Leary, M.R. & Kowalski, R.M. (1990). Impression management: A literature review and two component model. *Psychological Bulletin, 107*, 34–47.

Machiavelli, N. (1958). *Fursten*. Stockholm: Natur och Kultur.

Maccoby, M. (1976). *The gamesman*. New York: Simon and Schuster.

Maccoby, M. (1981). *Ledaren*. Malmö, Sweden: Liber Förlag.

Mantere, S. (2003, July). Champions of the strategy process. A structuration viewpoint. Paper presented at the 19th EGOS–European Group for Organization Studies Colloquium. Copenhagen, Denmark.

Markides, C. C. & Williamson, P. J. (1996). Corporate diversification and organizational structure: A resource-based view. *Academy of Management Journal, 39*(2), 340–367.

McCarthy, D. (2000). Interview with Henry Mintzberg: View from the top: Henry Mintzberg on strategy and management. *The Academy of Management Executive, 14*(3), 31-42.

Melin L., Ericson T. & Müllern, T. (1999) *Organizing is strategizing. Innovative forms of organizing means continuous strategizing.* Paper presented as part of the INNFORM.

Melin, L. (1991). Omorientering och strategiska synsätt. In G. Arvidsson and R. Lind (Eds.), *Ledning av företag och förvaltningar* (pp. 168-193). Stockholm: SNS.

Mintzberg. H. (1988). Opening up the definition of strategy. In J. B. Quinn, H. Mintzberg, and J. M. Robert (Eds.), *The strategy process: concepts, contexts, and cases* (pp. 13-20). Englewood Cliffs, NJ: Prentice Hall.

Müllern, T. & Stein, J. (1999). *Övertygandets ledarskap. Om retorik vid strategiska förändringar.* Lund, Sweden: Studentlitteratur.

Northouse, P. G. (2004). *Leadership. Theory and practice* (3rd ed.). Thousand Oaks: Sage Publications.

Palmer, R. J., Welker, R. B., Campbell, T. L. & Magner, N. R. (2001). Examining the impression management orientation of managers. *Journal of Managerial Psychology, 16*(1), 35-45.

Pearson, C.S. (1991). *Awakening the heroes within. Twelve archetypes to help us find ourselves and transform our world.* San Francisco: Harper Collins Publishers.

Pettigrew, A. (1973). *The politics of organizational decision-making.* London: Tavistock.

Picard, R. G. (2003). Environmental and market changes driving strategic planning in media firms. In R. G. Picard (Ed.), *Strategic responses to media market changes.* Jönköping: JIBS Research Reports No. 2004–2. Media Management and Transformation Centre, Jönköping International Business School.

Pralahad, C. K. & Hamel, G. (1990). The core competence of the corporation. *Harvard Business Review*, May-June, 79–91.

Radhika, A. N. (2003a). *AOL Time Warner: A merger gone wrong?* ICFAI Center for Management Research (ISMR), Hyderabad, India. ECCH Collection.

Radhika, A. N. (2003b). *Steve Case: The story of AOL's architect.* ICFAI Center for Management Research (ISMR), Hyderabad, India. ECCH Collection.

Radhika, A.N. (2003c). *Bertelsmann: Before, during and after Middelhoff.* ICFAI Center for Management Research (ISMR), Hyderabad, India. ECCH Collection.

Risberg, A. (1999). *Crossing the Baltic Sea in the name of the market. A post-colonial approach to the start-up of an Estonian newspaper.* Working paper. Department of Intercultural Communication and Management. Copenhagen Business School. Denmark.

Risberg, A., Tienari, J. & Vaara, E. (2003). Making sense of a transnational merger: Media texts and the (re)construction of power relations. *Culture and Organization, 9*(2), 121–137.

Rosenfeld, P., Giacalone, R.A. & Riordan, C.A. (1995). *Impression management in organizations. Theory, measurement, practice.* London: Routledge.

Sallot, L. M. (2002). What the public thinks about public relations: An impression management experiment. *Journalism and Mass Communication Quarterly, 79*(1), 150–171.

Samuelson, B. A., Galbraith, C. S. & McGuire, J. W. (1985). Organizational performance and top-management turnover. *Organizational Studies, 6,* 275–291.

Sánchez-Tabernero, A. (2003) The future of media companies: Strategies for an unpredictable world. In Robert G. Picard (ed.), *Strategic responses to media market changes.* Jönköping: JIBS Research Reports No. 2004–2. Media Management and Transformation Centre, Jönköping International Business School.

Sarvani, V. (2003a). *Vivendi Universal: In a strategic flux.* ICFAI Center for Management Research (ISMR), Hyderabad, India. ECCH Collection.

Sarvani, V. (2003b). *The rise and fall of Vivendi Universal's Jean Marie Messier.* ICFAI Center for Management Research (ISMR), Hyderabad, India. ECCH Collection.

Schlenker, B. R. (1980). *Impression management: The self-concept, social identity, and interpersonal relations.* Monterey, CA: Brooks Cole.

Scott, M. B. & Lyman, S. M. (1968). Accounts. *American Sociological Review. 33*, 46–62.

Sjöstrand, S.-E. (1997). *The two faces of management. The Janus factor.* UK: International Thomson Business Press.

Sjöstrand, S-E., Sandberg, J. & Tyrstrup, M. (Eds.) (2000). *Invisible management.* London: Thomson Business Press.

Sveningsson, S. (1999). *Strategisk förändring, makt och kunskap. Om disciplinering och motstånd i tidiningsföretag.* Dissertation. Lund Studies in Economics and Management 48. The Institute of Economic Research. Lund, Sweden: Lund University Press.

Tallman, B. (2003). The organization leader as king, warrior, magician and lover: How Jungian archetypes affect the way men lead organizations. *Organization Development Journal, 21*(3), 19–30.

Taylor, C. R. & Wheatley-Lovoy, C. (1998). Leadership: Lessons from the Magic Kingdom. *Training and Development, 52*(7), 22–24.

Tetlock, P. E. & Manstead, A. S. R. (1985). Impression management versus itrapsychic explanations in social psychology: A useful dichotomy? *Psychological Review, 92,* 59–77.

Tushman, M. L., Newman, W. H. & Romanelli, E. (1986). Convergence and upheaval: Managing the unsteady pace of organizational evolution. *California Management Review, 29*(1), 29–44.

Virany, B., Tushman, M. L. & Romanelli, E. (1992). Executive succession and organization outcomes in turbulent environments: An organization learning approach. *Organization Science, 3,* 72–91.

Westerberg, M. (1998). *Managing in turbulence.* Doctoral thesis. Luleå: University of Technology.

Yukl, G. (2002). *Leadership in organizations.* Fifth edition. Upper Saddle River, NJ: Prentice-Hall.

5

Clustering Media Operations: Rationales and Managerial Challenges

Hugh J. Martin
University of Georgia

As audiences fragment, and competitive pressures increase, managers in local media markets might consider bolstering their position by acquiring direct competitors. This strategy may allow media firms to extend their geographic reach, and their ability to reach different segments of the audience. Newspaper and broadcast firms in the United States have engaged in widespread clustering of similar properties within markets, suggesting this portfolio strategy has significant economic benefits (Asher, 1999; Bass, 1999; Brister, 2000; A decade of deals, 2000; Ekelund Jr., Ford & Koutsky, 2000; Martin, 2003b; Parsons, 2003).

Clustering is a form of horizontal integration because it merges firms in the same line of business that also operate in the same market. Clustering a firm's operations offers two potential advantages. First, the firm may lower costs by extending existing economies across multiple business units. Second, the firm may reduce or deter competition, allowing it to increase its prices, its market share, or both.

However, realizing the benefits from this limited form of diversification requires an informed understanding of potential complications. Clustering may appeal to managers hoping to extend core competencies to a newly acquired firm. Research suggests the importance of understanding the economic principles that come into play before a decision to create a portfolio cluster is made. Horizontal integration may also allow firms to monopolize a market, attracting attention from regulators. This chapter analyzes these issues in light of the concerns that managers might bring to the creation and operation of media clusters.

CLUSTERS AS PORTFOLIOS

Horizontal integration occurs when firms making the same product merge (Barney, 1997; Scherer & Ross, 1990). A cluster of media firms exists when the horizontal acquisition involves firms that might otherwise compete because they operate in the same or in adjacent markets (Martin, 2001). Horizontal integration may create new opportunities to reduce costs or deter competition (Barney, 1997; Scherer & Ross, 1990), allowing firms to stabilize or increase earnings. Horizontal integration is a form of "limited diversification" (Barney, 1997, p. 357).

Portfolio theory was developed to describe optimal diversification strategies in financial markets. Subsequent modifications suggest it provides a useful perspective for discussing media clusters. A portfolio is a mix of "assets that investors hold to maximize their wealth" (Litman, Shrikhande & Ahn, 2000, p. 57). Portfolios allow investors to maximize returns for a given level of risk. A well-designed portfolio of diverse assets gives investors a hedge against a broad set of contingencies (Litman, et al., 2000).

Portfolio theory describes how to structure financial investments to maximize returns for a given level of risk (Devinney & Stewart, 1988; Leong & Lim, 1991; Litman, et al., 2000). The theory was adapted to describe product investments made by individual firms (Devinney & Stewart, 1988; Leong & Lim, 1991). Portfolio theory has also been used to analyze television programming (Litman, et al., 2000). Leona Achtenhagen discusses some criticisms of portfolio adaptations in Chapter 3 of this book. Much of that criticism focuses on acquisitions involving firms in the same line of business. However, portfolio theory still offers useful insight into how managers can think about the potential advantages, and disadvantages, of clustering.

There are two important dimensions to consider. The first dimension is the expected return from an investment. Expected return is a function of the probability of possible outcomes, such as profit or loss, from investing in an asset (Litman, et al., 2000). Expected return from a portfolio is a weighted average of the expected returns from each asset in the portfolio.

The second dimension is risk. There are two kinds of risk. Variance in returns from an individual asset represents "idiosyncratic risk" (Litman, et al., 2000, p. 58). An asset's history of returns can be used to quantify and estimate anticipated idiosyncratic risk.[5] Markets also expose investors to "systematic risk" (Litman, et al., 2000, p. 59). Events in the market can influence returns

---

[5] Mathematically, idiosyncratic risk is the expectation of squared differences from the mean expected outcome (Litman, et al., 2000, pp. 58-59). If X_i is an outcome, and $E(X)$ is the mean expected outcome, then risk = $E[(X_i - E(X))^2]$.

from individual assets. Therefore, systematic risk is measured as the covariance between market events and returns from an asset.

Portfolios are intended "to diversify away some of the systematic risk" (Litman, et al., 2000, p. 59). This is possible only if the portfolio correctly balances assets that respond differently to market events. Losses from some assets can then be offset by earnings from other assets, resulting in positive earnings over time (Litman, et al., 2000).

An investor's optimal mix of assets is determined by his or her individual tolerance for risk. The optimum is the point where returns cannot be increased without increasing risk beyond the investor's tolerance (Litman, et al., 2000). At this optimum, risk cannot be reduced without reducing returns.

An analysis of television network programming used portfolio theory to examine how networks maximize audiences to attract advertising revenue. Litman et al. (2000) argued that programs are assets, and the anticipated size of each program's audience represents expected returns. Ratings from previous seasons provide an estimate of likely audience size for the next season. This makes existing programs less risky than new programs. Programming portfolios on three major broadcast networks in the United States were designed to minimize the risk of losing audience, not to maximize ad revenue (Litman, et al., 2000).

Mass Media Portfolios

This study (Litman, et al., 2000) suggests that portfolio theory can be extended to other forms of mass media. All firms that depend on advertising revenue must maximize audiences that advertisers want to reach (Shaver, 1995). Firms can differentiate their content to increase their audience (Lacy, 1992; Litman, 1992; Litman & Bridges, 1986). Advertisers target segments of the audience where there are potential consumers for the advertisers' products (Shaver, 1995). This suggests that media firms can diversify content to attract a broad audience, balancing returns from individual advertisers over time.

However, portfolio models have important limitations when they are applied to the horizontal integration of media firms. Litman, et al. (2000) point out that portfolio models describe investments in an unlimited number of stocks. Media firms do not usually select content from an unlimited range of choices. Firms are also constrained by their line of business, by their format, and by the demands of their audience and advertisers.

Some forms of clustering, such as the acquisition of radio stations with differing formats, may result in content diversification within a market. But acquisitions are strategic decisions because they require an irreversible commitment of capital (Rumelt, Schendel & Teece, 1991). This is also quite different from the tactical adjustments to diversification contemplated by portfolio theory.

Still, scholars (Devinney & Stewart, 1988; Leong & Lim, 1991) have developed portfolio models that apply to capital investments that change a firm's mix of products. Devinney and Stewart (1988) argue that managers have more control of variables affecting risk and return than do investors in financial markets. For example, managers can apply specific knowledge about a firm and its products when they change the mix of products (Devinney & Stewart, 1988). These same skills have little use outside the firm. If the profit from one set of products is a function of the amount invested in another set of products, portfolio theory can help managers decide how to allocate a firm's resources (Devinney & Stewart, 1988). Media managers may find clustering attractive precisely because it allows them to create a mix of content that attracts audiences and advertisers across multiple business units.

Leong and Lim (1991), however, argue the differences between financial and product portfolios expose firms to "enormous costs" if capital allocations are misdirected (p. 184). A firm's decision to substantially increase production in an oligopolistic industry can influence that firm's market share and profits (Leong & Lim, 1991). The relationship between different product lines may also be altered by changes in each product's stage of growth. Leong and Lim (1991) found that portfolio models for product investment decisions must account for changes over time, constraints on a manager's ability to change a product mix, and the financial requirements for making and sustaining an investment.

Media managers should therefore recognize that opportunities to apply skills across business units do not guarantee the success of a cluster. The acquisition of a competing firm will change the acquiring firm's position in the market. Changes in demand in different segments of the market—segments not previously controlled by the acquiring firm—will also influence the firm's growth and profitability. These variables may interact in unforeseen ways, with unforeseen consequences. The firm will require financial resources sufficient to meet these challenges.

Reducing Risk

An intuitive analysis suggests that creation of a cluster, which allows one firm to access audience segments previously served by competitors, might reduce the systematic risk associated with operating in a particular market. Potential increases in market power from horizontal integration are, after all, the reason some countries regulate such mergers. Clustering might therefore reduce the negative covariance associated with the presence of competition.

Managers might also expect reductions in idiosyncratic risk associated with the operation of their firm because the cluster allows them to apply specialized skills across multiple business units. Recall that expected returns are determined by an asset's history of performance in response to changing market conditions. There is some degree of variance in the performance of all assets, and the mean variance in performance over time defines expected returns.

Variance in performance is affected by a firm's fixed or capital costs, by a firm's variable or operating costs, and by the ability of managers to contain those costs. Idiosyncratic risk at media firms will also be affected by the firm's ability to attract advertising and subscription revenue. This, in turn, will depend on the mix of content used to attract an audience, and the prices that advertisers and audiences must pay. If clustering provides managers with opportunities to reduce variance in earnings associated with capital costs, operating costs, content, or prices, the strategy might be effective.

A study of some Fortune 500 companies, however, raises questions about clustering's effects on both kinds of risk. Lubatkin and Chatterjee (1994) studied stockholder returns over 12 years. They concluded that diversification can reduce both kinds of risk, but not when a firm diversifies within a single line of business. Firms that performed best at risk reduction diversified into related businesses so "that all of its (sic) eggs are in similar baskets—not in the same baskets or in different baskets" (Lubatkin & Chatterjee, 1994, p. 130).

Other studies focused on how advantages are created by the merger of related business. Robins and Wiersema (1995) argued that the key is exploiting opportunities across business units, lowering costs and improving customer service to increase the firm's stock of internal strategic assets. Brush (1996) studied horizontal mergers in manufacturing industries that allowed firms to sell buyers complimentary products, share distribution, or promote a common image across business units. Brush concluded that such synergies were positively associated with increases in market share.

Markides and Williamson (1996) argued that merely being in the same industry will not make merged firms more profitable. Too much variance in product marketing, product distribution, or the frequency of consumer purchases, will erode advantages from mergers. This (Markides & Williamson, 1996) was one of several studies that found evidence that businesses must adopt specific internal structures before they can realize the advantages from mergers of related firms.

The other industry studies suggest that firms that adopt clustering as their sole diversification strategy may realize fewer benefits than firms with broader strategies. For example, Picard and Rimmer (1999) described newspaper companies diversifying into other lines of business to provide a hedge against cyclical economic changes. Newspapers are particularly sensitive to economic changes because of their dependence on retail advertising sales (Picard & Rimmer, 1999). Companies that diversified into other media, reducing dependence on retail advertising, suffered less from a recession (Picard & Rimmer, 1999). This suggests managers might consider combining clustering with broader, but related acquisitions.

If a firm adopts clustering as its dominant strategy, managers should not expect the benefits available to rivals with a more flexible mix of diverse assets. However, properly managed clusters may represent an alternative form of diversification with similar, but limited, benefits.

IMPORTANCE OF MANAGERS' KNOWLEDGE

Even if clustering is part of a larger strategy, managers face the complexities of costs and customers in the markets in which the cluster operates. Leong and Lim (1991) warn of high informational demands (p. 190) for managers trying to determine an optimal product mix. Demands for information will be even higher in media clusters if interdependencies between audiences and advertisers vary within and across properties.

However, studies in a range of industries suggest that managers can coordinate the operations of multiple business units if they understand the limits beyond which coordination cannot succeed (Govindarajan & Fisher, 1990; Hill, Hitt & Hoskisson, 1992; Hill & Hoskisson, 1987). These limits may be reached when uncertainty about how to coordinate operations exceeds the manager's knowledge. Uncertainty increases as relationships between the activities of business units decrease. In other words, coordination is easier if a firm's lines of business are similar.

This argument is consistent with studies showing that firms with related lines of business are more profitable than firms pursuing unrelated diversification (Brush, 1996; Litman & Sochay, 1994; Lubatkin & Chatterjee, 1994; Markides & Williamson, 1994; Robins & Wiersema, 1995). Such studies are the basis for arguments that businesses can increase the probability of success by focusing on their core competencies.

For example, Litman and Sochay (1994) studied mergers that created large, diversified mass media conglomerates. Managers had difficulty reducing costs after these mergers (Litman & Sochay, 1994). This was partly because conglomerates had a diverse set of business units that duplicated, instead of sharing, resources. Media conglomerates also tended to diversify and decentralize operations at the expense of focusing on a single core business (Litman & Sochay, 1994).

Developments in media markets throughout the United States are consistent with arguments that diversification is more likely to succeed if lines of businesses are similar. Clustering is an increasingly important strategy for newspaper companies, radio broadcasting companies, and cable television companies (Brister, 2000; A decade of deals, 2000; Ekelund Jr. et al., 2000; Lacy & Simon, 1997; Martin, 2003b; Parsons, 2003).

Managers of media companies argue that clustering reduces costs by consolidating operations (Bass, 1999; Ekelund Jr., et al., 2000; Kuhl, 2000). A single press can produce content for more than one newspaper. One cable headend can do the same for multiple cable systems. Radio stations can share production facilities. Other benefits include sharing the work of various employees. Administrative costs can be shared across different business units. Advertisers may benefit from regional placement of ads at lower costs. In radio markets, a single company with a cluster of stations can offer programming in multiple formats, serving a variety of audiences and attracting more advertising (Hull, Greco & Martin, 2000). All of these are examples of how clusters might reduce variance in expected earnings.

Studies also show that clustering in newspaper markets is associated with reductions in competition and higher prices (Fu, 2000; Lacy & Simon, 1997; Martin, 2001, 2003b).[6] These are examples of how clustering might reduce systematic risk.

A survey (Loomis & Albarran, 2004) examined internal operations at clustered radio stations in the United States. Results showed the general managers spent 60% of their time on financial responsibilities, such as budgeting and sales. Most of the remaining time was devoted to dealing with other people at different levels of the company (Loomis & Albarran, 2004). General managers emphasized the importance of having competent department heads to ensure a cluster's success. They also reported spending more time at work than ever before (Loomis & Albarran, 2004). These findings are consistent with efforts to reduce idiosyncratic risk.

However, the study argued that the radio industry missed an opportunity by approaching "consolidation primarily as an opportunity to cut costs" (Loomis & Albarran, 2004, p. 65). Clustered stations could have restructured internal operations to flatten hierarchies. Teams could have been created to efficiently coordinate functions such as marketing the stations or creating programming across each cluster, the authors argued. The survey found little evidence of such restructuring (Loomis & Albarran, 2004). For example, programming decisions were still made at the corporate level, not by employees in a particular market.

---

[6] Reductions in competition from clustering may also reduce the number of independent media voices in a market.

These arguments are consistent with more general examinations of interactions between a firm's organization and its diversification strategy. Diversification can only succeed if a firm puts "organizational structures in place that allow it to share its existing strategic assets and transfer the competencies to build new ones between divisions in an efficient manner" (Markides & Williamson, 1996, p. 347). Markides and Williamson (1996) found that businesses with highly skilled work forces do best if they give individual business units autonomy to make operating decisions while the central office focuses on transferring knowledge between units.

Even if managers are competent, and organizational structures are designed to maximize potential advantages, clusters may not succeed. There are broader economic principles that come into play. Economists distinguish horizontal mergers that arise from normal business motives, such as attempts to reduce cost, from mergers intended to reduce competition and increase profits (Scherer & Ross, 1990). Managers of clustered firms must understand the implications and possible consequences of each.

ACHIEVING EFFICIENCIES IN PORTFOLIO CLUSTERS

A cluster is created when two or more potential competitors in the same or adjacent media markets merge. However, a merger alone is not sufficient to increase profits. Managers must efficiently coordinate the firm's post-merger activities to take advantage of the potential for reducing costs (Markides & Williamson, 1996).

When mergers involve firms of unequal size, the larger firm may enjoy lower capital costs. Such mergers can allow smaller firms to make otherwise uneconomical capital investments in new plants or equipment (Scherer & Ross, 1990). However, managers considering such investments must first decide if the anticipated returns will be equal to or greater than the cost of the merger. If the answer is yes, the firms might form a cluster that provides the smaller firm new equipment that improves its operations and profit margins.

Taking Advantage of Scale Economies

Horizontal mergers can also create or expand economies of scale. Economies of scale exist when a firm's long-run average costs decline as more goods are produced (Scherer & Ross, 1990). Economies of scope are a special subset of scale economies. When the cost of separately producing at least two goods is higher than the cost of producing those goods together, there are economies of scope (Teece, 1980).

Four kinds of scale economies might be associated with clusters. First are product-specific economies, which arise from the volume of production for a single product (Scherer & Ross, 1990). These economies are available if specialized production processes require substantial preparation before a production run begins. When firms pay substantial costs to set up production, average production costs decline as production increases. Product-specific economies of scale are also available when workers become more efficient as they learn more about how to perform specialized tasks.

Product-specific economies are available to media firms if the production of news or entertainment requires substantial initial costs for equipment and labor. For example, newspapers (Lacy & Simon, 1993) may enjoy economies if the costs of putting a single truck in service are spread across increasing numbers of newspapers delivered by that truck. Economies also exist for labor costs when a carrier delivers increasing numbers of newspapers on the same block. However, the economies will dissipate if circulation is less concentrated, and the truck and carrier must cover increasing distances to deliver the papers (Lacy & Simon, 1993).

Second is scale economies associated with the total output of an entire production plant (Scherer & Ross, 1990). Economies may be available if output increases with the size of equipment used by the plant. However, economies will only be available if costs of acquiring and operating the larger equipment are proportional. In other words, economies vanish if the ratio of cost to production capacity increases with size. Newspapers might realize plant-level economies of scale if they can expand presses and output without a disproportional increase in associated costs. The same might be true for broadcasters or cable companies if they can expand production capacity without disproportionate increases in costs.

Third are economies of scope. These result from interactions between the first two kinds of scale economies. This is because the cost of producing individual products is affected by the volume of production, and by the size of the production plant (Scherer & Ross, 1990). If a single plant does not produce enough volume to realize all available scale economies, then producing more than one product may result in economies of scope.

For instance, if a larger press run would not significantly increase overhead and other costs, economies of scope would be available. More than one newspaper could be printed on the same press. There might be similar economies available if broadcasters can distribute programming and advertising to multiple cable systems, or to multiple stations in a single market, without significantly increasing the costs associated with production facilities.

Fourth are scale economies associated with the operation of multiple plants. Firms might reduce average production costs if different parts of the production process are located in different plants (Scherer & Ross, 1990). Media companies might take advantage of multiplant economies by centralizing administrative functions such as payroll processing instead of having each unit perform these separately.

Requirements for Expanding Economies

Managers should be aware that creating scale economies is often easier said than done. Studies of mergers in a range of industries provide weak evidence that postmerger profits increase, even when there is specific intent to create economies of scale (Krishnan & Park, 2002; Litman & Sochay, 1994; Scherer & Ross, 1990; St. John & Harrison, 1999). Profits actually decrease in many cases (Scherer & Ross, 1990). Even horizontal mergers can fail to increase efficiency. In some cases, smaller firms become less efficient after they merge with larger firms.

This is not to say there are no economies available to media firms creating clusters. Empirical studies since Rosse (1967) have found evidence that newspapers enjoy scale economies. These include what appear to be plant-level economies associated with size (Blankenburg, 1989; Ferguson, 1983), economies of scope from producing news and circulation at the same plant (Dertouzos & Trautman, 1990), and possible economies associated with increases in circulation (Thompson, 1988). Martin (2003a) found higher workloads for news staffs at clustered newspapers when compared with non-clustered papers.

In the radio industry, clusters allow multiple stations to share a general manager and other personnel involved in production, programming, and clerical work (Ekelund Jr., et al., 2000; Loomis & Albarran, 2004). Ekelund Jr. et al. (2000) also found indirect evidence of efficiencies from bulk purchasing across stations, sharing operating facilities, and combining advertising and promotional expenses.

Many cable television companies began consolidating operations in particular regions of the United States during the 1990s (Parsons, 2003). This enabled them to create clusters intended to create economies in marketing, sales, personnel, and new distribution technologies (Parsons, 2003). However, this study did not examine whether new efficiencies were actually created.

Managers must understand why there are substantial risks that clusters might fail. For example, an acquiring firm may take possession of inefficient production facilities (Scherer & Ross, 1990). The creation of economies will then require the firm to take the costly step of replacing previously separate production facilities with new plants.

Media managers must be prepared to quickly make such replacements when they acquire capital equipment that has a limited capacity, or is obsolete. For example, a cluster of newspapers might require a new printing press. A cable television cluster might require new production facilities.

Managers should also be aware that efforts to create efficiencies can backfire. A merger study (Krishnan & Park, 2002) suggests that managers should be particularly careful about reducing the work force in newly created clusters.

Krishnan and Park (2002) examined 60 mergers, including 42 in which the work force was reduced. Reductions in the work force at the acquired firm, the acquiring firm, and the consolidated firm, all negatively affected postmerger profitability. These results challenge "the notion that consolidation of the work force in the aftermath of an acquisition can result in benefits for the organization" (Krishnan & Park, 2002, p. 290).

Krishnan and Park (2002) suggested that acquisitions may fail in part because workers are fired without regard for the skills the fired employees had. Reducing the work force can also increase internal stress, making post-merger integration harder while prompting valuable employees to leave on their own. Krishnan and Park (2002) did not argue that work force reductions should never be made, but they did warn managers to carefully consider such reductions first.

Two studies of media clusters have raised questions about work force size. Martin (2003a) found work loads at smaller clustered newspapers that were high enough to raise questions about whether their staffs were overtaxed. Loomis and Albarran (2004) found that managers of clustered radio stations worked longer hours than ever before.

Evidence on Efficiencies

Much of the evidence on efforts to lower costs in media clusters is anecdotal. For example, newspaper companies that operate clusters have reported printing more than one newspaper on a central press, or consolidating the production of news or advertising (Asher, 1999; Bass, 1999). Administrative functions for multiple newspapers have been consolidated, and companies also offer regional ad placement across clustered papers.

Clear Channel Communications reports its clusters of radio stations eliminate duplication in operating and overhead costs (Clear Channel Communications, 2002). The company owns stations in markets throughout the United States, and reports that clustering increases the diversity of programming formats in individual markets. This allows advertisers to efficiently reach a variety of listeners (Clear Channel Communications, 2002).[7]

---

[7] The report states that Clear Channel, which also owns outdoor advertising, television stations, and live entertainment production companies, regards its ability to offer advertisers diverse platforms in a single market as a strength (Clear Channel Communications, 2002).

Managers of cable television companies have stated that one long-term goal of clustering is to consolidate headends so costs can be reduced and new economies created (Kuhl, 2000).

There are few systematic studies of how media clusters affect costs. Ekelund Jr., et al (2000) looked for evidence that radio station buyers expected post-merger efficiencies from the creation of clusters. Buyers would pay more if this is the case, because a station's sales price "reflects all available information about its future profitability" (Ekelund Jr., et al., 2000, p. 167). An analysis of 549 radio sales in 1995 and 1996 showed prices increased 5% for each additional station in an average cluster. Prices increased just .07% for each additional radio station when a firm sold properties scattered throughout the United States.[8] Buyers anticipated higher earnings from clustered stations than from group-owned stations in separate markets.

Martin (2003a) surveyed United States newspapers about efforts to share resources and create efficiencies at clustered papers. The study compared responses from executives at clustered dailies with a random sample of nonclustered newspapers. Clustered newspapers reported sharing newsgathering resources, production resources, and administrative resources significantly more often than nonclustered newspapers (Martin, 2003a). The study also found higher daily workloads, equivalent to about two additional eight-inch stories per staff member, at clustered papers (Martin, 2003a).

These studies suggest clustering offers opportunities to create new efficiencies. However, neither study directly examined evidence showing that efficiencies translate into higher earnings.

CLUSTERING AND COMPETITION

Managers should also consider how clusters affect competition. For example, newspaper studies in the United States (Lacy & Simon, 1997; Martin, 2003b) showed that clustering reduces circulation competition, raising questions about potential violations of antitrust rules. Regulations vary from industry to industry and country to country, but managers should consult relevant rules before a cluster is formed. Barney (1997) reported horizontal integration is forbidden or controlled in most developed economies because of concern about the creation of monopoly power.

Newspaper clusters in the United States might be regulated under federal or state antitrust statutes. Federal guidelines (U.S. Department of Justice & Federal

---

[8] The average cluster in the study included 3.6 radio stations. The average national group included 21.8 stations (Ekelund Jr. et al., 2000).

Trade Commission, 1992) for determining whether horizontal mergers violate the law ask if a hypothetical monopolist in a horizontally integrated market can impose a "small but significant and nontransitory" increase in price. This is generally defined as a price increase of 5% lasting for the foreseeable future (U.S. Department of Justice & Federal Trade Commission, 1992). The guidelines require consideration of variables such as consumer reaction to price increases, and the creation of efficiencies necessary to keep a firm in business, before any action is taken. Lacy and Simon (1997) reported a federal challenge to the creation of a newspaper cluster in 1995. However, such actions are unusual.

The United States regulates broadcasting under a separate set of rules that date to the Federal Communications Act of 1934 (Hull et al., 2000). The Federal Communications Commission began relaxing restrictions on the number of broadcast outlets owed by a single company in the 1980s. This process culminated in the Telecommunications Act of 1996, which was passed by the United States Congress (Hull, et al., 2000). Current rules allow one company to acquire up to eight radio stations in a market with 45 or more stations. In markets with 30 to 44 stations, a company can own seven stations; in markets with 15 to 29 stations, a company can own six stations; and in markets with 14 or fewer stations, a company can own five (Hull et al., 2000). Changes in ownership restrictions allowed companies like Clear Channel to adopt clustering as a strategy.

Ekelund Jr., et al (2000) examined the possibility that firms pay higher prices for clustered stations because they anticipate colluding on prices in more concentrated markets. Support for this argument was weak. The authors concluded the price increases primarily reflected anticipated efficiencies available to larger firms (Ekelund Jr., et al., 2000).

The Federal Communications Commission also governs cable television ownership. However, federal ownership restrictions do not speak directly to local markets, where cable franchises are controlled by local governments. Regulations instead limit horizontal acquisitions by cable companies based on their share of the national market (U.S. Federal Communications Commission, 2000). For example, rules state that a single company may not control more than 30 percent of subscribers to cable, direct broadcast satellite, and other multi-channel video service subscribers throughout the United States (U.S. Federal Communications Commission, 2000).

EVIDENCE FROM A STUDY OF
CLUSTERING AND COMPETITION

Three studies (Lacy & Simon, 1997; Martin, 2001, 2003b) examined how clustering affects competition among daily newspapers in the United States. Head-to-head competition between daily newspapers in the same market is increasingly rare because the dominant newspaper usually enjoys a cost advantage arising from economies of scale. Rival newspapers cannot gain enough circulation to match the dominant paper's lower costs (Lacy & Simon, 1993; Rosse, 1967).

However, indirect competition still exists in layers, or rings, of newspapers (Bridges, Litman & Bridges, 2002; Lacy & Simon, 1993). Newspapers in these models are not perfect substitutes. Regional metropolitan dailies, one layer, compete with satellite-city newspapers that emphasize local coverage, a second layer. Regional dailies may also compete with suburban dailies, which are a third layer. A fourth layer of competition includes weeklies, shoppers, and specialized newspapers. National dailies are a fifth layer of competition, and group-owned suburban newspapers make up a sixth layer. Competition in these models is based on circulation and content (Bridges, et al., 2002; Lacy & Simon, 1993).

Newspapers can differentiate themselves by providing unique information or advertising (Lacy, 1989; Lacy & Simon, 1993), and may to some degree isolate themselves from competition so they can raise prices above costs (Scherer & Ross, 1990). However, relatively high prices still will convince consumers to accept the imperfect substitute of another newspaper firm's differentiated product. Firms also risk attracting new competitors if the difference between costs and prices is large enough (Scherer & Ross, 1990; Tirole, 1988). Therefore, even indirect competition may create pressure on newspaper managers.

Martin (2003b) argued that newspapers also face potential competition if they pay substantial transportation costs to distribute copies to more distant subscribers. This may force managers to increase subscription or advertising prices for copies circulating farther from a printing press. Competitors could then undercut prices at the edge of a newspaper's market (Martin, 2003b).

The dynamics of competition are also shifting. Bridges, et al. (2002) argued that larger papers once enjoyed scale economies and sophisticated information about readers that were beyond the reach of smaller rivals. Smaller papers have found ways to match those advantages, including sharing the production of news and advertising across multiple papers (Bridges, et al., 2002).

Martin (2003b) argued that a newspaper can cut its transportation costs by acquiring another paper near the edge of its circulation territory. This cuts high transportation costs. The firm can then extend its circulation without significantly increasing costs, creating barriers to the entry of competitors in other layers within its market. Clustered newspapers might then increase prices because readers and advertisers do not have substitutes available (Martin, 2003b).

Lacy and Simon (1997) studied newspaper clusters using random samples of counties in the United States. Clustered newspapers circulated in fewer counties outside their home county than nonclustered newspapers. Clustered newspapers also averaged less circulation penetration outside their home county (Lacy & Simon, 1997). However, this study did not measure prices. Fu (2000) found evidence that newspaper clustering is associated with higher advertising prices, but did not control for competition from other newspapers.

Martin (2003b) identified the population of clustered newspapers in the United States in 1988 and 1998 to study long-term changes in clustering and its effects. One-third of all United States dailies were part of a cluster by 1998.

I selected random samples of clustered newspapers for comparisons with samples of nonclustered newspapers. Results showed clustered newspapers face less competition from other dailies and have higher advertising and subscription prices than non-clustered newspapers (Martin, 2003b). However, the findings also suggest that managing newspapers clusters is complex.

Dynamics of Managing Clusters

Newspapers that merged into clusters often failed to stay there. A total of 127 dailies that were clustered in 1988 were not part of a cluster 10 years later. This raises two questions. First, what happened to the newspapers that left a cluster during the study? Second, what happened to those clusters?

I found that 81 of the papers either stopped publishing or converted to weekly publication. Managers apparently rearranged or closed production facilities at these dailies. However, another 46 of the 127 dailies removed from clusters were still publishing in 1998.

Additional analysis showed that the 127 dailies at issue belonged to 59 separate clusters in 1988. Changes in ownership were examined year by year to determine what happened to each cluster over the next decade.

Preliminary results show that 26 of the original clusters dissolved. Although the remaining 33 clusters still existed in 1998, almost half actually dissolved and reformed during the course of the decade. In many cases the clusters reformed under new ownership.

In 15 cases the original owner dissolved a cluster, and then continued to operate just one daily in the same market. In 10 of these cases, all of the other dailies in the cluster were closed. In four cases, a daily member of the cluster converted to weekly publication. In the last case, a firm closed 10 daily newspapers in a heavily populated county and replaced them all with one new daily. In each of the 15 cases, managers apparently took dailies out of business to operate more efficiently in the market with a single paper. Each of these clusters might also have been used as a step toward monopolization of a market.

Reconfigurations of clusters were common. Eighteen clusters were reconfigured. Owners sometimes closed dailies, but left other members of a cluster in operation. In other cases, owners added dailies to a cluster. Sometimes, both occurred.

In 11 instances, dailies were removed from one cluster, then acquired by another owner and added to a new cluster. In one case a two-paper cluster was dissolved when the original owner sold both papers. The same company later reacquired both papers, and then merged them during the creation of a new cluster of five papers.

These dynamic patterns indicate that successful operation of clusters can be difficult. Many companies formed clusters, and then apparently discovered the arrangement was not as profitable as expected. Some firms adjusted the makeup of the cluster. Others exited the arrangement. Other companies sometimes stepped in to create new clusters with characteristics that managers believe increased the chances of success.

A number of variables may have influenced these decisions. For example, creating efficiencies requires that newspapers in a cluster be relatively close so they can share resources. Clusters became smaller and more compact during the original study (Martin, 2003b), suggesting that there is an optimal combination of size and distance needed to realize gains from clustering.

Rearranging production processes also requires an investment that must be recouped over time. Some companies may lack resources to make such investments; other companies may decide earnings from such investments are not sufficient to justify continued operation of a cluster.

Prices in Clusters

This does not mean similar problems afflict all newspaper clusters. I found clustered newspapers charged higher advertising prices than their non-clustered counterparts (Martin, 2003b). When subscription prices were adjusted for circulation size, clustered papers also charged more than nonclustered dailies. However, differences in advertising cost per thousand declined from 78% in 1988 to 15% in 1998 (Martin, 2003b).

Additional analysis examined whether differences in circulation size account for some of this change. Picard (1998) found a curvilinear relationship between circulation size and newspaper advertising rates. Newspapers under

10,000 circulation priced advertising differently than larger newspapers (Picard, 1998).

My findings on competition and prices were reanalyzed for newspapers under 10,000 circulation, and for newspapers with a circulation of 10,000 or more. Larger clustered newspapers faced almost as much competition from other dailies as non-clustered newspapers did. Smaller clustered papers, however, faced significantly less competition than their nonclustered counterparts in 1998.

These differences apparently affected prices. Clustered dailies with a circulation of 10,000 or above had significantly higher advertising prices in 1988, but not in 1998. Smaller clustered dailies, however, had significantly higher ad prices in both years, although the difference declined from 78% in 1988 to 21% in 1998. Smaller clustered dailies also had significantly higher subscription prices both years.

This analysis suggests that identical strategies had different results depending on the size of the newspaper involved. Circulation size has significant correlations with the number of households in a market and total retail sales.[9] The smaller papers operated in markets where patterns of competition may be less complex. In these markets clustering may provide a competitive advantage, allowing papers to impose price increases.

In larger markets with complex patterns of competition, clustering may instead be a defensive strategy. This may be why larger clustered papers had difficulty raising prices. These markets may offer more substitutes for both advertisers and readers.

A final note on clustered newspapers: The Canadian-owned Thomson newspaper group was heavily invested in clustering its United States papers. The company owned 45 clustered newspapers in the United States in 1988, and 30 clustered papers in 1998.

However, Thomson's newspapers lost circulation and market share throughout the 1980s (Lacy & Martin, 1998). The company had stated that an emphasis on high profits hurt the quality of its papers and eventually affected its earnings (Lacy & Martin, 1998).

Thomson has exited the newspaper industry. All of its papers, clustered and nonclustered, were acquired by other companies. Clustering apparently failed to protect the company from long-run declines in profits, perhaps because managers neglected other important aspects of their business.

---

[9] Pearson's R for circulation and households, and circulation and retail sales, was .63 or higher in 1998 for clustered and control papers. The correlations were .48 or higher for clustered and control papers in 1988.

CONCLUSION

Media firms that adopt a strategy of clustering portfolio properties may hope to reduce variance in earnings by reducing systematic and idiosyncratic risk. The general business and economics literature suggests that diversification into similar lines of business is more likely to succeed than unrelated diversification. However, managers should not expect that the mere creation of a cluster will produce the desired benefits.

Managers should first explore financial requirements for acquiring and operating clusters. Managers must understand and apply relevant economic principles to their analysis of potential cost reductions from creation of the cluster. They should be sure they have an adequate understanding of conditions in the markets in which the clusters will operate, and how those conditions will change. Clustering is a form of horizontal integration that may attract scrutiny from regulators, so mangers must also be prepared for this contingency.

Once a portfolio cluster is created, managers must be prepared to meet high demands for information. The firm should select an internal structure that enables employees to apply their skills as efficiently as possible. Potential reductions in work force should be carefully studied to ensure that they will not negatively affect earnings.

Studies of clustered media firms (Ekelund Jr., et al., 2000; Lacy & Simon, 1997; Loomis & Albarran, 2004; Martin, 2003b; Parsons, 2003) also suggest that benefits may vary by medium, and by market. The analysis of newspaper clusters reported above suggested that in some markets newspapers clustered to lower costs so that they could keep operating despite competitive pressures. In other words, these may have been cases where clustering reduced idiosyncratic risk, but had little effect on systematic risk. However, in other cases newspapers apparently clustered to gain market power, presumably influencing both idiosyncratic and systematic risk.

The findings from clustered newspapers are instructive for managers throughout the media industry. Clustering may be an effective strategy for different reasons in different situations. However, managers who exploit the benefits of clustering without regard for their long-term position in the market – those willing to sacrifice the quality of their content for higher profits – may eventually be forced to exit that market as audience and advertisers seek substitutes that might not otherwise be attractive.

REFERENCES

Asher, D. (1999, December). Who owns what. *Presstime, 21*, 29–30.

Barney, J. B. (1997). *Gaining and sustaining competitive advantage*. New York: Addison-Wesley.

Bass, J. (1999, July/August). Newspaper monopoly. *American Journalism Review, 21*, 64–86.

Blankenburg, W. B. (1989). Newspaper scale & newspaper expenditures. *Newspaper Research Journal, 10*(2), 97–103.

Bridges, J. A., , B. R. & Bridges, L. W. (2002). Rosse's model revisited: Moving to concentric circles to explain newspaper competition. *Journal of Media Economics, 15*(1), 3–19.

Brister, K. (2000, November 8). Mergers in cable industry aren't to everyone's liking; Disagreement: Firms say efficiency and profits will be better, but critics abound. *The Atlanta Journal and Constitution*, p. 1F.

Brush, T. H. (1996). Predicted change in operational synergy and post-acquisition performance of acquired businesses. *Strategic Management Journal, 17*(1), 1–24.

Clear Channel Communications, I. (2002, 2002). *Form 10-K, Annual Report*. Retrieved Oct. 6, 2003, from http://www.clearchannel.com/documents/financial/ClearChannel_10k_2002.pdf

A decade of deals. (2000, February). *Presstime, 22*, 33–34.

Dertouzos, J. N. & Trautman, W. B. (1990). Economic effects of media concentration: Estimates from a model of the newspaper firm. *The Journal of Industrial Economics, 39*(1 September), 1–14.

Devinney, T. M. & Stewart, D. W. (1988). Rethinking the product portfolio: A generalized investment model. *Management Science, 34*(9), 1080–1095.

Ekelund Jr., R. B., Ford, G. S. & Koutsky, T. (2000). Market power in radio markets: An empirical analysis of local and national concentration. *Journal of Law and Economics, 43*(1), 157–184.

Ferguson, J. M. (1983). Daily newspaper advertising rates, local media cross-ownership, newspaper chains, and media competition. *Journal of Law and Economics, 26*(3), 635–654.

Fu, W.-J. (2000). *Three essays on the economics of networked and traditional information services.* Ph.D. Dissertation, Northwestern University.

Govindarajan, V. & Fisher, J. (1990). Strategy, control systems and resource sharing: Effects on business unit performance. *Academy of Management Journal, 33*(2), 259-285.

Hill, C. W. L., Hitt, M. A. & Hoskisson, R. E. (1992). Cooperative versus competitive structures in related and unrelated diversified firms. *Organization Science, 3*(4), 501–521.

Hill, C. W. L & Hoskisson, R. E. (1987). Strategy and structure in the multiproduct firm. *Academy of Management Review, 12,* 331–341.

Hull, G. P., Greco, A. N. & Martin, S. (2000). The structure of the radio industry. In A.N. Greco (Ed.), *The media and entertainment industries* (pp.76–98). Boston: Allyn & Bacon.

Krishnan, H. A. & Park, D. (2002). The impact of work force reduction on subsequent performance in major mergers and acquisitions—An exploratory study. *Journal of Business Research, 55*(4), 285–292.

Kuhl, C. (2000, November). The clock is ticking. *CED Plant Management Supplement,* 24–27.

Lacy, S. (1989). A model of demand for news: Impact of competition on newspaper content. *Journalism Quarterly, 66*(1), 40–48, 128.

Lacy, S. (1992). The financial commitment approach to news media competition. *Journal of Media Economics, 5*(2), 5–21.

Lacy, S. & Martin, H. J. (1998). Profits up, circulation down for Thomson papers in 80s. *Newspaper Research Journal, 19*(3), 63–76.

Lacy, S. & Simon, T. F. (1993). *The economics and regulation of United States newspapers.* Norwood, NJ: Ablex.

Lacy, S. & Simon, T. F. (1997). Intercounty group ownership of daily newspapers and the decline of competition for readers. *Journalism & Mass Communication Quarterly, 74*(4), 814–825.

Leong, S. M. & Lim, K. G. (1991). Extending financial portfolio theory for product management. *Decision Sciences, 22*(1), 181–193.

Litman, B. R. (1992). Economic aspects of program quality: The case for diversity. *Studies of Broadcasting*, 121–156.

Litman, B. R. & Bridges, J. (1986). An economic analysis of American newspapers. *Newspaper Research Journal, 7*(3), 9–26.

Litman, B. R., Shrikhande, S. & Ahn, H. (2000). A portfolio theory approach to network program selection. *Journal of Media Economics, 13*(2), 57–79.

Litman, B. R. & Sochay, S. (1994). The emerging mass media environment. In Babe, R.E. (ed.), *Information and Communication in Economics,* pp. 233–269. Boston: Kluwer Academic Publishers.

Loomis, K. D. & Albarran, A. B. (2004). Managing radio market clusters: Orientations of general managers. *Journal of Media Economics, 17*(1), 51–69.

Lubatkin, M. & Chatterjee, S. (1994). Extending modern portfolio theory into the domain of corporate diversification: Does it apply? *Academy of Management Journal, 37*(1), 109–136.

Markides, C.C. & Williamson, P.J. (1994). Related diversification, core competencies and corporate performance. *Strategic Management Journal, 15,* 149–165.

Markides, C. C. & Williamson, P. J. (1996). Corporate diversification and organizational structure: A resource-based view. *Academy of Management Journal, 39*(2), 340–367.

Martin, H. J. (2001). *A study of how a strategy creating clusters of commonly-owned newspapers affects prices, quality and profits.* Ph.D. dissertation, East Lansing: Michigan State University.

Martin, H. J. (2003a). Clustered newspapers operate more efficiently. *Newspaper Research Journal, 24*(4), 6–21.

Martin, H. J. (2003b, July 30-August 2). *Some effects from horizontal integration of daily newspapers on markets, prices and competition.* Paper presented at the Media Management & Economics Division, Association for Education in Journalism and Mass Communication Annual Convention, Kansas City, MO.

Parsons, P. R. (2003). Horizontal integration in the cable television industry: History and context. *Journal of Media Economics, 16*(1), 23–40.

Picard, R. G. (1998). A note on the relations between circulation size and newspaper advertising rates. *Journal of Media Economics, 11*(2), 47–55.

Picard, R. G. & Rimmer, T. (1999). Weathering a recession: Effects of size and diversification on newspaper companies. *Journal of Media Economics, 12*(1), 1–18.

Robins, J. & Wiersema, M. F. (1995). A resource-based approach to the multibusiness firm: Emperical analysis of portfolio interrelationships and corporate financial performance. *Strategic Management Journal, 16*, 277–299.

Rosse, J. N. (1967). Daily newspapers, monopolistic competition, and economies of scale. *American Economic Review, 57*(2 May), 522–533.

Rumelt, R. P., Schendel, D. & Teece, D. J. (1991). Strategic management and economics. *Strategic Management Journal, 12*, 5–29.

Scherer, F. M. & Ross, D. (1990). *Industrial market structure and economic performance* (3rd ed.). Boston: Houghton Mifflin.

Shaver, M. A. (1995). Application of pricing theory in studies of pricing behavior and rate strategy in the newspaper industry. *Journal of Media Economics, 8*(2), 49–59.

St. John, C. H. & Harrison, J. S. (1999). Manufacturing-based relatedness, synergy, and coordination. *Strategic Management Journal, 20*(2), 129–145.

Teece, D. J. (1980). Economies of scope and the scope of the enterprise. *Journal of Economic Behavior & Organization, 1*(3), 223–247.

Thompson, R. S. (1988). Product differentiation in the newspaper industry - an hedonic price approach. *Applied Economics, 20*(3), 367–376.

Tirole, J. (1988). *The theory of industrial organization.* Cambridge, Mass.: MIT Press.

U.S. Department of Justice & Federal Trade Commission (1992, April 8, 1997). *Horizontal Merger Guidelines.* Retrieved Oct. 6, 2003, from http://www. justice.gov/atr/public/guidelines/hmg.htm#0

U.S. Federal Communications Commission (2000, June, 2000). *Cable Television Information Bulletin.* Retrieved Oct. 6, 2003, from http://www. fcc.gov/mb/facts/ csgen.html

6
Product Platforms for the Media Industry

Thomas Hess
University of Munich

Automotive industries and hardware industries already use it with great success; the software industry tries to use it these days: the platform concept. Although platforms seem to be a very successful approach for efficient production, product innovation, and product diversification in many industries, the media industry so far has had little interest in product platforms. This is all the more surprising since the media industry typically exhibits enormous economies of scale which can be exploited through the re-use of content. Product platforms strongly enforce this re-use of content and thus are—theoretically—an efficient tool to increase economies of scale and scope. While economies of scale come along with the industry-specific first-copy-cost-effect, economies of scope occur when content modules are used in different content products and the media company can cheaply produce a wide set of different products through the bundling of a defined set of modules. Understanding and efficiently controlling platforms and the production capabilities they provide is an important aspect of managing product portfolios.

The attractiveness of this concept, however, seems to vary depending on some technical and economic conditions. Against this background, media managers show different attitudes toward the economic impact of content platforms. Florian Pütz of *Frankfurter Allgemeine Zeitung* considers it valuable in production and storage applications across media.

> The concept of product platforms in media business can especially be used for the media neutral production of editorial content. In modules itemized texts, graphics, photographs, audios and videos are suitable for the different utilization channels: newspapers and journals (print), digital newspapers (e.g. newspaper direct, satellite newspapers) archive databases (syndication), Internet (website, news ticker, e-paper, RSS), mobile services (e.g. i-mode, Vodafone live, t-mobile, text-to-speech). The data based acquisition of information and intelligent use of keywords is the basis for the efficient and flexible usage.

Bodo Thielmann of Bertelsmann Corporate Network sees additional value in product creation and customer service:

> By fostering product differentiation and customization as well as cross media publishing, the concept of product platforms generally comprises potentials to satisfy information and entertainment needs more efficiently. However, seeking to realize these potentials, media-specific patterns of consumption as well as different dynamics in the process of content creation have to be taken into account. As a result, the concept of product platforms of course is appropriate for the Internet and other digital media, but elements for example can be found in the production of daily soaps for television.

In order to assess the full potential of product platforms in the media industry, it is necessary to understand the mechanism of the concept and to analyze which impact a product platform would have on the production of media products and the management of product portfolios. Media companies have strong interest in operating media product portfolios because they allow for risk reduction, market exploitation and production efficiency, as Robert G. Picard indicates in Chapter 1 of this book. Because product platforms directly support the efficient and inexpensive creation and management of product portfolios, they indirectly enable media companies to reduce risk, exploit markets, and reduce costs of production. Consequently—at first sight—media companies could easily profit from portfolio concepts when implementing product platforms.

The remainder of this chapter is organized as follows. Section 2 introduces the platform concept and illustrates the basic idea of product platforms in the media industry. Section 3 provides insight into possible system support for media product platforms while section 4 analyzes the economic rationale behind product platforms from a cost and revenue perspective. The chapter concludes with an outlook for the use of platforms.

THE CONCEPT OF PRODUCT PLATFORMS

Platform concepts focus on the similarities of products and processes, and do no longer consider products and technologies of a company as independent from each other (Sawhney, 1998). Theory distinguishes product platforms, brand platforms, processing platforms, global platforms, and customer platforms as five different types of platforms. Most widely discussed are product platforms, which support the planning and realization of complex products and production concepts and can be compared to a construction kit that enables a company to create differentiated offerings based on modularized products. Products are manufactured by combining the modules on the basis of product architectures. Accordingly, Meyer and Lehnerd define a product platform as a "set of subsystems and interfaces that form a common structure from which a stream of derivative products can be efficiently developed and produced" (Meyer & Lehnerd, 1997, p. 210).

Using multipurpose modules in multiple products is possible through a sweeping unification of different product architectures in a company, resulting in a significant advantage of efficiency compared to monolithic approaches in both product innovation and production. In monolithic approaches, products are developed and produced as a single unit and not as modules. The exact extent of the efficiency advantage depends on the modules' multiple usability and is greatest when it is possible to reproduce modules very cheaply or nearly for free as in the case of software modules. The individual products of a product platform sum up to a product family as they depend on the same technologies and belong to the same group of products. Major technological drivers for product platforms are new technologies for content storage and content representation, such as the eXtensible Markup Language (XML) and multimedia databases.

In most cases, product platforms use the principle of modularization, an idea as old as the idea of division of labor. Tasks or problems are no longer treated as monolithic devices but are fractionalized in subtasks or subproblems, which possess clear-cut limited functions and interfaces, and can be looked at and worked with independently and combined with each other. The individual parts are called units or modules; the underlying principle is called modularization (process-related view) or modularity (condition-related view). Product platforms transfer these principles to products and create product architectures based on modules that are designed independently but still function as an integrated whole. The relation of products and components and the role of the product platform are visualized in Fig. 6.2.

CASE STUDY
Product Platforms at Ernst Klett

A first approach of a product platform in the media industry is used at the German publisher Ernst Klett that offers textbooks, teaching aids, learning software, and other educational materials for schools and adult education.

Because of different conditions made by the local authorities in Germany, the offers for schools have to be adapted for the sixteen German States. This was one of the reasons why Ernst Klett started to think about the re-use of content and the modularization of its products at the end of the 1990s. Their objective was to produce easily and cheaply adapted versions of their media products. The IT department of Klett was asked to design a software tool that supports modularization of media products and re-use of modules. The tool designed by the IT department and used by Ernst Klett consists of two main components (Fig. 6.1). The first component is a database in which all products that build up a package—generally named as textbooks—are stored in a modularized way. The second component is an editorial system which is used for different tasks. Authors and editors use the editorial system to create modularized content, to store the modules in the database, and to bundle the modules into products. IT specialists use the editorial system to create the technical components of media products—such as the technical parts for learning software—and to administrate the tool.

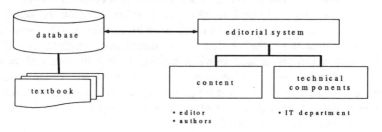

Fig. 6.1
IT-based Modularization Support Concept at Klett

Beneath the adaptation of their products the tool allows Ernst Klett also the re-use of content in several products and a faster innovation of new products. So the tool enabled Ernst Klett to save money by reducing the time for innovation and production.

products

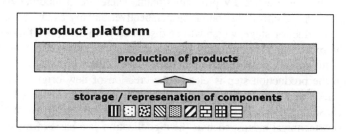

Fig. 6.2
The Relation of Components and Products and the Role of the Product Platform

However, the procedure is only beneficial if the partition is precise, unambiguous and complete. For this purpose the procedure is divided into visible design rules and hidden design parameters (Baldwin & Clarke, 1997). The visible design rules include all aspects that affect subsequent design decisions and therefore it is useful to establish all of them in an early stage of the design process and to communicate them to those involved. The visible design rules are split into the three categories: architecture, interfaces, and standards. The architecture specifies the modules of a system and their functions while the interfaces describe in detail how the modules interact, including how they fit together, connect, and communicate. The standards describe how the conformity of a module can be tested and how their performance can be measured. The hidden design parameters contain the decisions that do not affect the design beyond the local module. Hence, modules can even be changed, chosen, or substituted at a late stage in the design process without the necessity to communicate to anyone beyond the module design team.

From this rather broad perspective of product platforms we now want to approach the media industry and discuss modularization and platform usage in the production of media content. A starting point for the modularization of media content is the media value chain, which, in three generic stages, describes the production, bundling, and distribution of media contents. A form of modularized products already seems to exist when we relate these stages to the stages of modularization: media contents are first produced and then bundled into products to be distributed. Therefore, regarding media products, we can already talk about modularized products, which admittedly have a low degree of modularization because the products on the step of production are usually already marketable. An example is single TV shows that are distributed in a bundled form for economic as well as technical reasons together with other products as a entire TV program stream. Therefore, a modularized production, taking a view from the bundling perspective, already exists. Modularization in the production stage, which will be discussed from the view of modularization in the following, is traditionally very low, mainly because of technical restrictions. In this context we will talk about monolithic content production. The main effort on the production step is clearly the creation of new original content, the so-called "first copies" that are bundled and distributed in the succeeding steps and whose production costs are called "first copy costs" (Shapiro & Varian, 1998). New technical means, such as the digitalization as a basis of media-independent data management, low-priced storage, and duplication of content, allow a modularized production of the former monolithically produced content. Consequently, the first copy costs are therefore split into two components, according to the two steps of modularization. Original content modules (for example text modules of a book, which are not marketable on their own) are generated during stage one and bundled during stage two to create original content products (see Figure 6.3).

We can split the creation of first copies into two stages. While the activity of producing the "first" first copy is the same as in the production of original content (e.g., writing a text), the activity to produce the "second" first copy is a

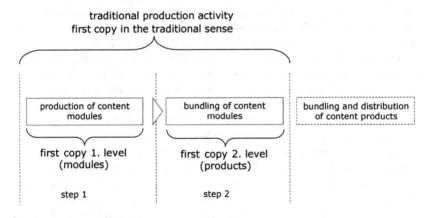

Source: Köhler, Anding, and Hess, 2003

Fig. 6.3
Production and Bundling of Content Products in Two Stages

bundling activity. Compared to monolithic content production, there is a higher degree of modularization. While in monolithic content production the major effort lies in the production of original content, in the modularized production of content the effort is shifted toward the bundling of content modules and the effort for production of original content is reduced. A higher re-use of modules accompanies a rising degree of modularization. The effects on the first copy costs are obvious. Minimizing costs to a level significantly below the cost of monolithic content production can be attained by an ideal proportioning of efforts in both steps of the content production.

SYSTEM SUPPORT FOR PRODUCT PLATFORMS

The following section will shed light on possible system support for product platforms. Firstly, the underlying concept of modules and construction plans is discussed in detail, and, second, a framework for a product platform system is presented. For details see Köhler, Anding, and Hess (2003).

Modules and Construction Plans

Product platforms allow for the creation of media products through the bundling of existing content modules. To create, store, and manage these bundles, the product platform has to handle specific information which is represented by "construction plans." A construction plan describes which and how content modules are combined to a specific product.

Thus, in the following discussion of the content platform, the term "module" will be used with respect to media content being stored and processed by the platform. Moreover, it will be illustrated how these modules can be bundled to products and how "construction plans" have to be designed for this purpose.

In other industries, modules are created by decomposing products into their individual parts. This decomposition can take place in different steps by deconstructing every part as often as possible. As a result, hierarchies develop between the modules on these different steps. Due to this procedure, modularization of products ends with screws and nuts for manufacturing goods or with single bits for digital goods. In this case, modularization of digital media contents could be extended to single bits. However, from an economic point of view such an extensive modularization is not reasonable. Therefore, the modularization of media products should not be based on a technical perspective; it should take place with respect to the human perception of content. The particular size of single modules, such as a single audio stream, can be determined according to the economic value of the module. This value results on the one hand from the difference between additional costs of producing an original module (which can be saved by reuse) and the costs of finding a re-usable module in a database, and on the other hand, from the value that customers assign to the module. For the technical representation of content, the markup language XML would be appropriate as it distinguishes between content, semantics and layout of media contents (see Fig. 6.4).

Following this approach, media content like texts, pictures, audio/video files, and applications are content modules and classified using meta data. For consumption, the content modules have to be bound to a semantic module and a layout module. The semantic module describes the structure of the content and can be compared to a grammar. A semantic module, for example, describes that a specific content consists of a headline, an abstract, a body text, and a number of graphics. These descriptions are stored in semantic modules, which in turn consist of meta data. To display the content, a layout is needed, which, with the help of layout modules, describes features such as the font, font size, resolution, or placement of a headline. Different layout modules result from different layout guidelines for different structures.

This principle of modularization can be used not only for textual content but also for pictures, videos, and audio content. For instance, a film could be structured according to a semantic module into trailer, intro, different chapters, credits, and "making of" products. The corresponding episodes are saved as independent, modular film sequences and are presented according to layout

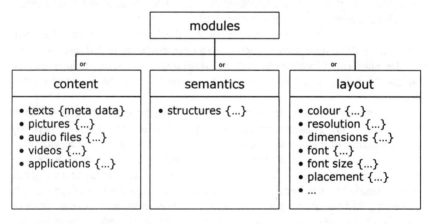

Source: Köhler, Anding, and Hess 2003

Fig. 6.4
Modules of Media Content

modules. As such, it is possible to realize—for example—different resolutions or picture qualities for different customer target groups or for different technical means of presentation (e.g. a television vs. a cell phone version).

Each of these modules is exactly described by meta data. The meta data could comprise names or descriptions of people and objects on a photograph, the date of the shooting, the name of the photographer, and the copyright of the picture. Copyright information is particularly important meta data for media companies because it enables the company to track the holder of a specific copyright and whether a module is free to be published or not.

According to the procedure described earlier, modularized media products consist of content, layout, and semantic modules. We further want to discuss how these single modules can be assembled into a marketable content product. The assembly is based on construction plans, which determine the modules contained by the product, the way these modules are linked, and the methods to be used for editing the product and the modules.

The concept of construction plans resembles object-oriented software development and follows the class principle, which contains the data used as well as the methods used to edit the data. Further, hierarchies can exist among different construction plans, similar to class hierarchies in object-oriented software development. Construction plans at a higher hierarchy level define the spectrum of modules and methods, which can be used in construction plans at a lower level. For example, the construction plan of a product line defines the modules and methods that can be used in the construction plans of products in this product line. The construction plan of the product in turn defines the methods and modules that can be used to produce an issue of this media product (e.g., an issue of a newspaper). The construction plan of an issue finally contains all elements and methods that are used in this issue. Therefore, it is reasonable to name the construction plan of an issue "logic first copy." The construction plan of an issue again can be compared to an object (or instance) of the product class. Later on, the "physical first copy" is assembled on the basis of the construction plan for the issue. The physical first copy in turn serves as a master copy for copies of the media content.

A Framework With Four Elements

The rather generic approach to modularization in the media industry shall now be transformed into a concrete design of a product platform.

The media industry is made up of several sectors with different companies using different media and running different business models. Because of these differences, it is not possible to develop just one product platform that fits all companies. Instead, it is useful to compose a framework that allows the design of customized product platforms, aligned to the specifics of each media company. To allow the design of individual platforms, the framework needs a modular design with independent system components that can easily be combined using standardized interfaces.

Content modules and construction plans are stored and managed by the platform. Thus, the core element of the product platform is a repository for content and meta data.

Besides the storage of media content, product platforms should also offer functions to support other activities. We will discuss some of these activities starting from the media value chain with its three steps: production, bundling, and distribution. The framework for product platforms in media companies must offer individually applicable system components that support these activities, even if some companies do not cover all value chain activities in their business model and do not need all of the system components. By analyzing the different value chain activities (production, bundling, and distribution) it is possible to identify more detailed activities, which are contained in the value chain activities but which should be offered independently by the framework.

The *production* activity can be divided into purchase, creation, and integration of media content depending on the business models of different media companies. Some companies just create their own media content; others only purchase media content from producers or syndicators. Some integrate media content from outside the company, such as media content from customers for other customers, and others use several ways to produce media content. Because of these differences in the business models, the framework should offer independent components that support each function and that can be chosen independently.

The second value chain activity represents the process of *bundling* separate content modules into products. For modularized media content as described before, we can differentiate between bundling single modules to larger units (e.g., combining pictures and texts with the help of construction plans to articles) and bundling these larger units into complete products (e.g., different articles to a whole newspaper). The media content produced and bundled within the first and second activity is stored in the repository of the product platform. In the case of modularized media products, content, semantic, and layout modules as well as the construction plans have to be stored separately from each other.

The third value chain activity covers all activities linked to the *output* of media content. These are activities of copying, marketing, distributing, and syndicating media content as well as after sales services. Each of these activities must be represented by a distinct system component within the framework. In this framework, the system component for copying media content supports the production of a first copy and the duplication of this first copy. Further, marketing, distribution, and syndication components support the delivery of the media content to customers. Finally, the component for after-sales services assists activities after the delivery of content, such as updates.

In addition to these activities, there are activities that belong to or influence all steps of the value chain. Product innovation, for instance, influences all activities because it determines the construction plans of product groups, product lines, or products. Furthermore, product innovation also has an impact on whether modules are acquired from other firms or created within the company and on the syndication of products. Hence, product innovation affects not just one activity, it influences all activities. As a further activity, relevant for the whole value chain, a controlling function collects data about all processes and units and generates information to manage all processes and units. According to the specific needs of media companies, product platforms should also support these functions by providing independent system components.

Finally, further components are needed to manage the product platform itself. With the help of these management components, system components can be integrated into the platform, updated, changed, or removed. In addition, management components support the administration of users and workflows.

To enable the design of individual product platforms aligned with the specific needs of a media company, a framework to develop product platforms is required. This framework is composed of independent system components, which can be combined and which interact using standardized interfaces. Within this framework, there is the product platform in the narrow sense, which solely represents the repository of the platform, and the product platform in the broader sense, which—besides the repository—comprises additional system components for further functions.

The product platform in the narrow sense consists of the content repository, which includes the content, layout, and semantic modules of a company and the construction plans of product groups, product lines, products, etc. The repository itself is divided into a multimedia database and a XML database. While the first stores different content modules, the second holds layout and semantic modules as well as the meta data describing content modules in the multimedia database.

The product platform in the narrow sense only provides the storage of media content modules. To extend the functionalities of the product platform, different system components have to be integrated using standardized interfaces. By integrating system components, the product platform can be individually adjusted and designed, according to the needs of a specific media company.

The product platform in the broader sense is designed according to the principles of component-based software development and comprises the product platform in the narrow sense and different integrated system components to expand the functionalities. The various system components can be categorized into three groups, which resemble the various value chain activities of a company (see Fig. 6.5). The first group of components supports the input of media content into the platform. The second group supports the output of media content, while the third group provides components for the platform management. In the following, the different components are further discussed.

Each group consists of several standard components, which can be combined according to the needs and the business model of a company. One of the input components is the purchasing component, which supports the process of buying media content from producers or content syndicators and which includes several functionalities, such as a billing system, a retrieval system, and a system to generate relevant meta data for the purchased media content. The next component supports the creation of new content by the company and provides editing functionality for different media systems to split content into modules as well as content mining systems. A further component enables the bundling of various modules with the help of construction plans. Thereby, the bundling does not need to take place manually by editors, but can be an automated process, based on personalized product configurations. These, in turn, could be generated manually by the customers or automatically by collaborative filtering systems. Another component to input media content could support the integration of media content from outside the company. This media content may be advertising content from advertising customers or media content such as comments produced by consumers.

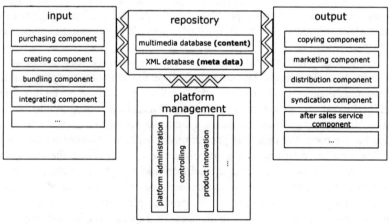

Source: Köhler, Anding, and Hess 2003

Fig. 6.5
Framework for Product Platforms in Media Companies

The group of output components also provides various functionalities. The copying component allows the physical production of the first copy, linking the construction plan of an issue to a medium. This component also supports the duplication of this first copy. The marketing component supports the advertisement and the sale of the product. Functionalities for analyzing customer target groups or producing the advertisements can be integrated in this component. The distribution of products to the consumers is supported by a distribution component, enabling the customization of the products (e.g., to fit the customers' technical equipment). The B2B distribution of products to other companies can be supported by a specific syndication component, which is customized to the particular features of these deals. Another component may support the after-sales services, including content updates after the sales process.

The third group of components aids the management of the product platform. Thereby, they support the administration of the platform and the management of the overall activities. To administer the platform, these components offer functionalities to plan and design the platform as well as to integrate, update, change, and remove components. The components also deliver functionalities for user and workflow administration. The second part of this group supports the overall activities of the company, such as product innovation or controlling. The component for product innovation offers, among others, functionalities to design construction plans for product groups, product lines, and single products. It also supports market testing of new products.

The different groups can be extended by new components, which may be customized for a specific company if the functionality of the standard components is insufficient.

THE RATIONALE BEHIND PRODUCT PLATFORMS

After having described the technical perspective on product platforms in the media industry, we want to analyze the economic rationale behind the usage of platforms and modularization (for details, see Anding & Hess, 2004).

Considering production and distribution, modularization and individualization cause a *cost effect* and a *revenue effect*. Whereas the cost effect is driven by modularization and implies that production costs are (potentially) lower with modularization, the revenue effect is caused by the fact that modularization increases the number of different content products (different first product copies) and consumers have a higher willingness to pay (WTP) for individualized content products.

Changes on the Cost Side

To analyze the impact of modularized, platform-based content production on production cost, we start from a multi-product cost-model, where the cost of the production of B different media products (B for "bundles"), each with an individual circulation n_i, is:

$$C = \sum_{i=1}^{B} C_{FCi} + \sum_{i=1}^{B} n_i * c_{Ri}$$

C_{FCi} is the first copy cost of product i, while C_{Ri} represents the reproduction cost of product *i* under the assumption that the costs of reproduction (can) differ for each product.

If content is produced on the basis of modules rather than monolithically, production costs change. Instead of a first copy for each product, a set of modules is created, which then is bundled together to different products. This requires a redefinition of the term "first copy." While the first copy in the traditional understanding describes a master copy of a content product ready for distribution, we in fact have two kinds of first copies: *first module copies* and *first product copies*. The character of a first module copy and the process of its creation are identical to the traditional first copy: it primarily involves creative and editorial work. The first product copy instead either simply describes a logical compilation of modules or represents new content, merged from a set of modules which are strongly interconnected (this means that new creative or editorial work is involved in the bundling activity). An example would be a news article, which is assembled from different existing text modules and some pictures. The text modules can either be simply put together in a specific order without changing the text, or the text itself could be edited in order for the modules to be better aligned with each other. For simplicity reasons we assume that a first product copy only represents a logical assemblage of modules which are not edited in the bundling process.

The distinction of first module copies and first product copies introduces a new component to the cost calculation in the first equation: the costs of bundling. The overall costs of bundling depend on the number of bundles which can be generated with a given number of modules. Thus, the numerical relation between modules and possible bundles is most important for the efficiency of modularized content production. This opens up a discussion of the requirements that content modules would have to fulfill in order for the content production to have a high bundling efficiency. We will not enter this discussion here but concentrate solely on the relation between modules and bundles, whereas the number of bundles B depends on the number of available modules M: B = B(M). If we understand the number of different bundles as the result of the content production process, we consider B(M) as the relevant production function.

Thus, the first equation changes into:

$$C = \sum_{m=1}^{M} C_{FCm} + \sum_{i=1}^{B(M)} C_{Bi} + \sum_{i=1}^{B(M)} n_i * c_{Ri}$$

The second term describes the costs of bundling with C_{Bi} being the costs that occur for the creation of bundle i.

To compare the costs of modularized production with the costs of traditional content production, the overall number of distribution-ready content units (i.e., the number of copies) and thus the value of the last term of equation must be equal to the value of the last term in equation one. Consequently, modularized production of content is favorable if the sum of first module copy costs and first product copy costs are less than the first copy costs in traditional monolithic production. This requires a certain minimum bundling efficiency.

When clarifying the impact of modularization on content production, it is important to consider a specific *ceteris paribus* condition. We can either assume a *fixed number of different content products*, which in modularized production are produced at different (preferably lower) costs by using modules, or we can *fix the production costs*, which in modularized production can generate a different (preferably higher) number of products (bundles). For simplicity reasons we stick to the first *ceteris paribus* condition and compare the costs occurring in monolithic and in modularized production of an equal number of different products. This allows us to exclude possible effects on the distribution side—primarily regarding the average willingness to pay of consumers—and to concentrate solely on cost effects in content production.

Thus, the cost effect of modularization can be described as the difference ΔC in production cost in traditional and modularized production:

$$\Delta C = \left[\sum_{m=1}^{M} C_{FCm} + \sum_{i=1}^{B(M)} C_{Bi} \right] - \left[\sum_{i=1}^{B} C_{FCi} \right]$$

The *ceteris paribus* condition forces the number of traditionally produced first copies B being equal to the number of new first product copies B(M). The distribution costs are the same in both cases, because the number of distributed copies does not depend on the production of the first copies. Therefore we do not have to consider them in ΔC.

Changes on the Revenue Side

To discuss changes on the revenue side, it is necessary to provide a more elaborate analysis. Media companies typically serve two markets: a consumer (or recipient) market to which the content is sold and which is used to generate an audience, and an advertising market to which this audience is sold. Considering these two markets, not only recipients have a higher willingness to pay for individualized content, but also advertising customers will potentially pay more if advertising is better aligned with consumer interests, because this increases advertising efficiency. Thus, we model the revenue side in a way that regards the interdependence of individuality of content and the willingness to pay of consumers and advertisers.

We start with a simple revenue model for the case of non-individualized content and modify it in a way that considers the effect of individualization and the increased willingness to pay of consumers and advertisers.

$$R = \sum_{i=1}^{B} n_i * (r_{Di} + r_{Ii})$$

The revenue of a multiproduct content producer R is calculated as the sum of the revenue of each product's number of copies, whereby the revenue of each copy splits into a direct component r_{Di}, paid by consumers, and an indirect component r_{Ii}, paid by advertisers.

To consider the effect of individualization in this model, we have to modify the direct and indirect revenues by some parameters that represent the degree of individuality of the content and thus the rise in willingness to pay of the consumers and advertisers. We expect the WTP to increase with an increasing individuality of the content and to be highest when the individuality is at its maximum. It is difficult, if not impossible, to measure the absolute individuality a consumer expects from a product and to determine when a product is at its maximum individualization level for a specific consumer. Thus, we have to employ a proxy and use a measure for relative individuality. While there are many ways to design such a measure, we use a simplified approach in order to keep the analysis simple. We can assume that the individuality of a product is positively correlated with the number of modules used for its production. If we compare monolithically produced content (which, in fact, consists of only one module) with content that is assembled from a large number of modules, the second one potentially exhibits a higher level of individuality than the first one. However, at the same time we have to assume that there is more than one version of the modularized content offered on the market or that the consumer can assemble a bundle by choosing from the set of modules.

Thus, we can derive a direct relation between the number of modules M used to produce the content and its level of individuality as well as an indirect relation of M to the WTP of consumers and advertisers. We specify this relation by a factor λ, with $0 \le \lambda \le 1$ such that:

$$WTP = \lambda * WTP_{max}$$

λ can be called the individuality-sensitivity parameter. Although we distinguish different WTPs for consumers and advertising customers, we can assume that this mechanism is the same for both customer groups while λ might differ.

λ is dependent on the number of modules M used for the production of bundles with $\lambda (0) = 0$ and $\lambda (M \to \infty) = 1$.

The form of $\lambda (M)$ might differ for consumers and advertising customers and even among different groups of these if the content provider has a diverse customer structure. For simplicity reasons again and without loss of generality we assume a single $\lambda (M)$ for all customer groups involved.

These considerations allow us to modify the simple revenue model and include the effect of individualization:

$$R = \sum_{i=1}^{B} n_i * (r_{Di}^{max} * \lambda_D(M) + r_{Ii}^{max} * \lambda_I(M))$$

In this modified model we replace the WTPs r_{Di} and r_{Ii} of consumers and advertisers for their maximum WTPs that they would have for a perfectly individualized product: r_{Di}^{max} and r_{Ii}^{max}. These maximum WTPs are exogenous factors and could be determined by empirical research on the consumer and advertiser markets. They are multiplied by the individuality-sensitivity parameter λ, which in turn is dependent on the number of modules M that are used to create the number of B bundles.

As for the cost effect, we can also calculate the revenue effect ΔR of modularization and individualization as the difference between the revenues of monolithically and modularly produced content:

$$\Delta R = \sum_{i=1}^{B} n_i * ([r_{Di}^{max} * \lambda_D(M) - r_{Di}] + [r_{Ii}^{max} * \lambda_I(M) - r_{Ii}])$$

CONCLUSION AND OUTLOOK

The production and management of media product portfolios can significantly be supported by content platforms, which in turn are strongly interconnected with modularized content production. As a consequence, the distinction of content modules and construction plans for media is an important prerequisite for the use of content platforms that benefit the differentiation and individualization of media products.

These content modules and construction plans need to be stored in a content repository that builds the core element of a content platform. For actually operation of such a platform, further elements need to be included that allow for the input of content into the repository and the output and distribution of content as well as the management of the platform.

Platform-based content production has impact on the profits of a media company from a cost and a revenue perspective. On the cost side, the content is produced more efficiently and with higher exploitation of re-use opportunities so that costs can be significantly reduced. From a revenue perspective, content modules can be bundled individually and differentiated for customer needs, which increases customer willingness to pay.

Applying the platform concept, media companies might realize significant synergies if some conditions are met. From a technical point of view, these conditions mainly refer to the modularization of content. Managers must deal with the following questions in this context:

1. What type of content are we dealing with in terms of its structure?
2. What is to be done in order to create and store the content as modules?
3. What type of meta data is required to manage the modules effectively?

Media companies can especially benefit from the concept of content platforms, if they are dealing with well-structured content (e.g., this is the case for educational and juridical content) that can be created and stored as modules. For management purpose, adequate meta data is required to address the content modules in a timely manner.

The modularization of content allows media companies to increase revenues by individualized and differentiated media products. At the same time, production costs might be reduced. However, the overall economic impact of product individualization and differentiation on profits is not clear at all. Thus, managers should also discuss the following questions:

1. How does the modularization of content affect production costs?
2. How much are customers willing to pay for new media products?
3. What is the impact on profits generated in the short run and long run?

The attractiveness of content platforms depends on their impact on net profits. For this reason, media companies have to evaluate how modularized content production and media products based on that affect production costs and revenues. Changes in both the short run as well as in the long run should be considered to rate the application of content platforms.

Further, academic research is needed on the viability of the implementation of content platforms and the theoretical relevance for media companies. Organizational factors and the adjustment of management systems might become a special matter of interest regarding the implementation and operation of content platforms. In addition, the economic rationale behind product platforms could be elaborated in detail and tested empirically. As a prerequisite, concrete scenarios as how to design product programs based on content platforms have to be developed as well. Based on that, the theoretical and empirical relevance of content platforms for media companies can be discussed and evaluated further.

REFERENCES

Anding, M. & Hess, T. (2004). *Modularization, individualization and the first-copy-cost-effect–Shedding new light on the production and distribution of media content*. Working Paper of the Institute for Information Systems and New Media, University of Munich, No. 1/2004.

Baldwin, C. Y. & Clark, K. B. (1997). Managing in an age of modularity. *Harvard Business Review, 5*, 84–93.

Köhler, L., Anding, M. & Hess, T. (2003). Exploiting the power of product platforms for the media industry–a conceptual framework for digital goods and its customization for content Syndicators. In Proceedings of the third IFIP Conference on e-commerce, e-business and e-government (pp. 303-313). New York: Kluwer.

Meyer, M. H. & Lehnerd, A. P. (1997). *The power of product platforms: Building value and cost leadership.* New York: The Free Press.

Meyer, M. H. & Zack, M. H. (1996). The design and development of information products. *Sloan Management Review, 1,* 43–59.

Sawhney, M. S. (1998). Leveraged high-variety strategies: From portfolio thinking to platform thinking. *Journal of the Academy of Marketing Science, 26,* 54–61.

Shapiro, C. & Varian, H. R. (1998). *Information rules—A strategic guide to the network economy.* Boston: Harvard Business School Press.

7
Cross-Promotion and Branding of Media Product Portfolios

Maria Norbäck
Jönköping International Business School

Cross-promotion and branding are critical for the creation and use of media product portfolios. The ability to cross-promote and extend a brand is an incentive for companies to develop product portfolios. The chance to engage in cross-promotion and branding is, thus, closely linked to the process of developing and managing a media product portfolio. When looking into cross-promotion, one soon discovers that it is closely connected to the brands of the products and vice versa. Cross-promotion and branding are therefore two interrelated concepts that are important to consider when looking into the use and development of product portfolios.

Cross-promotion and branding are not easily defined, however. These are broad concepts involving multiple practices which in turn produce different outcomes. Cross-promotion especially is a fuzzy concept which is incompletely understood and conceptualized. During the past several years, cross-promotion seems to have been a buzzword within the media industry. However, there has not been much academic attention paid to the concept. A search in the business papers and academic journals shows that the word cross-promotion is often used by the business media, but is seldom mentioned or conceptualized in any academic texts. This means that practitioners in the media business use, or at least try to use, cross-promotion strategies, but that the academic world has barely begun to investigate the issue. Many cross-promotion strategies are interrelated to the more established concept of branding and brand extension, which makes it important to try to conceptualize the differences and similarities. In contrast to cross-promotion, branding has been acknowledged both academically and by practitioners for quite some time.

This chapter aims at conceptualizing branding and cross-promotion in relation to media product portfolios. It will also look at the connection between branding and cross-promotion and the possibilities and problems these strategies pose for media companies with a product portfolio. The questions that this chapter will explore are as follows:

What are the definitions and characteristics of branding and cross-promotion, and how can they be used by media firms with a product portfolio? The ideas behind branding and brand extension will be explored, and examples of how they are being used in the media industry will be given. A typology of cross-promotion and examples of how these typologies are used in practice will be presented.

What factors affect whether, and in which ways, firms with a product portfolio can engage in branding and cross-promotion? A number of factors that play a part in whether a company is suited for successful cross-promotion and branding will be presented. These factors concern, among other things, the conditions and context of the specific company, the nature of the company's product portfolio, relationships of both an internal and external nature (e.g., employees and competitors), and the company's customers.

What opportunities and challenges can be connected to the branding and cross-promotion of media products within a portfolio? Some examples will be given of both the opportunities and challenges that a media company with a product portfolio might face when pursuing cross-promotion and branding.

Initially, the chapter will elaborate on what branding is and in what ways branding techniques such as brand extension and endorsement can be applied by media product portfolio companies. Next the discussion will turn to cross-promotion and look at how these strategies relate to branding strategies and the effect they will have on the development of product portfolios. This section will also feature a typology of different kinds of cross-promotion used by the media industry. Then, the chapter will look into some of the factors that influence companies' use of cross-promotion and what problems a firm might run into when pursuing cross-promotion strategies. The chapter ends with a summary of the most important aspects a media company must consider before it initiates branding and cross-promotion.

BRANDING

Branding and cross-promotion are closely related to each other. Media firms that own a portfolio of product lines with one or several brands can advantageously use these branded products as mediums for cross-promotion. As we will see below, there are several types of cross-promotion that are all connected to branding strategies. But before looking into the connection between branding and these cross-promotion strategies, we will turn to the concept of branding and the activities connected to it.

Branding and Brand Equity

Despite the heavy emphasis that the marketing community has put on the concept of branding in the past decades, it is a relatively new phenomenon for the media industry (Ha & Chan-Olmsted, 2001). The introduction of new products to the product portfolio could be a way to extend the brand for a media company, or at least make use of the value of their existing brand when introducing new products. In the competitive media market of today, in which the consumer has hundreds of magazines, television channels, radio stations, and other products to choose from, a strong brand can boost company products. Chan-Olmsted and Kim (2001) affirm that media companies need to establish a consistent brand image in order to succeed in today's noisy marketplace. Chan-a and Chan-Olmsted (2001) define branding as "the marketing strategy of giving value to the name of a product to distinguish itself from competitors and achieve a competitive differential advantage" (p. 202).

The purpose of branding is, thus, to create a high brand familiarity and a positive brand image. The branding process consists of the development and maintenance of sets of product attributes and values that are coherent, appropriate, distinctive, protectable, and appealing to consumers (Ha & Chan-Olmsted, 2001). Bellamy and Traudt (2000) quote a television promotion executive, who described brands as "signposts" for the viewer and stated that "a successful brand incorporates comfort, originality and awareness of how one fits into the overall media environment" (p. 128).

For the broadcasting industry, branding is used both in on- and off-air promotion efforts. Bellamy and Traudt (2000) describe how network brand logos, in the form of ubiquitous on-air "bugs," allow for cross-promotion within programs. Brand names can also be used to promote products such as news channels or other spin-off products (e.g., ESPN Zone sports bars in the U.S.). Marketing researchers argue that it will become increasingly important for companies to manage their brands like assets in order to increase their value over time. Branding should be a long-range strategy that all companies must engage in (Aaker, 1996).

A closely related issue when discussing branding is the question of how to assign value to a brand. Brand equity is the added value that a brand gives to a product or service. Aaker (1991) explains it as "a set of brand assets and liabilities linked to a brand, its name and symbol, that add to or subtract from the value provided by a product or service to a firm and/or to that firms' customers" (p. 15).

The difficulty of measuring brand equity has resulted in extensive research in the matter, and it seems that there is no one variable that covers the complex concept of brand equity. This is because the concept, in large, consists of two parts: one "hard" part of tangible and functional attributes, and one "soft" part of emotional and cognitive attributes. To complicate the matter, brand equity should be based on both present and potential value. However, Bellamy and Trandt (2000) argue that there seems to be a general consensus in the branding literature that brand equity to a large extent derives from brand knowledge, which consists of both brand awareness and brand image. Awareness is to what extent and what type of recalling and recognition a brand receives from the consumers. Image is is a bit more complex and difficult concept to measure, but it can be seen as the consumer's subjective conception of the brand, and the role the brand plays in the consumer's lifestyle (Bellamy & Traudt, 2000).

Because this book addresses product portfolios, it is of interest to look at whether there is a difference between the branding of a single product and the branding of several products like those in a portfolio. When it comes to product portfolios and branding, there are two major differences to take into account: portfolios of products with different brands and single-brand portfolios. We will first look into the rationale behind having a portfolio of different brands, and then turn to how one brand can be extended beyond the original product.

Brand Portfolios

Brand portfolios are product portfolios that include different brands and/or several branded product lines. The logic behind a brand portfolio is that a brand might be worth more as a part of a wider portfolio than standing alone. Barwise and Robertson (1992) maintains that the portfolio owner can leverage the brand and achieve a greater financial return than if the brand was marketed as a part of a narrower line. He concludes that the specific advantages for companies that create brand portfolios lie in the ability to develop global markets, pursue multiple market segments, counterbalance the increased power of the trade, and take advantage of marketing economies of scale. These four incentives for creating brand portfolios may also be applied to the media industry. The growth of international media conglomerates indicates how important global market shares are. These international media firms pursue multiple market segments, e.g., the record company EMI has myriad of sublabels for different customer segments with different tastes in music. Because media companies depend on advertisers and distribution- and sale-forces, their ability to counterbalance the power of these actors is vital for survival. Another reason for establishing a media product portfolio is the opportunity to create synergies in areas such as content production, marketing, and advertising. In addition, there is also the advantage of being able to use an endorsement strategy. Endorsement strategies are mostly used when the company name is used to endorse a brand (like CBS's 60 *Minutes*) but it could also be used when one brand endorses another. When an endorsement strategy works as planned, the value and image of the company or the original brand rubs off on the endorsed brand. The same phenomenon can be achieved when companies engage in the type of cross-promotion in which they cooperate with other companies in promoting each others' products. In a joint promotional effort between Coca-Cola and Walt Disney Co., these two brands' good connotations can rub off on each other. If one brand has stronger brand equity, the weaker brand will benefit more from the endorsement than the stronger one (Riezebos, 2003).

Brand Extension

The "opposite" of brand portfolios is brand extension, where one brand is extended onto several products. The idea is that if a brand is well managed, it can be more efficiently used for levering a brand's value by extending the brand to other related product categories. The product portfolio will then consist of products with the same brand. To successfully manage brand extension, it is important to establish a connection between the new and the old product. The transfer of the perceived benefit from the old to the new product cannot be too far-fetched, but must appear to be meaningful from the consumer's perspective (Chan-Olmsted & Kim, 2001). There are examples where brand extension has been a success, but there are also examples where it has been a failure. One must not forget that there is always a risk of damaging the brand if its image and connotation is diluted in the process (Barwise & Robertson, 1992). On the other hand, when the brand extension is successful, the benefits could be cost savings when launching a new product, and consolidation of the product line leading to stronger customer and distributor loyalty (Barwise & Robertson, 1992; Ha & Chan-Olmsted, 2001). Bellamy and Traudt (2000) conducted a study of people's awareness of television-network brands in the U.S. and found that the three major broadcasting networks ABC, CBS, and NBC had an advantageous position compared to many of their cable-competitors. They argued that ABC and CBS ought to take advantage of this and follow the example of NBC in extending the brands by developing new TV channels. Another implication of the study was that the U.S. television industry seems to be near the saturation point for the introduction of new brand names. This indicates that the companies with high brand equity will be able to extend their brands to exploit the television market in the future, something that will be increasingly difficult for new brands.

Another American brand extension example is the television host Oprah Winfrey, whose program has generated a book club, a magazine, a charity network, and an online clothes retailer. All these products use the Oprah brand and image, and of course all of them are heavily engaged in different sorts of cross-promotion. There are also examples of brand extensions going the other way around, starting with a magazine and extending into TV: the international fashion magazine *Elle* was extended into a TV format and broadcast in several countries in Europe. In both brand extension, as the Oprah example, and brand endorsement strategies, the transfer of an image from one product to another is the key issue. In the media industry this might be especially important for news media, where the reputation of journalistic integrity should be seen as a competitive advantage. The legitimacy of a news medium is one of the foundations for its operations—if people regard it as untrustworthy it will have no future. Brands that connote a high standard of journalism and have a long tradition of quality news reporting will, therefore, be a valuable asset when a company wants to introduce a new news medium on the market. Arrese and Medina (2002) take the *Wall Street Journal* and the *Financial Times* as examples of business press brands that have gone from one single journalistic product to become "journalistic brand names." These powerful brands made it possible for the companies to enter new geographical markets and launch new products under their respective brand name. A strong brand can, thus, reduce entry barriers (Aaker, 1996). Disney's ventures into sports-magazine publishing and the restaurant business were carried out by extending the brand identity of ESPN, the strong brand originally created in the sports television market (Bellamy & Traudt, 2000). Having a product with a strong brand and a strong differentiation can, in some cases, also be a barrier for competitors to enter the market. One such example is MTV, which, according to Bellamy & Traudt, "owns" the music video/lifestyle niche. MTV's strong niche strategy and branding has made them the one channel for their specific market segment.

One interesting question that arises is whether the product portfolio creates cross-promotion and brand extension, or whether the ability to cross-promote and extend a brand creates the portfolio? The answer to this question would probably be both—in some cases a company might happen to own a couple of products and then look for ways of achieving synergies between them. In other cases, a company might have a strong brand that they want to extend, which will lead to a creation of a product portfolio that could be used for cross-promotion.

Extending the Brand Online

In the late 1990s, many companies thought of the Internet as the Promised Land for business and advertising. Many of these companies came to realize how difficult it was to build a brand new online brand (due to low Internet penetration, among other things), and found that in many cases it was better to extend already established offline brands (Steinbock, 2000). Most media companies have followed this path: they have extended their already established brand to products on the Internet, such as newspaper publishers that have established a digital version of the newspaper. CNN uses their website as an extension of their cable brand and cross-promotes their channel and online operation. There are also promotional links to the *Time* magazine website from the CNN website, with tips on interesting stories to read (CNN and *Time* magazine are both products in the Time Warner product portfolio.).

Chan-Olmsted & Kim (2001) have studied U.S. television broadcasters and their Internet strategies. Their study shows that only a minority of television broadcast executives thought of the Internet as a strategic branding tool. Most of the managers saw Internet presence more in the light of tactical operations than as a long-term strategy to be managed. Many researchers argue that this will have to change because of the importance of the websites when it comes to cross-promotion in terms of complementary and in-depth information about a media company's other products such as television programs, movies or records. Television broadcasters are using the Internet to provide station and personality information, cross-promote news and other programs, and communicate with the audience (Chan-Olmsted & Suk, 2000). There are many examples of websites that work as a complement to the main product. In many cases the companies have taken advantage of the Internet's capacity for interaction, such as the U.S. television network ABC's *Who Wants to be a Millionaire* game site. On this site the audience can play the game at any time, or log on and play in real time with the same game that is on live TV. During the first six webcasts of the online show, one million people logged on to the site (Gruenwendel, 2000).

Apart from the cross-promotional opportunities, another important incentive for creating platforms online is the possibility to enhance customer loyalty by interaction and personalization (Chan-Olmsted & Jung, 2001; Ha & Chan-Olmsted, 2001). Many television broadcasters have created web-based fan forums for their television series, where the viewers can update themselves and exchange opinions about the show (e.g., forums for fans of the reality series *Survivor* (Chan-Olmsted & Jung, 2001)). This idea of creating Internet communities for consumers interested in the same products has been given increasing attention from marketers (Steinbock, 2000).

Ha and Chan-Olmsted (2001) found that websites played an important role in supporting television networks' programs. They state that even though a good website might not compensate for a mediocre program, it certainly adds value to programs already popular among the audience. Websites also increase the time that viewers are involved with the network brand. Another important implication from their study is that cross-product promotion on TV is the best way to attract an audience to the website, and the more familiar the audience was with the network, the more time she or he would spend on the site. This underlines the potential for television companies to create online content that can improve and support their brand-image (Ha & Olmsted, 2001). Others argue that even though most websites today are used as a supporting tool for the prime activities (e.g., newspapers, broadcasting, book publishing), it will be strategically wise for media companies to create unique products for Internet distribution in the future. Gilbert and Christensen (2002) show, in a study of U.S. newspapers' online editions, that there is a kind of dichotomy at work in the newspaper industry: half of the companies use a lot of original content for their online editions, and the other half is largely lifting the content from the print edition to their online activity. The major problem that has to be solved before it can be profitable on a larger scale for media companies to produce original content for online distribution is how to establish a satisfactory method of payment. Another problem is how to convince people to pay for something that has until now been free of charge in most cases (Dinkelspiel, 2001).

This chapter has so far dealt with the concept of branding, how these practices can be used by media companies, and what opportunities and challenges they present. It is now time to turn to the other concept in focus: cross-promotion and its implications.

CROSS-PROMOTION

When discussing branding, brand extension, and brand portfolios, cross-promotion is a strategy close at hand: when you have a portfolio of media products within one or a couple of brand lines, many of the cross-promotional activities come naturally. For most media companies it would seem like a good idea to use the brands they already have when pursuing cross-promotion—what would be more natural than to take the opportunity to promote the *Popstar* album in the *Popstar* television program commercial break? Another example is when Oprah Winfrey uses her TV show for cross-promotion of her book club, magazines, or Internet site. Because they all have the same brand, the book club, magazines, and Internet site are like an extension of the show, which makes the cross-promotion a strategy close at hand. The relationship between branding and cross-promotion is very much a reciprocal one; the brands can create cross-promotion possibilities, but the cross-promotional possibilities can also create incentives for branding activities such as extension or the creation of brand portfolios.

Using the Oprah example above, the opportunity to cross-promote must have been one economic incentive for the extension of the brand into the other media activities. But, as we shall see, cross-promotion is not one single consistent strategy. In order to further understand the relationship between branding and cross-promotion, a typology of cross-promotion will be presented next.

A Typology of Cross-Promotion

The term *cross-promotion* is popularly used by both practitioners and theoreticians for different practices. It is, in fact, an umbrella concept incorporating several different practices that create different outcomes. What they have in common is the "cross," which in all cases means that the promotion crosses some kind of boundary, be it company, product, media, customer groups, or content. To clarify what is actually meant by cross-promotion, a categorization of the different meanings/uses popularly called cross-promotion is presented below:

- Cross-company promotion: when a number of companies cooperate in promoting joint products or projects,
- Cross-customer promotion: when a company uses the information they have on their customers to promote to them other products they might be interested in,
- Cross-media promotion: when a company uses their advertising sales force to bundle advertising space in all their products and sell it as a package,
- Cross-product promotion: when one company owns several products and use their advertising space for promotion of their other products, and
- Cross-content promotion: when one company owns several products, the content of which they use for promoting their other products.

The elements of these are presented in summary form in Table 7.1. We will now turn to each of these concepts and look at their practical implications and the rationales behind them.

Type of cross-promotion	Cross-company	Cross-customer	Cross-media	Cross-product	Cross-content
Actors involved	Portfolio firm & other firms	Portfolio firm	Portfolio firm & advertisers	Portfolio firm	Portfolio firm
Customer targeted	All	Company's current customers	All	Consumer of the product in which the promotion occurs	Consumer of the product in which the promotion occurs
Outcome	Cross-promotion campaigns with several firms involved	Customized promotion to known customer segments	Bundled advertising packages	Promotion in portfolio media for products produced by the same firm	Promotion for products produced by the same firm "hidden" in content
Benefits	Cover areas the firm cannot cover alone	Promotion reaching the right customer segments; cost effective	Long term deals with advertisers; securing a critical resource	Targeting already caught customer's attention; cost effective	Catching the consumer off guard; cheap content; cost effective

Table 7.1
Types of Cross-Promotion

Cross-Company Promotion. Cross-company promotion occurs when two or more companies cooperate in a promotion effort for a joint project. An example is when Time Warner's New Line Cinema launched *The Lord of the Rings*: the videogames were produced by Electronic Arts and the toys were sold in kids' meals at Burger King. This sort of cooperation and networking is something that most companies today regard as an important strategy for reaching the customer in an ever-increasing competitive environment (Gardner, 1998) and this can be seen a lot today, both in the media industry and other industries. Cross-company promotion will probably have little effect on the internal management and creation of product portfolios, because this type of cross-promotion has to do with a company's cooperation with other companies.

A firm's ability to engage in cross-company promotion therefore depends on their relationships with other actors. Cross-company promotion is often used for endorsement purposes, when a brand or a company benefit from the association with another brand or company. However, because this book focuses on media companies' product portfolios, and not on media companies' strategic alliances with other actors, this sort of cross-promotion will not be explored in depth here.

Cross-CustomerPromotion. Cross-customer promotion occurs when a company uses their existing customer base of one of their products to promote their other products. One advantage of having a product portfolio is that a company with a good knowledge of its customer base can use this audience as a target group when adding new products to its portfolio. It can then design promotion activities for its new products that are targeted to the correct customer segments, using the company's previous knowledge of those customers' preferences. Customer clubs and other such activities have long been used by companies that want to gain a better knowledge of their customers. For example, the customer address register is a potential goldmine for cross-customer promotion of the other products in the portfolio for a magazine publisher with subscribing customers. A magazine subscriber interested in boats and sailing could be "bombed" with promotions for other related magazines. Another possibility for a product portfolio firm is to follow a customer through her or his life cycle and the different demands that different life stages create.

The opportunities for cross-customer promotion have made media companies aware of the advantages of having a good understanding of and contact with their customers. The record company BMG has begun to exploit the opportunities of offering its customers tips on music that fits their music profile. The customer knowledge should, thus, be seen as a competitive advantage, because it can be used for creating demands which the company instantly can satisfy. At BMG the customer data is gathered through artist websites, where a log-in function collects data on the visiting fan. Customer data could also be collected by their digital distribution, where the company can keep track of customer purchases, and by customer clubs which in the case of BMG so far have provided data on 10 million members (Wistein, 2001). The Canadian media group Can West Global Communications is another example of a media company that wants to get a better understanding of their customers. They have launched electronic versions of their newspapers in hopes of increasing their knowledge of the audience. They thus hope to collect data on their readers via the Internet (Precision Marketing, April 11, 2003).

Cross-customer promotion is an advantageous strategy for companies that want to reach a certain audience segment. By using customer data, the company can both reach "new" customers (such as former customers or a consumer of one of the company's other products) and retain old customers. If products are homogenous, it could be a cost-effective way of promotion since it enables promotion targeted to a specific segment instead of the randomness of mass-advertising. Here we can find a connection between brand extension and the use of cross-customer promotion, because the same brand often targets the same customer segment. Subscribers of the ESPN sports cable channel would be a good target for cross-customer promotion of the ESPN magazine, the ESPN radio channel, and ESPN retail stores. One obstacle for many product portfolio firms has been that they have, so far, not had any good data about who their customers are. This will probably change in the future, though, when companies realize what opportunities good customer knowledge provides. With the increasing importance of one-to-one marketing, good data on customers will be a competitive advantage. When it comes to the effect of cross-customer promotion practices on the development of product portfolios, it can be an incentive for the creation of both related and unrelated media product lines. One important implication of this practice could be that the products, related or unrelated, will be aimed at the same customer segment.

Cross-Media Promotion. Cross-media promotion occurs when a media company that owns multiple media products bundles advertising-space in all of these products and sells to advertisers as a package. One of the financial basics for most media companies is their dependence on dual customers: the audience and the advertisers. For a media firm producing multiple products, there can be lucrative cross-media promotion benefits in the companies' businesses with their advertisers. In recent years, the possibility of joint advertising, combined sales forces, and marketing efforts has been one of the goals for many media mergers, acquisitions, and alliances (Dignam, 2002). However, after the failures of the big mergers of AOL Time Warner and Vivendi Universal, among others, (Albarran & Gormly, 2003; Brundin & Melin, Chapter 4 in this volume) there has been an increased skepticism also toward cross-media promotion deals. Within the marketing and advertising communities, there are different opinions on whether cross-media promotion is beneficial or not. Some argue that from the advertising buyers perspective, the bundling of advertising space shifts the focus from quality to quantity. Instead of buying audiences especially targeted for their purposes, the advertisers end up with audiences whom they have no interest in reaching (Dignam, 2002). Others are skeptical about whether media companies really can contribute with any extra value to the advertisers that the advertising agencies have not been able to provide so far. Advertising campaigns distributed on several platforms existed long before it became fashionable for media companies to merge (Dignam, 2002; McCarthy & Rose, 2003).

But there are also voices that undividedly sing the praises of cross-media promotion, arguing that they have been a success both for the media companies and their advertising customers. A study of AOL Time Warner's ad deals made by the industry journal *Advertising Age* showed that the company did succeed in generating incremental advertising increases at the same time as the advertising buyers seemed pleased. Interviews with their clients indicated that most of them were satisfied with the deals. The study examined U.S. advertisers' spending on AOL Time Warner's traditional media, such as magazines, cable, and broadcast, and found an increased spending of 30.5%. It should be pointed out, however, that spending and revenue are not the same thing, and some of the advertisers confirmed that AOL Time Warner had given discounts to snare these big advertising deals (Johnson, 2002). Within the U.S. radio broadcasting industry, there are also optimistic prognoses for the future of cross-media promotion deals. Radio industry executives argue that network radio provides an effective reach and frequency for brand managers who want to make the most of their advertising money (Ditingo, 1999).

Cross-media promotion could be a way for companies to create synergies in their advertising and marketing departments. Instead of having separate units for the selling of advertisements and marketing, this function could be centralized. When looking into the rationale behind product portfolios, cross-media promotion could trigger a development of large-scale media portfolios in order to benefit from synergies of the kind discussed above. It can also stimulate the creation of product portfolios targeted to audiences whom advertisers would be interested in, such as product portfolios targeted to similar customer segments or a special geographic market. Companies having a series of products under the same brand would therefore have an incentive for engaging in cross-media promotion, because the same brand often targets the same consumers, making the products attractive to advertisers. Cross-media promotion would also be beneficial for brand advertisers who want to reach a big audience. Whether it would be beneficial also to advertisers interested in more specialized consumer segments has been a topic of much discussion lately. The ability of an advertiser to benefit from cross-media promotion will depend on both the type of cooperation with the media company and on the attractiveness of the consumers.

Cross-Product Promotion. Steinbock (2000) defines what he terms *cross-promotion*, but what is here categorized as cross-product promotion, as: "Promotion of a product to the buyers of another product sold by the same seller" (p. 218).

As consumers, we are used to cross-product promotion. During breakfast, we read about the new dairy product promoted on the milk carton, a message sent from the producer of both these products. When baking bread using the recipe on the flour package, we are told to use only the baking powder produced by the same company that sold us the flour. This is nothing new. But when the cross-product promotion concept is transferred to the media industry, new opportunities open. Because the media producers have a long tradition of using their products as a medium for promotion of others' products and services, it is natural that they are taking the opportunity of using their products for promotion of their own products.

Lately, when many media companies have diversified their operations into operating more than one media business, cross-product promotion's importance has increased. Eastman (2000) contends that the media business only recently has begun to realize the advantage of being able to "self-promote." She regards the television broadcasters' and cable stations' ability to send on-air spots promoting their own programs (so-called promos) as the most valuable kind of self-advertising possible. An estimated figure is that the U.S. broadcast networks collectively were airing more than 30,000 promos per year by the late 1990s. For the four biggest networks, this meant that they were forgoing about $4 billion in advertising revenue they might have earned if they had sold the space to advertisers. According to Eastman, these sums show how valuable the networks regard the cross-product promotion of their programs.

There are other rationales related to cross-product promotion for a company in the media business to create a product portfolio. For a media firm it makes sense to promote its products in its own media if possible. In that way the money is being kept in the firm, instead of going to one's competitors. One example of this is the Swedish media group Bonnier's free sheet *City*, in which 8 out of 10 of the biggest advertisers in the first 2 months after its launch were other Bonnier companies. In order to lure the jointly owned companies into placing their advertisements in *City*, all Bonnier-owned companies got a price reduction of somewhere around 30% to 50%, sometimes as high as 70%, of the advertising price (Rydergren, 2003). In addition to keeping the advertising money in-house, it is also advantageous to fill advertising time/space with advertising for jointly owned products. This enhances the flexibility for, for example, a newspaper in the production and planning process.

In the media industry there has been an ever-increasing selection of products, while customers' money and time available for spending on these products have not at all increased at the same pace. In the urban world there are innumerable media products from which to choose, which makes changing the channel or buying another newspaper an easy thing to do. The cost for the consumer of abandoning a product for a substitute is in most cases very low (Picard, 2002). This has led to a fragmented audience where companies need to find ways to retain their customers. The problem of audience fragmentation is thus another incentive for cross-product promotion. This indicates that once one has the attention of the audience, one should make an effort to promote one's other products. According to the marketing "Big-Bang" theory, a promotional spot has only 3 seconds to gain the attention of the viewer before she or he changes the channel (Bellamy & Traudt, 2000). This is an incentive for media companies to create a well-balanced portfolio with products that can be promoted to their present customers. A product portfolio could in this way help a company exploit market opportunities and make the firm grow.

Cross-product promotion is generally a cost-effective way for a product portfolio firm to promote products by using one's own promotion channels. The use of these promotion channels is in many cases without additional costs. This is often the case for magazine and newspaper companies. For other companies there is a cost associated with the use of cross-product promotion (assuming that the advertising space otherwise would be sold to outside advertisers), but in comparison it would be relatively cheap even for television, radio, and Internet firms. Cross-product promotion could also be a way to strengthen a brand, like in the examples of promotion between Internet sites and nondigital products of the same brand. Products within the same brand also allow for logical cross-product promotion, because it makes sense to advertise for the Internet edition of the newspaper in the print edition and vice versa. Portfolio owners will, furthermore, achieve a promotional effect just by owning different product types with the same brand, such as a film based on the book will lure book readers to the cinemas and moviegoers to the bookstands. Cross-product promotion can also be used for the creation of customer loyalty—when a customer is a consumer of one product, the promotion of other products is a way to strengthen this loyalty by getting the consumer interested in other products within the portfolio. As in the case of both cross-media and cross-customer promotion, cross-product promotion can therefore lead to a development of product portfolios with products aimed at the same consumer segments.

Cross-Content Promotion. Cross-content promotion is closely related to cross-product promotion in the sense that both concepts refer to when one company uses one of their products for promotion of their other products. The difference is that cross-product promotion is limited to advertisements or clearly defined promotion activities, and is not mixed with the content such as television programs or newspaper articles. Cross-content promotion, on the other hand, occurs when a media company within its content promotes some of their other products. This sort of cross-promotion tries to blend content with promotion (critics even argue that in the worst cases it is the other way around: that media producers try to cover their promotion with a thin layer of content). Be that as it may, it is evident that some media companies, to different degrees, use cross-content promotion and that this has been going on for decades. It is also getting increasingly difficult to separate the content from the promotion. In television this has been particularly frequent. Stars from TV series playing on the same or jointly owned TV channels have appeared in other shows and programs in order to promote their show. Documentaries or "behind the scenes" programs are shown in connection with the main program. This phenomenon can also be detected when a film/book/record is released: the entertainment shows are swamped by actors/writers/singers promoting their new product. Newspapers might publish the first chapter of a new novel released by the jointly owned book publisher to make people buy the book. Even the Swedish public service broadcasting company has launched a strategy of increased cross-content promotion between its channels and programs (Resume.se, April 9, 2003).

Cross-content promotion in this kind of entertainment context is something most of us are used to, and if we are asked about it, most of us might think this is of no ethical concern. But we might react differently to cross-promotion in the news. McAllister (2002) investigated how the last episode of the sitcom *Seinfeld* was covered in U.S. television newscasts and found a remarkable difference between those stations that had economic connections to the show and those who did not. This phenomenon is called *plugola* and is defined as: "when a person responsible for including promotional material in a broadcast has a financial interest in the goods, or ... the group being promoted" (p. 384).

The plugola problem has gained increased attention from journalism and media scholars (Alden & Bensen, 1995; McAllister, 2002) and adds fuel to the debate and theorizing about agenda setting and power over the news. News journalists have also raised a cry of warning that their ability for critical coverage of media companies is threatened because the media conglomerates often end up owning or being allied with the company where the journalists work. Another possible threat to journalistic news integrity is pressure from the employer that the journalistic work should be guided by promotional goals rather than aiming at being a "watchdog" or other such journalistic norms (McAllister, 2002).

From a company's perspective, cross-content promotion is a good way of achieving cost effectiveness since the company can use its editorial material for promotion and does not have to pay for other types of promotion. It also reduces costs for editorial material if the firm produces content from resources they have "in their backyard" or can get hold of relatively easy. Many media companies with product portfolios are specialists at coming up with concepts that can be used across their different products. Disney for example can use the same story in a comic book, movie, soundtrack, television cartoon series, and computer games. This practice can create synergies in the production of these products. The chance of pursuing cross-content promotion could therefore be an incentive for media companies to create product portfolios. If a firm already has a TV show on a topic, they might find it a good idea to make a magazine out of the same topic and cash in on the synergies. The extension of TV show brands into magazines on the same sort of topics and targeted to the same type of audience is an example of how media producers are trying to achieve synergies. (The creation of synergies in content production has been doubted, however. One reason is the difficulty of coordinating different norms of operation and different industry cultures (Croteau & Hoynes, 2001). The branded products are also often used for cross-content promotion.

Cross-content promotion may also be advantageous from a firm's view in the sense that consumers might not realize that what they actually are consuming is promotion, and therefore let their guard down. But this strategy may also backfire and cause consumers to feel cheated, something that probably would hurt the company in the long run. The plugola debate should also serve as a warning for companies with media product portfolios that aim at pursuing cross-content promotion. From a public welfare perspective it is important to keep in mind that product portfolios can lead to increased opportunities for media companies to engage in cross-content promotion and "plugging."

Factors Affecting Media Companies' Ability to Cross-Promote

So far, some order has been brought into the different uses of the concept of cross-promotion and examples have been given of how they are used by media companies today. There are as many varieties of media product portfolios as there are media companies, and all these companies operate under different circumstances that one has to take into account when dealing with the individual companies. The incentive for companies with a media product portfolio to use any of the cross-promotion strategies, and whether they turn out to be successful when used, depends on several different factors. For some companies one of the strategies might be preferred above others, and on other occasions it might be difficult to use any of them. The main factors affecting companies' ability to cross-promote are the following:

- Product portfolio
- Customer segments
- Company culture
- Company size/complexity and structure
- Organization of cross-promotion strategies
- Relationship with external actors

These factors' influence on media firms' cross-promotional opportunities will be explored in the following section.

Product Portfolio. The type of product portfolio is one important factor influencing whether a company will be able to cross-promote. The products in a media portfolio can be categorized by how they are integrated with each other:

they can be horizontally or vertically integrated. Vertical integration is when a company controls all (or some) of the parts in the production and commercialization process of a product. Vertical integration is pursued for two reasons: to avoid dependence on suppliers or with the aim of increasing profits (Sánchez-Tabernero & Carvajal, 2002). An example from the media world is a newspaper publisher who owns the printing presses, the content-producing units and the distribution outlets. Companies that pursue vertical integration, and thus have a product portfolio containing products at different levels of the production chain, have very few opportunities for cross-promotion, because they often have no common customer or audience base and no advertisers who are interested in more than one of their products. However, there is a possibility for vertically integrated companies to pursue a cross-company promotion strategy.

Picard, in chapter 1 of this volume, indicates that a horizontally integrated media product portfolio can be built upon related media product lines (the same type of product, for example, only newspapers) or unrelated media product lines (different types of products, for example, both newspapers and magazines). Another way to diversify is to go into different markets and thus diversify marketwise. These different strategies will obviously create different outcomes, but the overall rationale for diversification strategies is to diversify risk, pursue growth, and create synergies (Sánchez-Tabernero & Carvajal, 2002). From a cross-promotion point of view, a media company with a product portfolio consisting of related products could theoretically be suitable for all five types of cross-promotion. This would also hold true for a company owning an unrelated product portfolio. Whether these companies would really benefit from pursuing a cross-promotion strategy has to do with the specific nature of the products. It might work to cross-content promote (using content as promotion channel) a record through a TV program, but the other way around is more difficult to imagine. When it comes to companies that have diversified their products in different markets, both domestic and international, they could also pursue all sorts cross-promotion strategies. This, of course, also depends on the situation and the structure of their diversification. A magazine like *Elle*, which is published in many countries all over Europe, can take advantage of both cross-media promotion (selling advertiser packages to companies wanting to advertise their brand) and cross-company promotion (cooperating with other firms in promotion campaigns). However, *Elle* has few opportunities for cross-product/customer/content promotion because of the country and language barriers.

Customer Segments. The second influence on the possibility for a product portfolio company to pursue cross-promotion strategies is the customers/ audience (it is important to note that when discussing customers in this sense, it is the readers, viewers, and listeners and not the advertisers who are referred to). Media products are targeted to different segments of customers, some to wide segments and others specialized for a very small audience. According to marketing textbooks (Fill, 2002; Kotler, 1999), basic customer segmentation could be based on customer attributes such as demography, geography, geodemography, psychoanalytic, and lifestage. These segments could thus be created according to criteria ranging from "obvious" attributes such as sex and age, to more complex attributes such as lifestyle and personality.

Picard argues in Chapter 1 of this volume that it would be beneficial for media firms to diversify their products into different consumer segments in order to avoid cannibalization of their existing customer bases. If the products become too similar, they might start competing with each other. Another incentive for market diversification is discussed above—it can reduce risk. However, this could cause a problem for companies that want to cross-promote. If one wants to take advantage of the cross-promotional opportunities of having a product portfolio, the products cannot be too heterogeneous. Cross-company/product/ content/customer promotion require the same type of customers, or at least customers who might be interested in the other portfolio products. For cross-media promotion (packaged advertising deals) to be desirable from the advertisers' point of view, it is also important that the products are targeted to the kind of audience they want to reach. To make full use of cross-promotion of a product portfolio, it would be important to have a portfolio of products that are of interest to a homogenous customer segment. If a product portfolio is too widely spread over different segments, companies can end up promoting products to customers who have no interest in the product. A record company's cross-customer promotion of opera classics to their teen audience might not be such a good idea.

Company Culture. The company culture is the third factor that can influence a company's abilities to successfully pursue cross-promotion of a product portfolio. Schein (1985) has defined organizational culture as: "The pattern of basic assumptions that a given group has invented, discovered or developed in learning to cope with its problems of external adaptation and internal integration, and that has worked well enough to be considered valid, and, therefore, to be taught to new members as the correct way to perceive, think and feel in relation to these problems" (p. 6).

In short, company culture is shared basic assumptions that all members of the organization have been taught. In many cases the culture can be a hindrance to new ways of doing business, including such things as cross-promotion strategies. The history, mission and organizational behavior of a firm constrains and directs the opportunities for a company in its creation of a product portfolio.

The same can be said for their possibilities of cross-promoting these products. If a company has several subcultures within different departments, it might be hard to engage all these in a joint cross-promotion strategy. If a media company always has seen their products and the departments in which they are produced as separate entities, management might run into strong resistance if they try to get the company involved in a cross-promotion strategy. It is reasonable to assume that the different types of cross-promotion might be varyingly affected by the cultural factor, however. Cross-company/media/customer/product promotion might be less problematic because at least the editorial content is unaffected. Even so, it might prove difficult to get different marketing departments to coordinate their activities across different cultural barriers. For a newspaper company with a legacy of serious investigative journalism it might be unthinkable to descend to cross-content promotion. Even the other cross-promotional strategies might be unthinkable because of the history of journalistic integrity that the company rests upon.

The culture of a company does not necessarily have to impede cross-promotion, though. It could also facilitate cross-promotion efforts. In the case of the Swedish media group Modern Times Group (MTG), the company culture can be one reason why the group has been relatively successful in pursuing an overall cross-promotion strategy between their products and business units. A former MTG executive states that the vision of cross-promotion has permeated the whole company from an early stage (Engzell-Larsson, 2000). This idea of joint cross-promotion for financial gain has then become a part of MTG's corporate culture, which is an essential factor for any strategy to succeed.

Company Size and Complexity. The size and structural complexity of the company owning the product portfolio can influence its ability to pursue cross-promotion strategies. For a small company with only one business unit it might be easier to coordinate cross-promotion strategies, such as cross-product promotion between products within the same unit. For larger companies the same strategy would have to be coordinated between two or more business units, often with increased communication and bureaucratic complexities. The degree of hierarchy and control, and the degree to which the different departments are autonomous or strongly linked to each other, will also affect the cross-promotion ability. A company that has a structure that makes cooperation between departments easy might do a better job of coordinating all units for cross-promotion strategies. It is, however, not necessarily so that large companies per se are in a bad position for cross-promotion. The former executive from the MTG media group, mentioned above, claimed that the MTG was far ahead of its competitors when it came to cross-promotion, despite being a big corporation that includes many different businesses. According to him, MTG's hierarchic top-down structure has been an advantage when it comes to getting all units involved in the corporate cross-promotion (Engzell-Larsson, 2000). With all the business units controlled tightly by top management, it has been possible to "order" people into joint cross-promotion strategies. Whether this really is a good way of managing an organization could be doubted, but it might force people into thinking in directions of cross-promotion.

Other ways of creating incentives for employees to pursue cross-promotion strategies will be discussed next.

Company Capacity and Organization of Cross-Promotion Strategies. An important factor for whether media companies successfully can pursue cross-promotion strategies of their product portfolios is whether they have the proper resources to do so, and how these resources are organized. Pursuing a cross-promotion strategy requires, among other things, knowledge of one's customers, resources for the promotional activities, commitment and knowledge from both the management and the employees, and an advertising sales function that can bundle cross-media advertising packages. The financial capacity is consequently not the only crucial resource affecting a company's cross-promotion abilities. Just as important are the managerial skills, the employees' commitment and knowledge of the strategy, and a well-thought-out cross-promotion strategy. A cross-product promotion campaign can be a smaller campaign with a time limit or it can be a more comprehensive strategy involving the whole company. The degree of formality of the cross-promotion undertaken will also affect whether the company experiences difficulties when pursuing cross-promotion activities. As with any other organizational action and strategy, the outcome and success will depend on many factors. In either case it will be important to create incentives for all employees and business units involved so that they can see how they benefit from participating.

Relationships with External Actors. There are not only factors within the company or relationships with the customers that affect cross-promotion opportunities. For cross-company promotion, the relationships with a company's external actors, such as other companies, are also important. If two companies engage in a joint cross-promotional effort, it is essential that these companies have a good relationship. If a media firm has a questionable reputation and a history of failed joint operations, it can be hard to find a partner willing to take the risk of cooperation. When it comes to companies offering cross-media promotion deals, whether they can sell these depends on what the advertisers are looking for. It is not only of importance what kind of portfolio, and therefore customers, that a company has. What also is significant is how committed the company is to the cooperation, and how willing they are to work together with the advertiser to develop long-term strategies (Johnson, 2002). External actors, such as the society at large and public opinion, may also be significant, especially if a company sets out to pursue cross-content promotion. Because this practice can collide with journalistic norms of ethics and integrity, cross-content promotion could cause problems for the company concerning its social and journalistic legitimacy. Consequently, the price a company might end up paying for an excessive use of cross-content promotion could be high.

CASE STUDY:
The Story of a Magazine Publisher

The case involves a small Swedish magazine company in the niche-magazine business that wishes to remain anonymous. The company is actively engaged in mainly cross-product promotion (but also cross-customer and cross-advertising promotion are of interest to the company). The company publishes magazines targeted at men (who constitute more than 80% of their readers) interested in motor vehicles and information technology. In order to make their product portfolio more suited for cross-product promotion, a couple of years earlier they had sold off a music teen magazine targeted towards young girls. The Magazine Publisher figured that they thereby had a good chance at reaching a large number of men aged thirty and above with what was now a niched product portfolio.

This strategy was put to the test when they launched a new boat magazine and figured that they could make use of their other magazines to promote the new launch. In the campaign for the new magazine they used half of their portfolio of magazines to carry special advertising offers for the new product (e.g., the customers were offered to subscribe to three issues of the new magazine at a discount). The turnout was a disappointment. The response-rate on the offers was as low as 0.18% of the total circulation of the magazines participating in the launch. This weak result showed that the publisher's hope for cross-product promotion benefits was harder to realize than expected. Their conclusion was that in the case of niche-magazines, it could be more difficult than generally expected to benefit from cross-product

Continued next page

SUMMARY

The growth of media companies into multimedia conglomerates during the last decades has brought to the fore the interest in media product portfolios. This raises the question of what kind of marketing and promotion possibilities this development will bring. This chapter has looked at media product portfolios and shown how media companies can use cross-promotion and branding strategies in the marketing of their product lines. The chapter has also outlined some of the critical factors that need consideration if these strategies are to be successfully pursued.

Continued from previous page

promotion. One possible explanation could be that the customer segments really were too heterogeneous. Despite the demographic similarities of the magazine consumers (mostly men in a certain age) they had such specific interests that were not interested in another type of niche product. The Magazine Publisher had thus underestimated the psychoanalytic differences in their customer segments. The outcome of the campaign indicated that men interested in specialized computer and car magazines were not that interested in specialized boat magazines after all.

The Magazine Publisher also had experienced how difficult it could be to organize other promotion activities of their product portfolio. Despite their seemingly good opportunity of coordinating the promotion of their different magazines, this turned out to be more difficult than it looked on paper. The company was made up of a couple of autonomous groups, in which the editorial and marketing staff was responsible for the different groups of magazines published. These autonomous groups had histories and cultures of their own, some of them having published magazines for decades, others being initiated by enthusiastic journalists interested in their special area and then bought by the larger publishing company. This meant that the editorial staffs on the different magazines often identified more with the readers of their magazines than with their owner, and that they were relatively uninterested in cooperating with the other magazine groups. The physical structure was another obstacle to cooperation between the units. Even though they all worked in the same building, they sat on different floors with distinct territorial boundaries between them. The management at the Magazine Publisher understood the benefits of letting the groups remain relatively autonomous in order to remain creative and enthusiastic, but they were still a bit frustrated by not being able to benefit from synergies coming from coordination.

The portfolio characteristics will influence the cross-promotion and branding abilities of a media portfolio company. Brand extension strategies depend on the connection between the old and the new product. If there is no natural connection between two products, there is a great risk that the extension attempt will fail. Therefore, it would be wise to only attempt brand extensions when products are in some way related to each other, or perceived to fulfill the same needs for the customer. For certain media firms, like news companies, the brand is a valuable asset, which, if extended wisely, will be a competitive advantage for the company. The sorts of products that make up the portfolio are also pivotal when it comes to cross-promotion activities. Certain products can be efficiently used for the different kinds of cross-promotion, while other products are less suited for these strategies. A vertically integrated product line will probably be less effective for achieving cross-promotional benefits, whereas a horizontally integrated range of products provides a better opportunity for cross-promotion. Branding strategies can work for both vertically and horizontally integrated product portfolios.

The second important issue is company characteristics. The size, structure, and corporate culture will have a great influence on the outcome of any strategy. Because coordination is essential, it might be easier for smaller companies of a simpler structure to pursue different kinds of cross-promotion. A smaller-sized company will in many cases communicate in a simpler and more effective way, which is crucial when pursuing a new strategy. Small size usually also makes cooperation between units and departments easier, and employees involved in the operations might find it easier to cooperate across boundaries in a small organization. With the increase in size often comes an increase in rigidity because the specialization of personnel and departments hinders cooperation between departments. On the other hand, as empirical examples have shown, the size and structure of the company is not the only factor that plays a part in cross-promotion strategies. Another important factor is whether the people involved in cross-promotion and branding are actually committed to being involved. If they do not understand or agree with the objectives, or lack the incentive to participate in the strategy process, the company will have difficulties in engaging successfully in cross-promotion and branding. As Ots argues in chapter 8 of this volume, it is vital to create incentive systems and structures that promote and facilitate synergy-seeking behavior and cooperation. The corporate culture will also be of importance. A firm's culture and history can be both an incentive and a hinder for people within the organization to invest their time and energy into pursuing cross-promotional strategies. Some media firms might have difficulties in engaging in certain cross-promotional efforts because of the journalistic legacy of the company. Others might have a culture of autonomy between different units that impedes cross-unit strategies. On the other hand, some companies might have a culture that facilitates cooperation and synergy-seeking operations. It is, therefore, vital that the strategy pursued is chosen not only because it fits the company product portfolio; the nature of the company must also be taken into consideration.

Knowledge of external factors, such as customers, competitors, possible allies, legislation, and public opinion, will also matter for the outcome of branding and cross-promotional activities. The impact that negative public opinion can have on a company heavily engaged in cross-content promotion should be ·taken into consideration if a firm is considering pursuing such a strategy. Also brand extension is a strategy best used with moderation. Croteau and Hoynes (2001) argue that the media conglomerates may cause a consumer backlash against the media "Big Brother" if they use the same brand for all their products. They argue that the big portfolio owners are wise to have several brand product lines instead of having the same brand on all their products, so that the origin of all these products is disguised.

A good relationship with other possible allies is vital for companies wanting to pursue cross-company promotional deals and engage in brand endorsement activities. Many of the cross-company deals involve a great deal of cooperation over a long period of time. Therefore, it is important that companies choose their allies with care and are committed to this cooperation. An issue of increasing strategic significance for media companies is customer knowledge. Media product portfolio owners can direct their current customers toward other products in their portfolio. This will prove to be a valuable resource in an increasingly competitive market, where one-to-one marketing will come to play an important role. The development of customer databases that enable cross-customer promotion will be one of the challenges for media portfolio companies in the future.

The implications of branding and cross-promotion on media product portfolio companies will also concern global media firms. In fact, in the global context, many of these issues will be even more important for global media companies to handle if they are going to succeed in their cross-promotion and branding strategies. Global markets require a complex organizational structure, with all the implications that will have for the coordination of cross-promotion and branding activities. The importance of understanding and anticipating cultural differences, both within the company and marketwise, will be a key factor for the success of a global portfolio product company.

Taken together, the factors outlined above all matter for product portfolio companies when they consider pursuing cross-promotion and branding-related strategies. As has been stated, these strategies are complex and there are several factors affecting the final outcome. On the other hand, a product portfolio firm will have a lot to win if they are able to master these processes. The growth of global multimedia companies and the increasingly competitive markets in which they operate will force the media business into thinking of new and improved ways of promoting their products. The strategies discussed in this chapter will surely be increasingly important in the future.

REFERENCES

Aaker, D. A. (1991). *Managing brand equity: Capitalizing on the value of a brand name.* New York: Free Press.

Aaker, D. A. (1996). *Building strong brands.* New York: Free Press.

Albarran, A. B. & Gormly, R. K. (2004). Strategic response or strategic blunder? An examination of AOL Time Warner and Vivendi Universal. In R. G. Picard (ed.), *Strategic responses to media market changes* (pp. 35-46). JIBS Research Reports Series No. 2004-2. Jönköping: Jönköping International Business School.

Alden, B. & Bensen, J. (1995). The plugola problem. *Columbia Journalism Review, 34*(1), 17.

Arrese, A. & Medina, M. (2002). Competition in Financial News Markets. In R. G. Picard (Ed.), *Media firms: Structures, operations and performance* (pp. 59–76). Mahwah, N.J.: Lawrence Erlbaum Associates.

Barwise, P. & Robertson, T. (1992). Brand Portfolios. *European Management Journal, 10*(3), 277–286.

Bellamy, R. V. & Traudt, P. J. (2000). Television branding as promotion. In S. T. Eastman (Ed.), *Research in media promotion.* Mahwah, NJ: Lawrence Erlbaum Associates.

Chan-Olmsted, S. M. & Jung, J. (2001). Strategizing the net business: How the U.S. television networks diversify, brand and compete in the age of the Internet. *International Journal of Media Management, 3*(4), 213–225.

Chan-Olmsted, S. M. & Kim, Y. (2001). Perceptions of branding among television station managers: An exploratory analysis. *Journal of Broadcasting & Electronic Media, 45*(1), 75.

Chan-Olmsted, S. M. & Park, J.S. (2000). From on-air to online world: Examining the content and structures of broadcast TV stations' web sites. *Journalism and Mass Communication Quarterly, 77*(2), 321-339.

Croteau, D. & Hoynes, W. (2001). *The business of media: Corporate media and the public interest.* Pine Forge Press.

Dignam, C. (2002). Cross media: Hype or Hope? *Marketing,* September 5, 22.

Dinkelspiel, L. (2001). Den stora utmaningen: ta betalt för nätinnehåll. *Vision* April 26, 4.

Ditingo, V. M. (1999). *Radio broadcasting and cable, 129*(1), 38.

Eastman, S.T. (2000). *Research in media promotion.* Mahwah, NJ: Lawrence Erlbaum Associates.

Engzell-Larsson, L. (2000). Intervju: Casten Almqvist—med blick för resultat, *Veckans affärer,* January 17.

Fill, C. (2002). *Marketing communications. Context, strategies and applications.* Harlow, UK: Financial Times Prentice Hall.

Galbi, D. (2001). The new business significance of branding. *Journal of Media Management, 3*(4), 192–198.

Gardner, E. (1998). Forget 'value added' think 'integrated media.' *The magazine for magazine management, 27*(16), 28.

Gilbert, C. & Christensen, C. (2002). Newspapers and the internet. *Niemen Reports,* Summer 2002.

Gruenwendel, E. (2000). Who wants to be a millionaire: Best multiplatform marketing efforts-enhanced TV. *Brandweek, 41*(23), IQ64.

Ha. L. & Chan-Olmsted, S. M. (2001). Enhanced TV as brand extension: TV viewers' erception of enhanced TV features and TV commerce on broadcast networks web sites. *International Journal of Media Management, 3*(4), 202-212.

Johnson, B. (2002). Ad deals pay off for AOL Time Warner. *Advertising Age,* *73*(49), 1.

McAllister, M. P. (2002). Television news plugola and the last episode of Seinfeld. *Journal of Communication, 52*(2), 383

Mc Carthy, M. J. & Rose, M. (2003). *Wall Street Journal,* May 14, B1 (Eastern Edition).

Picard, R. G. (2002). *The economics and financing of media companies.* New York: Fordham University Press.

Precision Marketing (2003). April 11, 9.

Resumé.se (2003) April 9. www.resume.se

Riezebos, R. (2003). *Brand management.* Gosport, UK: Prentice Hall.

Rydergren, T. (2003). Varannan annons I City är betald av Bonniers. *Resumé* January 30, 7.

Sánchez-Tabernero, A. & Carvajal, M. (2002). *Media concentration in the European market. New trends and challenges.* Media market monographs. June 2002 Pamplona: Servicio de Publicaciones de la Universidad de Navarra.

Schein, E. (1985). *Organizational culture and leadership.* San Francisco: Jossey-Bass.

Steinbock, D. (2000). *The birth of Internet marketing communications.* Westport, CT.: Quorum Books.

Wistein, E. (2001). Britney-fansen kartläggs—One-to-one-marknadsföring framtiden för skivbranschen i USA. *Dagens Media Sverige,* December 4.

8
Strategic Direction and Control of Portfolios: Can Standard Models Create Cross-Media Benefits?

Mart Ots
Jönköping International Business School

In increasingly competitive markets, media companies are forced to continuously develop new products, target new customer segments, and create new revenue streams. For the historically stable media corporations, future product portfolios are at risk of growing wilder and harder to manage. In order to maintain control over complex structures and the direction of multiple processes, an increased use of formalized, analytic methods to measure and evaluate portfolio performance is needed to help improve activities. This paper examines existing theoretical portfolio models from a corporate-level perspective to determine how well-suited they are for doing the job in the specific environmental settings facing the media business. Do they evaluate the right things? It appears that many underlying assumptions do not hold, creating a need for a more specialized perspective that takes into account both internal and external characteristics of media corporations.

Within each sector of the media industry, increased competition, customer fragmentation, and advertisers' shift to specialized and personalized media have forced media corporations to hold larger sets of more distinct niche products. In the meantime, *between* media sectors, new technologies are breaking down the barriers separating different forms of distribution among media actors, allowing channels with complementary content to join forces. Target audience is therefore a more important separation between media businesses than where and how the customers consume the products.

These considerations are leading major media companies to rapidly increase the scope of their operations, to broaden the media their activities involve, and to seek benefits through cross-media activities. Arthur O. Sulzberger Jr., New York Times Company chairman and publisher of the *New York Times*, has argued that "the future of media is convergence, and the New York Times Company has been acquiring other media outlets that will allow the *Times* to tell the same story in print, online and on television....Broadband is bringing us all together.

You can combine all three elements. News is a 24/7 operation, and if you don't have the journalistic muscles in all three fields you can't succeed in broadband" (Damewood, 2004).

Similar efforts have led other companies to seek benefits across their portfolios. Tom Curley, president and publisher of *USA Today*, says that the paper has begun positioning itself as a network. "Gannett's television stations now have instant access to *USA Today*'s deep editorial resource and daily morning inserts [have been added] to the AM newscasts at the Gannett stations....The project has gone beyond a corporate push at synergy to a smarter use of content resources that benefit viewers and readers, which is the goal" (Gannett, 2000).

Developments such as these have fundamentally altered the basis for constructing product portfolios in the media business. While the opportunities for achieving economies of scale decrease within each medium, economies of scope increase between media. What yesterday was considered a relevant group of related media products is not anymore. The widespread multidivisional form of organizing is not built for cross-divisional synergies and horizontal interactions. Existing product portfolios often reflect old logic, forcing media companies to implement new cross-media strategies with a given organizational structure based on past rules of the game. For example, radio, print, and television are by tradition placed in separate divisions of media corporations with different management, each with its own production capacity and profit targets, providing little incentive to cooperate. Businesses and products that today are closely related in terms of audience and content are in fact placed in remote parts of the physical organization, while products that only have their channel of distribution in common are managed together as one unit.

For this reason, there needs to be a revision, a questioning of the present construction of portfolios. There also needs to be a new way of organizing, evaluating, and monitoring products and businesses that acknowledges the strategic needs for cross-media synergies. Direction and control of media portfolios will hence be increasingly complex, multifaceted, and crucial to successful media corporations.

This chapter aims at highlighting the characteristics of the media industry and their effects on portfolio management and control. An initial review of portfolio literature identifies the situational shortcomings of several established models. It includes two case studies involving Vorarlberger Medienhaus and Bertelsmann that illustrate factors separating successful synergetic portfolios from unaccomplished attempts. Although diverse in size and scope of operations, the two cases show how size, structure, and management practices affect feasible outcomes, when analyzed from a corporate-level perspective. This allows us to make some recommendations as to which direction management practices need to be developed if cross-media synergies within the product portfolio are to be achieved.

A RAPIDLY CHANGING MEDIA ENVIRONMENT

As new titles and new channels are introduced, competition increases in European and American media markets. Television, for example, shows exponential growth in the number of channels while the amount of time spent on media consumption remains fairly constant (Van Cuilenburg, 2000). From another direction, advertisers voice criticism that mass media channels do not have the same impact on customers as they used to. The reason why many media businesses have survived so far is due to niche strategies (Dimmick, 2003) and barriers to competition created through legislation, languages, and cultures, national advertising markets, and consumer preferences for local media content (Sánchez-Tabernero & Carvajal, 2002).

Some products with standardized content formats such as magazines and capital intensive productions such as pay-TV and movies compete to a larger extent in international arenas. Others, such as daily newspapers and public television, still act on mainly national markets (Sánchez-Tabernero & Carvajal, 2002). The introduction of new technologies has changed customers' consumption patterns, opened up old barriers to entry, and at the same time questioned the construction of present media product portfolios. Because of the stable technologies and barriers to entry, industries such as the newspapers and music recording have hitherto enjoyed the enviable paradox of both exceptionally high returns and low risks (Picard, 2003). However, the very same firms are now facing a new situation, where they may remain market leaders, albeit of a rapidly vanishing slice of the consumer's total media consumption. In order to survive in this turbulent environment, firms must increasingly examine how their product portfolios are constructed and managed and how well their exploitation of existing profitable markets are balanced with exploration of new business opportunities. When capital resources are scarce, this balancing act requires both sensitivity and control.

The Goals of Portfolios

Portfolio management is about operationalizing the corporate strategy within a multi-business organization. It is a system for continuous decision-making including the emphasis on different products, markets, and technologies in order to keep the corporate direction (Cooper, et al., 1999). Aims of portfolios should be to support the overall corporate strategy, thus maximizing market share, share holder value or profits, for example.

There are three main arguments for holding a portfolio of media businesses: companies can maximize returns and available market opportunities, spread the overall risk of the operations, and gain economies of scale and scope (Picard, 2002; Van der Velten & Ansoff, 1998).

The concept of *synergies*, related to economies of scale and scope, is based on the idea that a certain combination of businesses produces better results when coordinated than they would if they remained independent of each other (Campbell & Luchs, 1992). This does put larger organizational requirements on the management techniques to create and exploit linkages between the businesses in the portfolio. Normally, more integration requires more central control and makes the organization react slowly to external changes (Lorsch & Allen, 1984). On the other hand, if there are few synergies to be made from coordination or the costs of achieving synergies are higher than the gains, the businesses can rather be treated as a portfolio of independent financial assets. Corporate top management can then, to a greater extent, leave the decision-making to the managers of each business unit (Van der Velten & Ansoff, 1998).

The usefulness of different management models is thus largely determined by the relatedness of the products and businesses and how profitable or desirable synergies and cooperation between the units is regarded. Multibusiness corporations employing unrelated diversification are likely to use different portfolio management tools than those with a related set of assets.

PORTFOLIO MANAGEMENT MODELS AND TOOLS

Three elements are important in making portfolio choices—the *balance* of the portfolio, the *attractiveness* of the included businesses, and the potential *synergies* between the products and businesses (Johnson & Scholes, 2002). The respective weights of these elements are in turn determined by the strategic intent of the portfolio.

A financially driven portfolio values the attractiveness of the businesses in terms of expected profit at a chosen risk level. However, a corporation looking for economies of scope emphasizes synergies. Both of them look for balance, but possibly from different angles—balanced financial risk in the first case and balanced match with corporate capabilities and resources in the second.

Finance-Oriented Models

Finance-oriented models use measures such as the net present value of future cash flows to determine the attractiveness of an investment. The strategic value of a product or business is here judged by its ability to pay back the investment with an interest that exceeds the expected risk level. Monthly EBIT can be the return rate, while variance of the returns normally is used as the risk variable. This builds on the assumption that it is possible to decrease systematic risk by holding a diverse set of portfolio assets. In this sense, finance-oriented models are tools for creating overview, comparability, and concrete limits as to when a unit meets certain requirements. Its primary use is for investment and divestment decisions. On the other hand, it gives little guidance for selecting portfolios that explore core capabilities or economies of scale and scope.

Financial models would work best for companies who only have the strategic intent to act as financial investors, acquiring undervalued businesses, divesting unprofitable parts, and improving performance through clear financial targets. Expectations and rewards are merely financial, and strategic decisions are left to the business managers as long as they meet the short-term targets. It is an extreme empowerment of the business unit, which maintains its creative freedom to explore new business opportunities. Also, the corporate strategic unit can be kept small despite holding a large number of diverse businesses (Johnson & Scholes, 2002).

Financial approaches are the most commonly used category of methods (Cooper, et al., 1999). Under stable environmental conditions, where the different units or products included in the portfolio are easily comparable and no synergies between the units are sought, financial models may help to increase overall business performance (Van der Velten & Ansoff, 1998). However, when uncertainty is high, valuation by discounting cash flows has the tendency to understate the value of projects (Bowman, et al., 2002). As a tool for project selection, compared with all available portfolio models, financial methods have proven to yield the poorest performance in terms of value of the projects, fit between projects and resources, and creation of bottlenecks and time losses (Cooper, et al., 1999).

Product-Based Models

Product-based models can to a greater extent be customized to fit a certain market or portfolio. The consequence is that not only are they more flexible to each firm's environment, but it is also difficult to construct, measure, and interpret their parameters. The two most significant product-based models are the mapping and strategic approaches.

Mapping Approaches. This is the first and perhaps most well-known group of product-based models, also called bubble diagrams. Examples include the growth/share matrix (also known as the BCG matrix) and the General Electric/McKinsey grid. These use diagrammatic pictures to map variables against each other, most commonly market growth versus market share or industry attractiveness vs. business strengths, but the dimensions could be selected by preference. A central obstacle is therefore how to select relevant and yet generalized, comparable parameters that suit the business (Wind & Mahajan, 1981).

The BCG matrix is a tool to create a balanced portfolio with a sufficient amount of cash to generate products to support a growing businesses. The outcome is a classification of the businesses into four categories. Businesses acting in early, high growth markets can have either large market shares (stars) or low market shares (question marks). Similarly, businesses in low growth markets have either high or low market shares (cash cows and dogs, respectively).

Mapping approaches have been shown to have an average capability of selecting valuable projects (Cooper, et al., 1999). One problem with regard to the media industry is that the growth/share matrix assumes an experience effect, lowering the unit costs with increasing volumes, thus rendering the "star" and "cash cow" positions highly favorable. The way to reach these positions is through quick and early growth. However, this size effect is offset among other things by differentiation strategies or innovation strategies (Lambin, 2000) that tend to become more critical in the maturity and the decline phases of the product life cycle (Anderson & Zeithaml, 1984; Wensley, 1982). By not allowing their products to turn into commodities, innovative firms can in this way keep high profit margins even in stagnating markets (Zeithaml & Fry, 1984). Thus, for smaller, creative, or technologically driven media companies serving niche markets, mapping approaches are not optimal. In fact, the trend indicates that competition drives media companies to specialize in narrower target audiences and to differentiate their products.

As technology changes and consumers embrace content variety, mere size is not directly transferable into profits, despite a position as a "cash cow." On the contrary, evidence suggests that especially in periods of change, size may in fact be correlated with inferior performance in the media business (Kolo & Vogt, 2003; Picard & Rimmer, 1999). At the same time, consumer preferences for regional content and language barriers make some small local newspapers highly profitable. But no matter how profitable, they would still be indicated as low market share, low-growth "dogs" in the grid. As a consequence, the models do not give any deeper understanding into when or what businesses to divest or invest in, and on what basis.

Strategic Approaches. These approaches have become increasingly important and are largely driven by the corporate strategy, looking to achieve "fit" between strategy and operations. Tools may include "strategic buckets" or categories to which resources are allocated in line with the overall strategy. Despite the lower emphasis on revenue, strategic methods produce the best-performing portfolios in terms of selecting projects with the highest value (Cooper, et al., 1999).

Other related methods are *checklists/scoring models*, paired comparisons such as *expert choice* and behavioral/consensus approaches such as *Delphi*. These can be based on more qualitative criteria such as perceived market attractiveness, core competencies, and synergies. Of all portfolio tools, the qualitative approaches are the most flexible and adaptable to the specific circumstances, which also make them possibly harder to formalize and more time-consuming.

Qualitative and Dynamic Tools

Strategic planning and portfolio management in the 1980s largely focused on markets and competition (Bowman, et al., 2002), which is well illustrated by the introduction of the mapping approaches and bubble diagrams. In the 1990s, academics such as Prahalad and Hamel (1990) shifted the interest towards the internal capabilities and core competencies of the firm.

The dominant Swedish media player, Bonnier, promoted all through the 1970s and 1980s the idea that the conglomerate structure was the way to spread the risk from their core activities in media. This strategy led the corporation into such diverse areas as real estate, capital investment, shipping, furniture, sports equipment, and medical research, just to mention a few. However, among other reasons, top management's lack of understanding of the specific strategic mechanisms of each of these diverse and highly competitive markets led to poor performance. In 1990, the deregulation of the Swedish media market opened new opportunities. Bonnier financed these investments through divestment and concentration of its operations into its area of core competence—media. Pure judgments of risk and return were no longer seen as enough to ensure long-term success in highly competitive markets (Larsson, 2001).

The multidivisional form of organizing (M-form), for which financial and mapping approaches were developed, was based on few assumed horizontal interactions between divisions (Hill, 1988). Recent interest in "synergies" and "strategic fit" has altered the perspective on portfolio management and control. Empirically it has been shown that high-performing firms use no one single tool, but rather a range of different portfolio management tools—including financial and mapping approaches—and are more committed to portfolio management than the average firm (Cooper, et al., 1999). Portfolio management now emphasizes the selection of products and businesses that complement each other in terms of present cash generation and strategic implications *as well as* future opportunities.

Dynamic Portfolio Models. Some researchers suggest that firms should increasingly look for a portfolio that represents a balanced blend of human resources and capabilities. Because innovation is a scarce good in many businesses, more resources will have to be put into developing entrepreneurial and expansion capabilities. The resources allocated to rigid financial portfolio steering will be limited to mature projects in stable environments. In this way, multiple products in different stages in the life cycle—entrepreneurial, expansion, and maturity—should be within the scope of the corporation's combined knowledge. It also means that the portfolio model does not have to rely on stable environments and stable competition in order to work. Different teams will use portfolio tools appropriate for their specific projects, thus developing internal dynamic capabilities of the organization (Lorange, 1998).

Synergy Tools. There are two main perspectives of synergy creation; that synergies are either found *horizontally* between the businesses in the portfolio, or that they emerge in the *vertical* exchange between corporate parent and each individual business.

Corporations employing the horizontal perspective seek to create value in the interaction between the businesses in the portfolio. Their success is determined by the ability to effectively identify markets, areas, and businesses activities, resources, and skills can be shared. If well managed, the shared pool of resources will then be a distinct competitive advantage in certain areas. As reward systems and portfolio evaluation benchmarks must be tailored to encourage cooperation and sharing of resources and knowledge, the corporate management needs to be determined and closely involved in creating synergies. In media businesses, this can be related to, for example, efficiencies in ad sales force, ad bundling, cross-promotion, and marketing, thus converging content production, printing, and distribution as well as infrastructure.

Corporations exploring vertical synergies believe in the existence of distinct value-adding competencies embedded in the central organization that can be induced in new portfolio objects (Campbell & Goold, 1999). Models such as the Ashridge Portfolio Display (see, e.g., Goold, et al., 1994), show that this requires corporate management to truly understand the success factors critical to the individual businesses. Outsourcing activities that may not fall into these competence fields, such as sales and printing in the case of Vorarlberger Medienhaus, may be one way to optimize efficiency and add maximum value with the given resources. All businesses that cannot gain added value from the parent should be divested from the portfolio even though the business itself may be profitable. If not, the parent will only be an overhead cost, adding bureaucracy, destroying successful structures, and lowering the value of the individual business.

In practice, evidence suggests that there may in fact be limited coherence between corporate-level strategies and product portfolios (Nayyar, 1993). In order to realize synergies in portfolios, companies should therefore identify not only physical relatedness, but also strategic similarity, routines, and culture—the dominant logic through which managers understand their business (Prahalad & Bettis, 1995). A low-cost, free sheet operation may for instance have few synergies with a market-leading morning daily even if they both are created in the same building and printed on the same paper. The strategic intent of the corporate parent thus dictates many of the rationales in the portfolio planning procedure.

Many large media corporations have indeed attempted to create synergies through cross-media and international diversification of their portfolios. More than just synergies, growth opportunities and risk reduction have motivated this action (Sánchez-Tabernero & Carvajal, 2002). The efforts have shown notable problems in generating meaningful value, and studies have shown that most functions in practice tend to remain duplicated (Litman & Sochay, 1994). In the case of mergers and acquisitions, it has been indicated that limited understanding of where and how efficiencies are going to be realized has resulted in lower return on equity than before the activities (Krishnan & Park, 2002). Portfolio planning has in this respect failed to generate internal growth and new business development opportunities (Hamermesh, 1986). Time Warner/ AOL and Vivendi Universal are two well-known but not unique examples where culture and dominant logics have clashed, cases where the parties may have produced greater value separated than combined (Albarran & Gormly, 2004). Suggestions have been made that it is in fact the size of these mega-mergers that fails to create synergies—the strategic visions are too grandiose, overestimating possible synergies and underestimating the difficulties of integration (Orwall & Peers, 2002).

Theory predicts that the changing game rules of the media business will increasingly force a shift in focus from external growth through mergers to internal growth through product innovation (Sánchez-Tabernero & Carvajal, 2002). Now, the multifaceted practices needed to excel in management of internal resources and capabilities of the organization will be even more critical (Lorange, 1993).

Arguments Against Traditional Portfolio Management Models

As the number of businesses and products in a corporation grows, so does the complexity of decisions concerning the allocation of resources among them. Portfolio models provide formalized tools to track, distill, and visualize information. They are constructed to assist management in deciding which products and businesses to include in the portfolio, which not to include, and how to allocate available resources between them. However, traditional models fail to provide any firm guidelines or accurate measurement of products' and businesses' strategic performance (Wind & Mahajan, 1981). Being standardized tools that aim at improving comparability, portfolio models by definition generalize and simplify. The aim is to reduce complexity, but by doing so, as critics claim, these tools also fail to account for specific characteristics of each product or occasion. The result can be erroneous conclusions, bad investment/divestment decisions, increased organizational rigidity, and missed opportunities. From this perspective, there will always be a trade-off between the amount of resources spent on detailed information gathering and the risk of aggregating data in a way that makes all products in the portfolio end up in a misleading average position (Wind & Mahajan, 1981).

Arguments have been raised that standardized portfolio models may constrain managements' motivation to try strategic alternatives, such as repositioning, innovating, or exploring new internal capabilities and new product markets. Further, premodeled solutions may mean that strategic moves are quite easily predicted by competitors. Most portfolio models only look at historical data and present product markets and have little capacity to guide changes in corporate direction. The more turbulent and uncertain the environment is, the less help can portfolio models provide to managers.

Some important characteristics of the media markets influence the tools and approaches that media companies use to control their portfolios.

- Media businesses are often *niche players* and survive because there is no perfect substitution between media, content-wise or geographically.
- They act on a *dual market*—what they do for readers influences the advertising market. For products relying on advertising, penetration within a certain audience niche, rather than mere size, gives competitive advantage. It should however be noted that not all media act on dual markets. For single-market products like music CDs, size matters more.
- The market environment is characterized by *radical technological change* through digitalization and legal change through *deregulation*, which will affect just about all media, making fixed long-term strategies highly uncertain.

- Many media *markets are in stagnation or decline*, as audiences fragment and advertisers tend to increasingly favor personalized and innovative channels compared to mass media.
- Strategies of many media corporations include visions of *closer interaction* between the businesses in their portfolios.

Under each of these circumstances, financial methods or mapping approaches to portfolio management have proven to be inadequate. The situation calls for innovation rather than standardization, for differentiation strategies rather than mass market dominance, for risk-taking rather than risk reduction. In order to manage innovation and risk reduction in a changing environment, firms will need to manage product portfolios on a more proactive and long-term basis.

CAUGHT BETWEEN SYNERGIES AND STRATEGIC FLEXIBILITY

We have now analyzed the appropriateness of various portfolio evaluation tools, without discussing the intent of the control system itself. How close corporate control of each business in the portfolio should be is to a large extent a trade-off between the values that are added (e.g., efficiencies, synergies, and knowledge) versus the values that are destroyed (e.g., bureaucracy, rigidity, and lack of management focus) through that relationship. Synergies often require integration and relatively close control, but as Lorsch and Allen (1984) argue, integration also implies increased rigidity. How do we then create a system that allows quick reactions to new market opportunities like financial approaches, while maintaining corporate direction like the strategic tools? A system that creates motivated individuals while encouraging a behavior that promotes the coordinated performance of the corporation as a whole (Goold & Quinn, 1990)? A system that is specific and understandable on all managerial levels while yet flexible and adaptable to strategic changes?

Media corporations are today caught in this tension between specialization, flexibility, and synergies. To deal with this paradox of closer centralization of portfolio decisions and quicker responses to market opportunities, many companies cut hierarchical layers in the organization. This, in turn, pushes increasingly more important decisions on to lower-level managers. A study by Loomis and Albarran (2004) shows that U.S. radio managers today are responsible for as many as eight different channels compared to one or two ten years ago.

CASE STUDY:
Synergies for Survival at Vorarlberger Medienhaus

In Vorarlberg, a small Austrian region near the Swiss border, the CEO and owner Eugen Russ has created a rapidly growing media corporation, yet tiny compared to Bertelsmann. Facing increased competition, Russ felt that he needed to reposition the regional daily *Vorarlberger Nachtrichten* (*VN*), which has been in his family's ownership for more than 100 years. Inspired by *USA Today*, the move has shifted the formerly political profile into a popular, 4-color, picture packed 20-minute read, that today has a 75% reach in a region of 365,000 inhabitants. The strategy is to be truly regional, minimizing coverage of national and foreign politics, but focusing on the ordinary person on the street. Within a year, *VN* estimates that about 100,000 readers will figure on picture either online or in print, showing that the paper and its related media channels are shaped by and about the local people. The newspaper subscription is the gate to value-added services, while the internet operations create something similar to a virtual version of the local town square, displaying numerous pictures of people, public documents, and local gossip and debate. In fact, Russ often uses the word "community" and "utility" to describe the relation between the products and their audience. Unlike many other media corporations, this indicates that Vorarlberger Medienhaus sees their customer relations rather than content production as their core competence.

Although the new strategy has received harsh criticism for being too market-oriented and profit-focused, Russ has managed to create a portfolio of media products with the paper as the nexus creating the customer relations. The reason for creating synergies, he argues, is above all to make the production of new products more cost effective. More specifically, the threat from the German WAZ company, which today has outmatched local competition in five other Austrian regions, has fueled the need for synergies as barriers to competition. While a number of journalists and editors in Austrian newspapers see him as degrading journalistic integrity, many managers consider Russ as a true innovator, showing the way through the economic downswing of the news industry.

Vorarlberger Nachtrichten is the original cornerstone and the cash cow of a portfolio that today has a turnover of 100 million euros, employing 400 people. To that has been added a small format boulevard paper *Neue Vorarlberger Tageszeitung* (with a reach of 75,000), in response to competition especially from the boulevard papers of WAZ. Further, there is an online paper and portal Vorarlberger Online (150,000 visitors per day), the weekly free youth magazine *Wann & Wo* (79% reach in Vorarlberg among ages 14-49), a printing operation, radio channel Antenne Vorarlberg, a telephone operator named 1036hallo! and an Internet service provider, Teleport. More recently, operations have been expanded to cover other parts of Austria—with Radio Arabella, the online paper/portal Vienna Online, and Austria.com—as well as parts of Hungary and Romania.

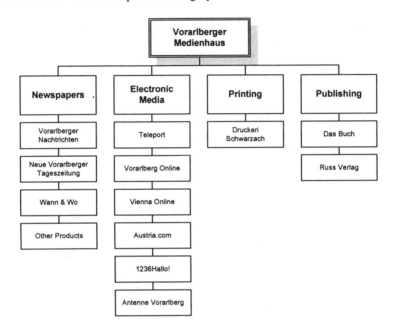

Fig. 8.1
Vorarlberger Medienhaus Organizational Chart

While community spirit is the driver behind customer relations and cross-media traffic, product bundling is a central part of the revenue model. The close connection between media and nonmedia operations has given *Vorarlberger Nachtrichten* the epithet "a customer club with a newspaper." When paying the yearly fee of 208 euros for the subscription (circulation is 100% subscription-based), one also gets the opportunity to use the 1036hallo! telephone services at a discounted rate, of which 35,000 (more than 50%) of the subscribers have chosen. You can also sign up for discounted electricity (45,000 customers), insurance, or, if one wants more serious in-depth news, a discounted subscription to Swiss daily *Neue Zürcher Zeitung*, delivered every morning together with *VN*.

> The success of the concept, building barriers to competition by monopolizing on local customer media relations, has made Eugen Russ look at possibilities to export the model. However, the degree of success that Vorarlberger Medienhaus will have on the Vienna market and in Romania and Hungary is yet to be seen. As a case, Vorarlberger Medienhaus is worth studying because they have succeeded in creating a synergetic product portfolio whereas numerous media corporations have tried and failed.
>
> First, Vorarlberger Medienhaus is under constant threat from financially stronger competitors entering the market. Therefore, they have to create barriers to entry in order to survive. Economies of scope of owning multiple media is this barrier, forcing the company to constantly maximize its synergies and lower costs in every operation. Operations that can be more efficiently performed outside the portfolio are outsourced. External forces give in this case a very clear incentive for businesses to cooperate.
>
> Second, Eugen Russ is, in his role as CEO and owner is a strong and entrepreneurial leader, making the flat organization of Vorarlberger Medienhaus flexible to adapt to strategic changes.
>
> Third, due to the small size, there are (as yet) no major economies of scale to be realized within each media. Vorarlberger Medienhaus is small enough not to distance the 400 employees either from each other, or from the management that placed together with operations.
>
> Finally, the organization is built and has grown to function horizontally. Therefore there has been no need to try to alter the formal structure or the dominant logic of the organization. The flat hierarchy further decreases the risk for conflicts between divisional and corporate interests and targets.

Lampel, et al., (2000) raise the question of whether a centralized M-form structure will kill creativity, which is the competitive advantage and the source of future opportunities in media companies. In contrast to what was suggested above, Eisenmann and Bower (2000) warn that in this period of uncertainty and rapid technological change, even a truly decentralized organization will react too slowly to emerging opportunities. The Bertelsmann and Vororlberger Medienhaus examples included in this chapter support the solution suggested by Eisenmann and Bower, emphasizing the role of a strong entrepreneurial and visionary CEO. In order to keep creative freedom while allowing synergies, the CEO drives strategy in a top-down manner in an "Entrepreneurial M-form," while allowing the business unit managers to shape, interpret, and implement. In a scale larger than Eugen Russ in Vorarlberg, News Corporation's Rupert Murdoch can serve as an example of such a leader.

Goold and Campbell (1987) put forward similar ideas of a strong corporate framework, defining where synergies should be achieved, but leaving the creativity to the businesses. In this way the corporate centre is more about creating processes than detailed planning. Within this framework, it is important to create relevant reward systems that encourage the desired behavior of cooperation, not only based on the sales or profits of the individual businesses (Paasio, 2004). Because short-term goals have been shown to be more motivating for managers (Hrebiniak & Joyce, 1986), existing tools have had the problem of not looking beyond annual budgets and measurable output (Argyris, 1977) when transferring strategy into rewards and performance measures.

CASE STUDY:
Organizational and Control Changes
at Bertelsmann

The turmoil in Bertelsmann in 2003 provides an example of how strategic changes should be reflected in the portfolio control systems and how synergies fail to be reached without the appropriate incentives. With the entry and exit of Thomas Middelhoff as CEO, the German media giant has moved from a decentralized business strategy to centralization and then back once again to a system of decentralized cost centers.

According to theory, the more decentralized a corporation is, the fewer synergies it seeks and the more it can rely on strict financial control measures. On the contrary, when centralization is high, synergies can be exploited and softer measures of competencies and strategic fit between the businesses should be used. The failures to gain synergies in Bertelsmann can be traced to the misfit between strategic intent on one hand and organizational structure and control practices on the other. Excessive use of financial portfolio tools can send the wrong signals to the organization, overestimate the value of financial variables, chose the wrong mix of projects, and ignore rewards for synergetic behavior.

In 2003, Bertelsmann's business divisions were cut from seven to six as Bertelsmann Springer, which only accounted for 3.9% of the total reported 18.3 billion euro profit, was divested. Even though the divestment of Springer had been on the agenda for quite some time, the event signaled the end of a period during which strategy was driven by the belief in content-centered synergies, and the return to one where bottom-line results count. The remaining six divisions are: TV division RTL (23% of total profits), Random House book publishing (10.5%), Grüner & Jahr magazines and newspapers (14.7%), music division BMG (14.3%), Arvato printing and multimedia

---

operations (19.3%) and direct sales group Direct Group accounting for book clubs, music clubs and e-commerce (14.3%).

For Bertelsmann which, through its different divisions, covers a large part of the media spectrum, content synergies across its divisions have been a tempting way to leverage the opportunities of the combined business units and product portfolios. Digitalization has opened new electronic distribution channels, and media convergence promises new products and opportunities to efficiently exploit the content produced. However, it should be noted that Bertelsmann's organizational structure by tradition has been characterized by highly decentralized divisions, where strategic direction, focus, and culture have developed independently.

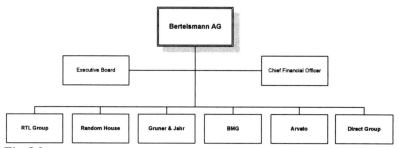

Fig. 8.2
Bertelsmann Organizational Chart

During the Middelhoff era, the spirit was one of centralization and portfolio synergies. As a result a corporate strategic center and a corporate executive council were formed to manage the strategic direction and identify synergies between the divisions. Further, the 20-people-strong strategic unit Bertelsmann Content Network (BCN) was established in 2000 to promote cross-media synergies from the content producing divisions: Random House, BMG, Grüner & Jahr, RTL, and Bertelsmann Springer. Later, also Bertelsmann Arvato and Direct Group were included in the project.

The new strategic initiative was based on the belief that content is the critical core competence of media companies and that the long-term success of media companies is the ability to network its content. This could take the form of exchange of content and business ideas between divisions and distribution channels, joint content creation, and finally cross-media brands with centralized brand management.

One example of this is the 25th anniversary of Elvis' death, which in 2002 was exploited through coordinated music releases (BMG), books, TV specials (RTL), magazine articles and special book club offers (Direct

Group). However, a precondition for the success of this kind of portfolio management was that BCN could control a portfolio independent of the decentralized divisional cost centers and that the customers would perceive the value of the products.

These synergy efforts were part of the corporate plans for a public listing in 2005. With the ending of Middelhoff's period as CEO, so ended also many of the synergy projects. The corporate executive council, along with most of the staff of BCN and the corporate strategic unit, was cut. The new target is a strict 10% return on sales for each division, perfectly in line with a decentralized portfolio strategy with no horizontal synergies. Projects are selected from decentralized decisions on a divisional profit maximizing basis. Over time, as corporate strategic intention has changed from decentralized structures to centralized and back to decentralized, portfolio management practices remained surprisingly intact. Even though the Middelhoff era was characterized somewhat by different products, cross-divisional cooperation, digital formats, and e-business, the portfolio management of the existing businesses did not change. The headquarters for the individual businesses remained as always at Bertelsmann, situated at the division level.

The difficulties in establishing synergies are illustrated by the failure of Bertelsmann to provide convincing incentives for the divisions to cooperate. From a portfolio management perspective we can see that there were several difficulties with creating synergies stemming from the way Bertelsmann was organized.

First, there were no convincing incentives or rewards for the divisions to cooperate where they had not before. Because the divisions still were evaluated on individual returns, there was no reason to join projects that were profitable for the corporation as a whole if they did not meet the separate divisional targets. As a consequence, it was more rational for the internal customer, for example a magazine editor, to use the best, profit-maximizing content available from all sources and not limit himself to the best in-house content. For the internal supplier it was rational to overcharge if he knew that the internal customer in another division was obliged to buy. Profit maximization on the business level, even when it meant deteriorating the profit margin of other divisions, was in fact the true incentive to cooperate.

Second, there were no good measures or benchmarks to quantify the value added through the synergies. And because synergies could neither be measured nor defined, they could not be fit into the reward system.

Third, BCN did not have the power needed to impose pressure on the divisions to coordinate their activities. In fact BCN was subordinated to the division managers and could only rely on their goodwill in order to commit the divisions to the synergy projects.

DISCUSSION

Whereas maximization of profits and minimization of risk was the focus of portfolio management in the 1970s and 1980s, the period from 1990 until today has focused on new technologies and increased portfolio economies through synergies. However, the failures of corporations like Bertelsmann, AOL Time Warner, and Vivendi Universal to gain value from huge mergers illustrate the difficulties that media still face when trying to capitalize on synergies.

Innovation, flexibility, and synergies will all be important elements in future media portfolio strategy. In the earlier sections we showed why the choice of portfolio tools must follow the choice of corporate strategy and structure. But even then, a purely financially driven, decentralized structure will not achieve synergies, while an integrated, centralized corporation is likely to be too slow and rigid. The dilemma is yet to be solved and better practices for portfolio management will be a precondition for future success in increasingly competitive markets. Given the turbulent environment of media corporations, this chapter has argued that financial and mapping approaches to portfolio management are unlikely to optimize the performance of media portfolios. As synergies need multifaceted and intertemporal competencies, the tools and practices used to evaluate and direct portfolios are likely to incorporate a range of different techniques. The discussion above suggests some further issues that these multiple approaches will need to address.

Leadership, Incentives, and the Control Practices of Portfolios Matter

Eisenmann and Bower (2000) suggest that the middle road between synergies and flexibility could be that of a strong and proactive CEO. Although the Entrepreneurial M-form seems to work well in the case of Vorarlberger Medienhaus, it should be noted that Middelhoff at Bertelsmann and Messier at Vivendi failed despite visionary leadership.

There appear to be other elements in play than just the role of the CEO. Larger corporations must increasingly rely on control systems that complement the top-down directives. If synergies are to be achieved, cooperative behavior must be acknowledged and rewarded. Developing benchmarks and incentive systems that detect and reward synergies in media corporations as a whole, while making sense for the individuals in their work, will be an important factor for future success. Incentive systems are from this perspective firm-wide issues that must be coordinated and developed for the best of the corporation rather than the short-term financial goals of businesses.

Just as synergy requires merging different perspectives on operations and strategies, controlling and evaluating them requires a merger of different portfolio tools and control systems. The successful media manager should have a broad understanding of the range of areas affected by cross-media integration and the dominant logic that makes the businesses fit in the portfolio. Then they can start to understand what behavior is relevant to control and evaluate and what areas traditional portfolio tools actually fail to account for.

Company Size Matters

Kolo and Vogt (2003) point out that size may not give the assumed competitive advantage. Rather, this chapter argues that because larger portfolios greatly increase complexity, top management is at risk of losing the overview and understanding of the operations. The comparison between Bertelsmann and Vorarlberger Medienhaus illustrates that with size and divisionalization, rigidity grows in the organization as individuals and departments are specialized. The difficulty of unlearning old logics (Prahalad & Bettis, 1995) appears to increase with size, complicating large and radical integrations such as the recently failed mega-mergers. Size also tends to bring both geographical and mental distances between the different businesses. Multinational operations may require taking into account parallel strategies and differing legal obstacles and accounting standards. As a result, individuals within the organization may have little natural horizontal contact across business boundaries and there may be drifts in the dominant logics of specific businesses, making synergies difficult to achieve. The portfolio management tools used should be able to identify which linkages are most important to encourage.

Company Structure and Strategy Matters

Because many portfolios are based on past strategies they may not, as Hill (1988) explains, be built to achieve horizontal synergies. As vertical value chains diminish in importance, past successes can be a burden. Making the new portfolio logics work may require a structural change in the way included businesses are organized. There may be several different strategies at different levels and different times in the product life cycle. Some products are needed to standardize and compete on cost, while others compete on creativity, innovation, and differentiation. Managing this in a portfolio may create considerable problems when realizing synergies and encouraging cooperation. Organizations thus need to be increasingly flexible, yet ordered and structured. The portfolio management tools should be able to logically follow these new structures. It is also worth noting that the focus on cross-media portfolios may be misguiding when, as in the Vorarlberger case, business models based on synergies do not have to be limited to media products.

Taken together, portfolio direction and control for the media corporation need to be undertaken by strong leadership to establish strategic direction and allow the businesses to maintain creative freedom and specialization. The ways in which individuals and businesses are evaluated and rewarded will ultimately determine their incentives to adopt the behaviors needed to successfully direct the media portfolio. However, the horizontal synergies will not appear by themselves, and managers need to acknowledge the shortcomings of the most well-known portfolio models on this matter. In addition, media firms increasingly need to evaluate the structure of their organizations—how size and the organizational structure of the corporation decreases the natural exchange of ideas, cooperation, and knowledge between businesses in their portfolios.

REFERENCES

Albarran, A. B. & Gormly, R. K. (2004). Strategic response or strategic blunder? An examination of AOL Time Warner and Vivendi Universal. In R. G. Picard (Ed.), *Strategic responses to media market changes* (pp. 35–46), Jönköping: Jönköping International Business School.

Anderson, C. R. & Zeithaml, C. P. (1984). Stage of the product life cycle, Business strategy and business performance. *Academy of Management Journal, 27*(1), 5–24.

Argyris, C. (1977). Organizational learning and management information systems, *Accounting, Organizations and Society, 2*, 113–123.

Benini, F. (2003). Das pressewunder von Vorarlberg. *Neue Zürcher Zeitung*, 29 Feb.

Bettis, R. A & Prahalad, C. K. (1995). The dominant logic: Retrospective and extension, *Strategic Management Journal, 16*(1), 5.

Branck, M. (2003). Der sanfte revolutionary. *Brand eins*, No 9.

Bowman, E. H., Singh, H. & Thomas, H. (2002). The domain of strategic management: History and evolution. In A. Pettigrew, H. Thomas & R. Whittington (Eds.), *Handbook of strategy and management* (pp. 31-51). London: Sage Publications.

Campbell, A. & Goold, M. (1999). *The collaborative enterprise*. Reading, MA: Perseus Books.

Campbell, A. & Luchs, K. (1992). *Strategic synergy*. Oxford: Butterworth/ Heinemann.

Cooper, R. G, Scott, J. E. & Kleinschmidt, E. J. (1999). New product portfolio management: Practices and performance, *Journal of Product Innovation Management*, *16*, 333–351.

Damewood, A. (2004). *New York Times publisher shares his vision for the future of journalism*. Lecture at Medill School of Journalism, Northwestern University, 2004–02–23. Available at http://www.medill.northwestern.edu/ inside/2004/sulzberger.

Dimmick, J. W. (2003). *Media competition and coexistence: The theory of the niche*. Mahwah, NJ: Lawrence Erlbaum Associates.

Eisenmann, T. R & Bower, J. L. (2000). The entrepreneurial m-form: Strategic integration in global media firms, *Organizational Science*, *11*(3), 348–355.

Friedl, D. (2004). Unkonventionell zum erfolg. *HandelsZeitung*, Nr. 8, 18 Feb.

Gannett (2000). Press release, Credit Suisse First Boston Media Conference, Conference presentation by Tom Curley 2000-12-06. Available at http:// www.gannett.com/go/press/tcmediaconference00.htm.

Goold, M. & Campbell, A. (1987). *Strategies and styles*. Blackwell.

Goold, M., Campbell, A. & Alexander, M. (1994). *Corporate level strategy: Creating value in the multibusiness company*. New York: Wiley.

Goold, M. & Quinn, J. L. (1990). The paradox of strategic controls. *Strategic Management Journal*, *11*, 43–57.

Hamermesh, R. G. (1986). Making planning strategic. *Harvard Business Review*, *64*(4), 115-120.

Hill, C. W. L. (1988). Internal capital market controls and financial performance in multidivisional firms, *Journal of Industrial Economics*, *37*(1), 67–83.

Hrebiniak, L. G. & Joyce, W. F. (1986). The strategic importance of managing myopia, *Sloan Management Review*, *28*(1), 5–14.

Hymowitz, C. (2002). In the lead: Arrogance and refusal to work with others led to many failures. *Wall Street Journal*, Dec 17. (Eastern Edition).

Johnson, G. & Scholes, K. (2002). *Exploring corporate strategy* (6th ed.). Essex, UK: Pearson Education.

Kolo, C. & Vogt, P. (2003). Strategies for growth in the media and communications industry: Does size really matter? *International Journal on Media Management*, *5*(4), 251–261.

Krishnan, H. A. & Park, D. (2002). The impact on work force reduction on subsequent performance in major mergers and acquisitions: An exploratory study. *Journal of Business Research*, *55*(4), 285-292.

Lambin, J.-J. (2002). *Market-driven management*. London: Macmillan Press.

Lampel, J., Lant, T. & Shamsie, J. (2000). Balancing act: Learning from organizing practices in cultural industries. *Organizational Science*, *11*(3), 263–269.

Larsson, M. (2001). *Bonniers—en mediafamilj; Förlag, konglomerat och mediekoncern 1953-1990*. Gjøvik: Albert Bonniers Förlag.

Litman, B. R. & Sochay, S. (1994). The emerging mass media environment, pp. 223-280 in Babe, R.E., ed., *Information and communication in economics*. Boston: Kluwer Academic Publishers.

Loomis, K. D. & Albarran, A. B. (2004). Managing radio market clusters: orientations of general managers. *The Journal of Media Economics*, *17*(1), 51–69.

Lorange, P. (1993). *Strategic planning and control*. Cambridge: Blackwell.

Lorange, P. (1998). Strategy implementation: The new realities, *Long Range Planning*, *31*(1), 18–29.

Lorsch, J. W. & Allen, S. A. (1984). *Managing diversity and interdependence: An organizational study of multidivisional firms* (3rd ed.). Boston: Harvard Business School Publishing.

Nayyar, P. R. (1993). On the measurement of competitive strategy: Evidence from a large multiproduct U.S firm. *Academy of Management Journal, 36*(6), 1652–1669.

Orwall, B. & Peers, M. (2002). Rocky marriages—The message of media mergers: So far, they haven't been hits. *Wall Street Journal,* May 10 (Eastern edition).

Paasio, A. (2004). *Accounting issues for media product portfolios.* Working paper, MMTC Media Product Portfolio Seminar, Jönköping, Sweden.

Picard, R. G. (2002). *The economics and financing of media companies.* New York: Fordham University Press.

Picard, R. G. (2003). Cash cows or entrecôte: Publishing companies and disruptive technologies. *Trends in Communication, 11*(2), 127–136.

Picard, R. G. & Rimmer, T. (1999). Weathering a recession: Effects of size and diversification on newspaper companies, *Journal of Media Economics, 12*(1), 1–18.

Prahalad, C. K & Hamel, G. (1990). The core competence of the corporation. *Harvard Business Review,* May-June.

Reuters News Service (2002). Bertelsmann scraps ex-CEO's initiatives in pursuit of growth. *Wall Street Journal,* Aug 23 (Eastern Edition).

Sánchez-Tabernero, A. & Carvajal, M. (2002). *Media concentration in the European market; New trends and challenges.* Pamplona: Servicio de Publicaciones de la Universidad de Navarra.

Thielmann, B., Sieprath, S. & Kaiser, S. (2003). BCN—Synergies and new businesses for a content powerhouse. In A. Vizjak & M. Ringlstetter (Eds.), *Media management, Leveraging content for profitable growth* (pp. 141-146). Berlin-Heidelberg: Springer Verlag.

Van Cuilenburg, J. (2000). On measuring media competition and media diversity: concepts, theories and methods. In R.G. Picard (Ed.), *Measuring media content, quality and diversity* (pp. 51–84). Turku: Turku School of Economics and Business Administration

Van der Velten, T. & Ansoff, H.I. (1998). Managing business portfolios in German companies, *Long Range Planning, 31*(6), 879–885.

Wensley, R. (1982). PIMS and BCG: New horizons or false dawn? *Strategic Management Journal, 3*(2), 147–158.

Wind, Y. & Mahajan, V. (1981). Designing business portfolios: Steps leading to construction of a portfolio model for planning strategy, *Harvard Business Review*, Jan-Feb.

Zeithaml, C. P. & Fry, L. W. (1984). Contextual and strategic differences among mature businesses in four dynamic performance situations, *Academy of Management Journal, 27*(4), 841–860.

9
Issues and Strategies in Managing Product Portfolios across Borders and Cultures

Min Hang
Jönköping International Business School

Media industries are in the midst of rapid change as we step into the twenty-first century. To smooth sales and profits fluctuations, and to stimulate growth more rapidly than if they concentrated on a single product or service, a large number of media firms have diversified their products. Rather than narrowly improving the performance of a single core business, they are moving toward a multiple products and services solution. Large firms often diversify into a wide spectrum of media and communication products and services, or even explore outside media sectors, whereas medium and small firms usually diversify into related areas. Newspaper firms, for example, diversify into other print media or extend their publications online (Picard, 2002). The creation of product portfolios has provided good opportunities for media firms to spread business risks across different product lines and to realize their economies of scope.

Meanwhile, to achieve economy of scale, and to deal with saturated domestic markets or competition regulations that hinder growth, an increasing number of media firms are moving across borders to capture the international market with product portfolios. They tend to take regional and global approaches, either serving nations within their region or expanding beyond them.

Although having a global reach is nothing new to the media industries (Hollifield, 2001), managing portfolios in an international environment still adds large complexities to the operational practices of media firms. Managers are required to have understanding and mastery not only of different media businesses but also of dynamic international environments. However, for many medium and small media firms, managerial staff usually take a comparatively narrow view of their products and services and, more unfortunately, they are not familiar with the issues associated with international business either. Even large firms engaged in international operations have often been confronted with difficulties in maintaining their focus, allocating resources, selecting appropriate products and activities, targeting the global market, finding sustainable business models, and managing their growth (Picard, 2003). Moreover, cultural differences and conflicts increase uncertainties when media firms conduct business across borders. All of these issues make the management of cross-border and cross-culture media product portfolios a great challenge to the firms who are seeking or conducting an international move.

Hitherto, there have been some studies conducted on the managerial issues and problems raised by the global expansion of media firms (e.g., Demers, 1999; Gershon, 1997; Smith, 1999). Yet, rare attention has been paid to the management of product portfolios in an international environment. Questions and issues arising from the internationalization of media portfolios still require careful study by both academic researchers and practitioners.

This chapter addresses issues arising from the internationalization of media portfolios and strategies for managing them. It also presents a model for formulating and implementing such strategies. This chapter first gives a general description of the internationalization of media product portfolios, in which the rationales of business portfolios, media product portfolios, and an international transformation of media portfolios are presented. Specific questions and issues arise from the internationalization. These issues are further examined and analyzed with regard to cultural issues, barriers to trade, policy control, media environment, managerial competencies, and resource allocation. Following this analysis, strategy decisions about portfolio decisions, entry selection, and methods for international development are studied. A model is offered to illustrate the formulation and implementation of these strategies.

MEDIA PRODUCT PORTFOLIOS AND INTERNATIONALIZATION

A portfolio is a set of different assets that investors hold to maximize their wealth (Litman, et al., 2000). Modern portfolio management theory draws on the early writings of Harry Markowitz. This theory states that an optimal portfolio is one that maximizes returns for a given level of risk (Markowitz, 1959). Portfolio concepts have been applied in business since at least the 1960s. Following the trends of divisionalization, many firms started to diversify their business in order to counter slowing growth rates and to spread business risks across different sectors. Rather than improving performance in a single area, firms entered into different markets, introduced new technologies, and developed multiple products and services (Velten & Ansoff, 1998).

Studies on business diversification and product portfolios converged thereafter. Four years before Chandler (1962) published his seminal work on diversified firms, Ansoff (1958) developed his proposals for diversification strategies (Velten & Ansoff, 1998). Following these groundbreaking efforts, diversity and other aspects of product portfolio management were studied by numerous researchers in a variety of academic fields. Although findings from these studies vary and views of the effect of product diversification on the performance of firms are still contradictory (e.g., Datta, et al., 1991; Grant, 1987; Grant, et al., 1988), the proliferation of product diversification in firms and the emergence of product portfolios in markets are definitely beyond dispute.

The media industries have witnessed increased creation of product portfolios in recent decades. Portfolios are appearing in almost every field, either inside the same media unit—magazine firms publish hundreds of titles, broadcasting firms operate multiple channels, and newspaper firms produce multiple titles and different types of newspapers—or across different media sectors—newspaper firms move into the broadcasting sector, and broadcasting firms get into program and motion picture production, as was shown in previous chapters.

Business diversification and product portfolios can help media firms to complement their resources, reduce risks, and maximize their sales and profits. According to U.S. media scholar Robert McChesney, for example,

> When Disney produces a film, it can also provide programs on pay cable television and commercial network television, it can produce and sell soundtracks based on the film, it can create spin-off television series, it can produce related amusement park rides, CD-ROMs, books, comics, and merchandise to be sold in Disney retail stories. Moreover, Disney can promote the film and related material incessantly across all its media properties. In this climate, even films which do poorly at the box office can become profitable (Demers, 1999, p. 48).

In contrast to the great research efforts made on the general concepts and issues of product portfolios, studies on specific media portfolios are rather limited. Only a few works have been done, for instance, that apply portfolio theory to the media network program selection (Litman, et al., 2000), that measure and analyze diversification in certain media industries (Albarran & Porco, 1990; Dimmick & Wallschlaeger, 1986; Picard & Rimmer, 1999), or that examine global media conglomerates' diversification strategies (Chan-Olmsted & Chang, 2003). Generally, there has not been sufficient and systematic examination of media product portfolios, and moreover, many managerial issues concerning cross-border management of media portfolios have remained unexamined or not even mentioned.

Moving Across Borders and Cultures: Internationalization

The international expansion of media firms has been significant in recent decades. In November 1988, Time Inc. Chairman Richard Munro said,

> Every player in the media/entertainment business—at least every smart one—will try to do the same thing: to build enterprises that can lay off the risk of increased production costs over as many worldwide distribution systems as possible....Thus, internationalization serves as a way of maximizing the economies of scale (Croteau & Hoynes, 2001, p. 130).

By the late 1980s and early 1990s, a combination of at least three factors helped lift many of the barriers that had previously restricted the international expansion of media corporations: (a) the emergence of new electronic distribution technologies; (b) the opening of viable new markets such as eastern Europe as the result of global political and economic change; and (c) the move toward deregulation of media and telecommunications industries at both the national and international levels (Hollifield, 2001). These changes led to an increasing trend of internationalization among media firms.

According to Hitt, et al. (1997), reasons for internationalization lie in three areas. First, the international market can provide greater opportunities for firms to achieve optimal economies of scale and to pay back investments in critical functions such as R&D and brand image. Second, international firms can gain competitive advantages by exploiting market imperfections (e.g., differences in national resources), and cross-border transactions can gain increased flexibility and greater bargaining power resulting from a multi-national network (Kogut, 1984). Economies of scale gained through internationalization allow firms to increase their efficiency. Third, increased learning and innovation can also occur from internationalization (Kochhar & Hitt, 1995).

Several researchers suggest that there is a positive interaction between internationalization and product diversification. Building multiple products can help managers to create capabilities that allow more effective management in an international environment (Hitt, et al., 1997). Firms holding multiple products may have advantages over single-product firms in their international operations. To further advocate this proposition, Tallman and Li (1996) argue that product diversity has a positive effect on multinational performance. Hitt, et al. (1997) achieved more fine-grained findings: international diversification is negatively related to performance in nondiversified firms, positively related in highly product-diversified firms, and curvilinearly related in moderately product-diversified firms.

These arguments have helped to accelerate the ongoing trend of internationalization of product portfolios. Media firms have kept pace with this trend. Large media corporations are increasing their range and scope of international products and services. For example, News Corporation now provides international products ranging from newspapers, television and film, magazines and inserts, to book publication. It has also cashed in on the global love of sports by owning valuable broadcasting rights to sporting events, sports channels, and even some professional sports teams. Nowadays, the businesses of News Corporation, according to the CEO, Rupert Murdoch, can reach more than three-quarters of the global population (Croteau & Hoynes, 2001). In addition, such global reach is not limited to the big media behemoths (Smith, 1999). Even smaller and more specialized media corporations have also ventured into cross-border product portfolios. For instance, the two radio station group owners Clear Channel Communications Inc. and Saga Communications Inc. have both made international moves. In 1998, Saga bought a 50% interest in a radio station group in Iceland to promote additional radio programs, and in 1999, Clear Channel operated different radio and advertising activities in 36 countries on six continents (Hollifield, 2001).

However, many media firms' efforts at international portfolio management appear not to have been strategically effective. Underlying issues appear within the internationalization of media portfolios and the complexity in handling them has generated great demand for study. It is beyond the scope of this chapter to deeply investigate all of the variety of issues arising from the internationalization of media portfolios. Instead, the following sections will address those issues that appear to have the most significant implications for firms considering expansion into international markets.

Issues in Managing International Media Portfolios

Cultural Issues

Cultural issues are of great importance in managing international media portfolios. This section discusses the importance of cultural influences from three aspects: national culture, corporate culture, and other cultural characteristics including, among others, language, religion, attitudes, social organization, and education.

National Culture. When moving beyond national borders, the management of media portfolios faces challenges of interpreting needs of local customers, communicating between different markets, and negotiating with local agents or managers. Understanding the target country's national culture is therefore crucial for success.

National culture is a totality of values and lifestyles in a particular society. It plays an important and enduring role in shaping the assumptions, beliefs, and values of individuals. National cultures differ markedly and these differences may provide vast new market opportunities for media firms. For example, when broadcasters enter into the Italian market, they may have a chance to deliver more midday content and services, as the country's culture makes people consume more media products during noontime.

However, portfolios could also encounter failures if cultural differences are misunderstood. This is demonstrated by the difficulties of exporting the TV format *Big Brother* to the Middle East and the United States. Originating from the Netherlands, this reality television format was successful in many countries including the UK, Germany, and Australia. However, it failed in the U.S. and the Middle East, as this live-TV format which exposed people's real private lives was very much opposed to the Muslim culture and American cultural perceptions and recognitions of people's right to privacy.

Similarly, national cultural differences regarding propriety produce different reactions to portrayals of family interactions, relations between young persons and older characters, disrespect for authority, violence, and nudity in films and television programming.

National cultural differences have been studied in several works. One of the most important studies was conducted by Geert Hofstede, starting in the late 1960s, and continuing through the next three decades. Hofstede identified four dimensions by which countries differ: *power distance, uncertainty avoidance, individualism/collectivism,* and *masculinity/femininity* (Hofstede, 1980). Michael Bond (1988) added a fifth dimension in a later work: *Confucian dynamism. Power distance* deals with the perceived hierarchical structuring of society; *uncertainty avoidance* focuses on the way society deals with risks; *individualism/ collectivism* centers on the importance of the group as opposed to the individual; and *masculinity/femininity* deals with the types of traits that are most valued by society. The last dimension of *Confucian dynamism* focuses on attitude toward time. Countries that rate high on this dimension are more focused on the long term and value commitment and persistence.

National cultural differences thus have strong impact on organizational processes in firms that internationalize their operations. In the process of decision-making, for example, who makes the decision, who is involved in the processes, and where decisions are made reflect different cultural assumptions.

Other organizational processes, such as planning and controlling, information processing and communication, are also heavily influenced by national cultural factors.

Considering these cultural differences and their impact on organizational processes, there are two implications for the management of international media portfolios. First, culture differs across borders. Managers should adjust their management when moving abroad; they need to know that they will be more successful if they are culturally flexible and try to adapt to new situations and ways of doing things. Second, cultural differences may also affect the success and failure of portfolio operations. Customer tastes and preferences, as rooted in their cultures, may vary in different countries, and firms must decide their portfolios by tailoring their offers to meet the unique requirements in each national market.

Corporate Culture. Corporate culture plays another crucial role in the management of international media portfolios. Media firms with different corporate cultures could encounter resistance or constraints when they create portfolio products or services.

Corporate culture represents the "basic assumptions and beliefs that are shared by members of an organization, and that operate unconsciously and define in a basic taken-for-granted fashion an organization's view of itself and its environment" (Schein, 1992, p. 6). Corporate culture influences internationalization processes and the achievement of strategic goals in media organizations.

A study conducted by Lucy Küng (2000) has provided evidence on the strategic role of corporate culture in pursuing global firm strategies. The study uncover the corporate cultural differences in the BBC and CNN, and how cultural beliefs support each organization's strategic goals. The research concluded that corporate culture can act as a powerful restraint to the global development and strategic plans of broadcasting organizations, as the culture exerts significant influence on the perceptions of environmental developments, the appropriateness of strategic responses, and the levels of organizational commitment to achieving those responses. At the same time, the study highlighted how corporate culture determines the style and variety of content and services offered by the companies. Different corporate cultures foster and support their different diversified products and services.

In the cases of both BBC and CNN, their cultures are emotional engines of their success. However, the cultural factors within an organization may also hinder the development if cultural conflicts are dealt with inappropriately. In the example of Vivendi Universal, a number of problems were reported after it was created by the merger of Vivendi (France) and Universal (U.S.) in December 2000. One of the main concerns was the cultural conflict among senior managers. CEO Jean Marie Messier adopted the U.S. culture, and his American-style "personality" riled many French who dominated the board of directors. Messier was accused of overspending at the peak of the tech boom, and was forced to resign only a year and a half after the merger of Vivendi and Universal. It was believed that the reasons for his removal were not only Vivendi Universal's share price loss, but unresolved cultural conflicts within the organization. Though Messier might be seen as a charismatic leader, his American management style was not coherent with the firm's French-biased organizational culture, which eventually created dissention in the firm and laid his grand vision in ruins. (Albarran & Gormly, 2003)

Cultural conflicts within an organization do not merely come from the executive level. When it comes to the management of international portfolios, more corporate culture resistance and conflicts may occur between different geographical and product divisions. While seeking to provide multiple products and services, different media divisions may pursue different business-level strategies, thus subcultures may be required or created. These subcultures can sometimes be very powerful, to the extent that they can be self-perpetuating and exclusive. It is therefore critical for managers of international media portfolios to align the pervading organizational culture and subcultures. In addition, they also need to align the corporate culture with their senior decision-making, and the creation and direction of their portfolios.

Other Cultural Characteristics. Other cultural characteristics that influence the international management of media portfolios include language, religion, attitudes, social organization, and education. Some countries, such as India, are characterized by linguistic pluralism, meaning that several languages exist there. Other countries rely heavily either on spoken or written language. Religion includes sacred objects, philosophical attitudes towards life, taboos, and rituals. Attitudes toward achievement, work, and time can all affect organizational productivity. An attitude called ethnocentrism means that people have a tendency to regard their own culture as superior and to downgrade other cultures. Ethnocentrism within a country makes it difficult for foreign firms to operate there or may lead to an attitude of superiority among personnel in the corporate home office toward counterparts in offices across the globe. Social organization includes status systems, kinship and families, social institutions, and opportunities for social mobility. Education influences the literacy level, the availability of qualified employees, and the predominance of primary or secondary degrees.

Media products by their very nature fall into ideological and cultural sectors; thus, all these cultural characteristics have impacts on the international planning and operation of media portfolios. For example, the literacy level of a country will determine the utilization of media content, because many media products and services, such as print media and information technologies, are effectively useless without literacy.

Given these cultural characteristics, media firms planning to internationalize their products and services must consider the necessity of adapting materials to local cultural conditions. They may need a content strategy to accommodate for language in national markets in which a firm operates. Moreover, as the driving force for use of media products is local and domestic information, they may also need another strategy of content localization (Picard, 2003). The successful portfolios are those that include a good deal of content that reflects the cultural characteristics of users in the target country.

Barriers to Trade and Policy Control

Media products are vehicles for conveying and preserving cultural values, but at the international level they also raise social, political, economic, and trade considerations. To protect national cultural identity, to reduce national media industry's dependency on foreign content, and to create and support domestic producers, many countries impose trade barriers to foreign media products.

Trade barriers influence the internationalization of media products and they limit or hinder the entry and development of media production. In the audiovisual sector, for example, barriers for foreign trade exist at almost every stage of trade. At the production stage, there are requirements to print films locally for them to be shown in some countries; in other nations local dubbing and subtitling obligations are present. In film distribution, quotas or import licenses are sometimes used to limit the number of foreign films imported annually, and some nations set annual ceilings on remittances of revenue from all foreign films. In addition, censors—which review and approve foreign films—may discriminate in favor of national products. At the video sales and rental stage, regulations may necessitate local reproduction and distribution as opposed to more cost-efficient regional distribution of products. In the area of television programming, a large number of countries on all continents limit programs that do not originate in local production firms. In radio broadcasting, local content requirements are imposed—as in France and Canada—and such requirements may differ for private or public broadcasters, pay audio, or cable broadcasting (UNCTAD Source, 2003).

Foreign ownership restrictions also constitute barriers to trade. To protect national identity, many countries impose foreign ownership restrictions on media products. In Korea, for instance, only 49% of foreign investment or contribution of property is allowed for cable operators, program providers and network operators. Foreign investment or contribution of property is strictly prohibited for terrestrial broadcasters, relay-cable operators, comprehensive programming channels, and the specialized news programming channels.

In addition to these trade barriers, differences in media policy requirements exist worldwide. Countries and regions impose different measures and standards for rating systems and censorship of films and TV programs; even within the European Union, there is a wide divergence among content rating systems, which strongly affects exports of film and television programs. The textbook publishing industry is affected by content requirements because national authorities in many countries officially approve and select textbooks—especially for primary and secondary schools—and these limit exportability as well.

Barriers to trade constrain the extent of the internationalization of media portfolios and their range of diversification. National media policy differences create more challenges for media portfolio managers to set and adjust standards to meet different market requirements. Because of these barriers, managers need to make corresponding plans for their product portfolios based on such impediments.

Media Environment

The media environment of a host country presents another delicate issue for portfolio management (Chan-Olmsted, 2003). The general availability of media products is affected by the media infrastructure development and people's consumption capacity in the host country, and the dependence on the local communication or media environment limits portfolio management in international markets.

Four kinds of basic factors have impact on the media environment in a host country, according to Picard (2001). First, urbanization is typically necessary to support the building of infrastructures required for modern communication systems. Second, the infrastructure, such as electricity and telephony, is critical to support portfolio products and services. Electricity is needed for all electronic equipment and for the efficient production and distribution of nearly all media and communication products and services. Telephony provides a means of overcoming time and distance through telephone services, fax, data transformation, and Internet access and operation. Third, income is also an important factor for media consumption and communication technology availability because of the costs of acquisition of equipment, content, and services. Fourth, hardware/service acquisition capacity, which includes literacy, costs of use, and desire to use is also a component critical for whether media and communications products and services are utilized once they are available.

To make sure that the host country has real capacity to support and consume portfolio products, media firms need to conduct a careful scan of the host country's media environment before they move to the chosen country market.

Managerial Competencies

International media portfolios are difficult to manage as they deal with diversification of both product and geographic dimensions. The large number of complex transactions across borders and sophisticated decisions concerning portfolio products require managers to have competencies to efficiently process a significant amount of information. These information-processing demands are similar to those identified by Chandler (1962) in his classic work on product diversification. However, information-processing demands are more complex and greater when firms move into new international markets than when they move into different product markets within the same domestic setting.

Managers' competencies in processing complex information are also closely linked to their capabilities and knowledge in other aspects, for example, their knowledge of portfolio products, their abilities to understand foreign target markets, and their skills at managing complex organizations.

Managers need to have knowledge of portfolio products. Because a portfolio includes multiple products and services, managers cannot be focused on a single product and a certain technology, but should rather have broad cross-field technical knowledge required by those multiple products and services.

Managers also need to understand their international target markets. Countries differ significantly in terms of cultural norms, content requirements, and media consumption habits, as previously stated. Appropriate portfolio design and composition in an international market is very much dependent on managers' understanding of the foreign target countries. Only with such understanding can managers make informed judgments about what products and services will succeed and how they will be perceived and accepted.

In addition, some tacit managerial skills (Johnson & Scholes, 2002) are required by the management of a complex organization. For example, managers need to know how to deal with cultural conflicts caused by the internationalization, how to negotiate between business units, and how to communicate between geographic markets. In addition, they are also required to have certain managerial skills in leading, motivating people, and controlling each stage of management processes.

Resource Allocation

Resource allocation is a basic issue encountered in product portfolio management, because managers must secure adequate resources to produce and support all products. Running product portfolios raises questions of how to evaluate the significance of various elements of portfolios and how to allocate resources among different product lines. In an international context, some new concerns have been raised relating to resource allocation.

First, for international media portfolios, there is a need to analyze and balance not merely the importance of alternative products but the significance and desirability of alternative international markets. Factors such as costs (e.g. wages, capital charges, and taxation) may vary considerably across countries, and these differences substantially increase the risks associated with decisions to allocate resources across various product markets. Managers should consider the costs and potential rewards of launching specific markets, the costs and requirements of market development, and market maintenance. Also, decisions about which geographical markets will bring the greatest benefit need to be made for strategy development.

Second, because of differences in the levels of consumer spending and in the stages of industrialization and urbanization, similar products are likely to be at very different stages of their life cycles. For example, using the growth/share matrix approaches, a product that is a "Cash Cow" in the home country's business segment may be changed into a "Dog," or a "Star" may become a "Problem Child" when introduced in other markets. Or, to be specific, in some countries, broadcasting products are in a mature part of their life cycle, and newspaper distribution is in a decline; whereas in others, the printing industry might be mature and broadcasting is growing. Thus, how to reposition different types of products based on new market situations and how to allocate resources in accordance with their changing international product life cycles are great challenges facing media firms.

Third, resources include not only those relating to finance and facilities, but also human resources. To allocate human resources across borders raises questions of understanding culturally rooted human behaviors and of managing people of cultural diversity. Educating managers for global cultural awareness and building teams with different managerial styles are also challenges to international human resource allocation. These challenges and other resource allocation issues require extensive and sophisticated control and management very different from that applied in the domestic firms.

STRATEGIES AND METHODS FOR MANAGING INTERNATIONAL MEDIA PORTFOLIOS

To manage the variety of issues generated by the internationalization of media portfolios, firms need to identify and adopt appropriate strategies. For media firms offering multiple products and services internationally, strategies are concerned with portfolio decisions and the way to launch portfolios in foreign countries. Strategists must also consider methods for developing portfolios in the international market.

This section examines several strategies and methods for portfolio development required by the management of international media portfolios. The strategy for portfolio decisions section looks at the creation of international media portfolios. It discusses the extent and direction of portfolio diversification. Upon the creation of portfolios, the strategy for entry selection illustrates how to choose a mode of entry in view of different product features and different market conditions. After getting into the foreign market, methods for development introduce ways to sustain portfolio development in an international environment.

Strategy for Portfolio Decisions

The strategy for portfolio decisions considers the extent (i.e., products are more or less diversified in the portfolio, and target markets are more or less diversified geographically), and the direction (i.e., products in the portfolio are related or unrelated diversified) of portfolio diversification.

Extent of Product and Geographical Diversification. International media portfolios involve geographic and product diversifications. Some researchers suggest that when portfolios go international the combination of diverse locations and diverse businesses will give rise to a level of complexity beyond which benefits are not gained (Johnson & Turner, 2003). There is also evidence that while international diversity grows, the level of a firm's internal innovation will decline, as the focus is more and more on coordination of portfolios and diversified growth (Hitt, et al., 1997). Therefore, moderate geographic and product diversification is advocated by many scholars (e.g. Hitt, et al., 1997; Tallman & Li, 1996).

However, a diversification strategy of moderate extent is not suitable for all firms, as the size and the capability of a firm may also affect the extent of diversification and the choice of geographic markets. Large firms usually have abundant resources supporting their increasing extent of both product and geographic diversifications; they may achieve a substantial market presence abroad, and hence obtain significant economies of scale in the international market. Nevertheless, medium and especially small firms always face difficulties with international growth because they have inadequate or limited resources (Liesch & Knight, 1999). It is more difficult for smaller firms to spread their operations over a sufficient number of countries to diversify their capabilities, or to set up their value-added activities in a number of different product units. Hence, to what extent to diversify is also dependent on the size and capabilities of firms.

In media industries, research on the relationship between the extent of diversification and the firm's performance has been done, for example, on media conglomerates (Chan-Olmsted & Chang, 2003). By examining the diversification strategies of large conglomerates, researchers attain results showing that "a high degree of product diversification with a fair level of overall international diversification was somewhat associated with a better overall performance" (p. 227).

There is no study yet on medium and small media firms. Generally speaking, most of these firms employ a deep niche strategy, that is, their market presences are likely to be accompanied by pursuit of market dominance in particular segments or niches (Dimmick, 2003). For internationalization, they usually satisfy the needs of a well-defined and specific segment or niche of the foreign market. And for product diversification, they do not go far beyond their traditional area, core products, and services.

Direction of Product and Geographical Diversification. The direction of diversification has been investigated and categorized as either related or unrelated (Qian, 1997; Rumelt, 1984). These two directions differ from each other by whether or not the organization is moving beyond its current system or industry. Strategic related diversification is strongly advocated by the resource-based view, as the use of core skills, know-how, and management resources is necessary for reducing uncertainties in the process of internationalization (Qian, 1997). Many other studies also stress that the internationalization of portfolios can help to exploit economies of scale and scope, resource sharing, and core competencies across related business units (Hitt, et al., 1997; Sambharya, 1995). Although there are also heated debates on the unrelated direction of diversification (Ramanujam & Varadarajan, 1989), it is believed that the type of diversification one would expect to result from resources depends on its specificity within a particular industry (Chatterjee & Wernerfelt, 1991).

In the media industries, a related product/geographic diversification as well as complementary resource alignment is preferred (Chan-Olmsted, 2003). This means that media product portfolios will more likely be profitable if managers pursue the related international market and if resource alignment among different media products is achieved.

The rationale of related diversification draws from characteristics of media products, according to Chan-Olmsted (2003). First, media firms offer dual complementary media products of content and distribution. They can aim at having their distribution products complement their content products and vice versa. For example, broadcasters provide content programs for audiences and distribution products for advertisers, which leads to the creation of a related diversified and complementary portfolio.

Second, many media content products are nonexcludable and non-depletable, meaning that media content products can be consumed by one individual and still be available to others. Thus media firms can reproduce and redistribute products in related content format to pursue superior performance. For instance, many media firms own both a newspaper and an online content site; news content is translated into several languages and distributed through both paper and Internet to different international markets.

Third, many media content products are distributed through a windowing process. Content such as film can be delivered sequentially to consumers through multiple channels in different time periods. This reinforces the advantage of diversifying into multiple related distribution sectors in various international markets to increase revenue potentials for such a product.

Fourth, media products are highly subjective to cultural preferences and regulatory policies of the host country. Diversifying into related product or geographic markets could help media firms to take more advantage of their acquired local knowledge and relationships. In addition, media products are subject to the existing communication infrastructure of the host country. This may also lead to a diversification strategy which is geographically related, because countries in a region are often at the same stage of infrastructure development, and the related geographic diversification may realize cost- and resource-sharing benefits (Chan-Olmsted, 2003).

Strategy for Entry Selection

Having decided what products should be included in an international portfolio, which kind (*related or unrelated*), and how many international markets to launch (*extent*), media firms are now faced with another decision: what entry mode should they select? The most commonly used entry modes are exporting, licensing, and foreign direct investment.

Exporting. Exporting is the simplest way to enter a foreign market. Firms can still keep the manufactoring in their home countries, and produce or just slightly modify products to the demand of the foreign markets. In the magazine business, for example, the most common form of export is the so-called overspill between markets with the same or very similar languages. In a bilingual country like Belgium, with overspill from both the French and the Dutch markets, this is possible. Also, there is some degree of overspill of Swedish magazines from Sweden to the Swedish-speaking population of Finland. Apart from the overspill, it is possible to export by agents. In Sweden, the import agent Interpress can offer an assortment of over 700 different titles (Hafstrand, 1995).

Exporting has both advantages and disadvantages. It is superior for limiting investments abroad, creating economies of scale, operating within current organizational structures, and relying upon existing production, marketing, and distribution systems. But it may also cause potential misunderstanding between the audience and advertisers in the new market, and induce competition from local entrepreneurs (Picard, 2003). In addition, for some media products (especially newspapers and other weekly magazines), exporting is challenged by the problem of durability because of their time sensitivity. Moreover, the issue of language is a limit to exporting. The need to translate, to dub and subtitle, also affects exportability and the means used for internationalization.

Licensing. Licensing essentially permits a firm in the host country to use the property of the licensor. Such property is usually intangible, such as trademarks, patents, and production techniques. The licensee pays a fee in exchange for the rights to use the intangible property and possibly for technical assistance. As little investment by the licensor is required, licensing has the potential to provide a very large return on investment (ROI). However, because the licensee produces and markets the product, potential returns from manufacturing and marketing activities may be lost.

The Walt Disney Co. is a well-known example of the use of licensing. It holds a name that distinguishes it from all other entertainment products and services. Through its consumer products division, Disney has licensed more than 16,000 items of merchandise worldwide. Similarly, the formation of Tokyo Disneyland is based on a limited partnership agreement. The Disney firm leases its name and characters in exchange for 10% of all gate fees and 5% from food and merchandise sales (Gershon, 1997).

Foreign Direct Investment. Foreign direct investment (FDI) is the direct ownership of facilities in the target country. It involves the transfer of resources including capital, technology, and personnel. FDI includes three basic methods: greenfield, merger and acquisition (M&A), and joint venture. Greenfield FDI involves starting a new operation from scratch. The firm buys or leases land, constructs new facilities, hires and/or transfers its managers and employees, and then launches the new operation. M&A deals with merging with or acquiring an existing firm that is conducting business in the host country. Finally, joint venture is a jointly owned separate firm, created to promote mutual interests (The M&A and joint venture approaches will be explored further as methods for international development later in this chapter). In general, FDI provides a high degree of control over the operations and the ability to better understand the consumers and a competitive environment. However, it requires a high level of resources and a high degree of commitment.

Foreign direct investment has been widely used by many media firms, and it is predominant, especially among large media conglomerates. Media firms engage in FDI in order to pursue proprietary assets and natural resources, obtain foreign market penetration, improve product and distribution efficiencies, and overcome regulatory barriers; as for the media conglomerates, they use FDI to build their media empires (Gershon, 1997).

Selection of Entry Mode. Each of the main modes of entry into a foreign market has pros and cons, and different modes may be appropriate under different circumstances. In selecting entry modes for specific firms and products, numerous theories and models provide insight. Among the most widely recognized are the stage of development (SD) model (Johnson & Wiedersheim-Paul, 1975), the transaction cost analysis (TCA) model (Anderson & Gatignon, 1986; Hitt, et al., 1990), the ownership, location, and internalization (OLI) model (Dunning, 1977, 1980, 1988, 1995, 1998, and 2000), the organization capacity (OC) model (Aulakh & Kotale, 1997; Madhok, 1998), and the decision making process (DMP) model (Root, 1994; Young, et al., 1989). Taken together these models show that four kinds of factors may affect the decision and selection of entry modes: country-specific factors (cultural distance, institution, exchange rate, etc.), industry-specific factors (market size, market structure, industry type, etc.), firm-specific factors (firm capacity, firm size, etc.) and product-specific factors (product type, maturity, sales service, etc.).

The selection of entry mode for international media portfolios can be drawn from a careful consideration combining all these factors, but special attention needs to be paid to a variety of factors.

The market size of the home country may affect the mode of entry. For example, most American media firms have made little direct investment and have relied upon direct export, joint venture, and licensing to move products worldwide. The size of the U.S market, with its internal opportunities and linguistic limitations, has kept many media firms from making significant efforts to globalize their operations (Picard, 2002).

The extent of trade barriers and national policy control also has influence on entry decisions. Media products are often subject to more regulatory control and barriers to trade from the host market due to their pervasive impact on individual societies. In a host country with high import restrictions, for example, FDI may be more favorable; and in a host country with strict limitation on the establishment of foreign entities, exporting or licensing can be a better choice.

A firm's size and capabilities are important determinants as well. Large media firms, having sufficient resources and experiences, are more likely to adopt a high equity entry mode, because they believe that this entry mode can offer high profit potential and opportunities. In contrast, medium and small firms possess comparatively limited resources; they may be short on capital or thin in terms of executive talents. Therefore, an incremental framework is often used as experiential knowledge is acquired (Bell & Young, 1998).

Product characteristics affect the entry mode decision by the way that product type, maturity, and content requirements vary across countries. Some embedded technology—such as telecommunication products—are often best transferred through an equity mode, whereas firms whose competitive advantage is based on a well-known brand name, such as the magazine *Reader's Digest*, often enter foreign markets through a licensing mode. Content requirement can limit the entry choice because audiences want media content that involves domestic citizens, cultures, and personalities. Thus, much media content, such as game shows, is produced worldwide under format licenses from the original producers (Griffin & Pustay, 2002; Picard, 2002).

The level of transaction costs in international operations is another critical determinant for the entry decision. If such costs are high, a firm may rely on FDI and joint venture for entry modes. If costs are low, the firm may use franchising, licensing, or contract manufacturing. In deciding which choice is appropriate, the firm must consider both the nature of the resources and capabilities it possesses and its ability to ensure productive and harmonious working relations with any local firm with which it does business. The firm also needs to consider the extent and directions of its business diversification, as these have a major influence on the level of transaction. Portfolios with a high degree of diversification may require significant efforts by managers facilitating internal transactions within diverse in geographic and product units and external transactions with government officials and agencies, suppliers, and customers.

To sum up, appropriate entry strategies must be made by considering both internal and external factors. Attention needs to be paid to, among others, market size, extent of barriers, the firm's size and capabilities, product characteristics, and transaction costs. Also, it is crucial to be aware that the selection of the mode of entry for international media portfolios often needs to be tailor-made, as each product in the portfolio might be best served by a different strategy. Even when the same product is involved, entry choice might vary according to different conditions of the target countries.

Methods for Development

An even greater challenge than creating portfolios and introducing portfolios to the foreign markets is sustaining portfolio development after getting into the international market. This section illustrates the methods required by media firms to develop their portfolios in an international environment. In general, media firms can develop their international portfolios through two basic methods: internal development and strategic alliances.

Internal Development. This development method describes situations in which the firm's capabilities are developed by building up an organization's own resource bases and competencies (Johnson & Scholes, 2002). For media firms holding international portfolios, internal development can be very important, as the sustainable development and competitive advantages of portfolios are built on a firm's unique resources and core competencies, which could be enhanced through internal development.

As discussed before, cultural awareness, environmental knowledge, and managerial competencies are required. This knowledge can be acquired through internal development, either by strengthening the organization's abilities to respond to a changing environment or by improving managers' capabilities in managing international activities. The knowledge achieved through internal development may be more of a competence in the sense that it is created and learned internally, and it is more difficult to imitate by the firm's competitors.

Media firms also choose to develop their portfolios through internal development when they do not have resources available for major investment. A favorable and realistic choice especially for small and medium-sized firms, which cannot conduct acquisitions and joint ventures because of their limited size and capabilities, is to develop their abilities to innovate and produce portfolio products internally.

Strategic Alliances. Beside internal development, media firms can enhance their portfolios via strategic alliances, including mergers and acquisitions, joint ventures, and other kinds of strategic agreements such as research and development, marketing, and production agreements. In addition to being the modes of entry, M&A and joint ventures are applied widely by media firms to support the development of their international portfolios.

Mergers and acquisitions have been very popular in recent years, because developing new products internally and successfully introducing them into the marketplace is often time-consuming, and because it is also difficult to earn a profitable return quickly (Shank & Govindarajan, 1992). Moreover, it is harder for firms to develop products that differ from their current lines for new geographical markets in which they lack experience (Hitt, et al., 1990). Thus, many firms develop their portfolios through M&A. In media industries, firms rich in resources are more likely to conduct M&A. In addition to the above reasons, these firms also hope to enhance their market powers through an increase in firm size.

Joint ventures and other kinds of strategic alliances can offer opportunities for media firms to acquire complementary resources for portfolio development. This kind of complementary resource is especially important to the success of media firms. For example, in the purchase of Universal Studios by Vivendi, the content was owned as an intangible asset and was highly complementary to the tangible distribution media. Strategic alliances may also share risks and reduce costs, as seen in the cases of international co-production of motion pictures and alliances of multiple U.S. cable system operators with new cable ventures in South America. In addition, because much of media content products are public goods, alliances are an effective approach for increasing economies of scale in production and, consequently, reducing costs. International alliances are also commonly formed to reduce competition and to reduce uncertainty, including uncertainty in local knowledge, technology, or standards (Chan-Olmsted, 2003).

Both internal development and strategic alliances can help firms sustain their development in the international markets. However, the method chosen is quite dependent on a firm's capabilities and associated circumstances. Internal development may be more favorable to firms that are thin in resources and capabilities to conduct heavy international investment. The advantage of internal development is that the capabilities achieved internally are more difficult for other firms to copy. On the other hand, strategic alliances are good for rapidly creating new products and achieving benefits. They can also help to complement portfolios, share risks, and reduce competition and uncertainties. Adopting a resource-based view of strategic management (Lockett & Thompson, 2001), sufficient and successful strategic alliances need to be built on unique resources of the firm and complement their core competencies. Only through full utilization of a firm's unique resources and core competencies can media portfolios sustain its competitive advantage and constant development in the international markets. This will be further illustrated through a resource-based portfolio decision and development model presented in the next section.

A MODEL FOR PORTFOLIO DECISION AND MANAGEMENT STRATEGY

In the preceding sections, issues raised by the internationalization of media portfolios and management strategies have been examined. To address the formulation and implementation of such strategies, a model for portfolio decision and management strategy is proposed here.

This model is based on the resource-based view. Previous research suggests that a related diversification would be preferred by media firms pursuing both geographic and product diversification. This preference is determined primarily by the special features of many media products, such as their dual product, nonexcludable, nondepletable characteristics and their cultural and environmental reliance. Research in connection with the resource-based view and corporate diversification argues that "the related diversification enhances performance only when it allows a business to obtain preferential access to strategic assets—those that are valuable, rare, imperfectly tradable, and costly to imitate" (Markides & Williamson, 1996, p. 351). Thus, it is assumed that for media portfolios to succeed in related diversification, firms should first be aware of their valuable, rare and hard to imitate resources. Even in unrelated diversification, exploring core competencies and fully utilizing unique resources are also critical for success, as these unique resources and core competencies might "provide the basis of creating opportunities in new arenas where the same CSFs (critical success factors) would be valued above those that currently prevail" (Johanson, et al., 2002, p. 305).

The unique resources of a media firm could be traced through an analysis of the firm's internal resources. Media firms have both general resources and specific resources. General resources include the firm's financial performance and stability, asset management teams, marketing systems, and related alliances; specific resources include the firm's access to content products, branded properties, reliance on content or distribution, repurposing/content transfer expertise, windowing capability, internationalization expertise, multi-stream revenue system, and so on. Unique resources are those that are valuable, rare and hard to imitate, and they may create the core competencies that underpin the firm's competitive advantage. The unique resources of a media firm, for example, could be a contracted veteran producer or brand name with a good reputation, and the core competencies, might be high expertise in producing certain programs or great capabilities in using a well-known brand name (see Fig. 9.1).

After identifying a firm's unique resources and core competencies, managers should identify and locate the foreign country and market in which the advantages of these resources and competencies could be fully utilized and applied. To do so, a scan of the target country and market is required, and this can be done in four steps. The first should be to scan the target country's external environment. Factors such as the target country's legal and cultural environment, barriers to trade, policy control, economic and technological advancement, and its social development should all be viewed. Second, the

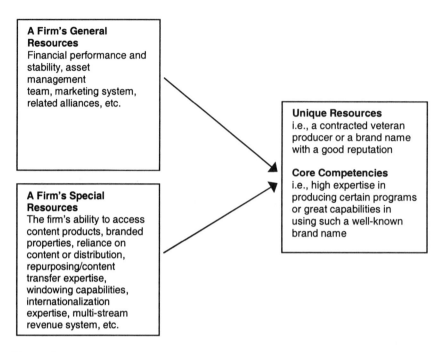

Figure 9.1
Unique Resources and Core Competencies

target country's media environment needs to be scanned. This scan is made to identify the target country's demand for multimedia products and communications/media infrastructure. Third, the target industry's characteristics are scanned, which may include market size, growth rate, profitability, competition, and product lifecycle. In the fourth step, the target industry's attractiveness needs to be determined. This step is critical for ensuring effective portfolio decisions, because a firm needs to examine the geographic relatedness between target and home countries, and the product relatedness between target and home firms. Managers also need to examine the alignment between home and target firm's content and distribution products (Chan-Olmsted, 2003; see Fig. 9.2).

Based on the above, portfolio decision and management strategy can then be formulated in the next stage. Firms need to decide the extent of their product and geographic diversifications, and the degree of product relatedness. While doing so, they should take factors such as the firm's size and capabilities into

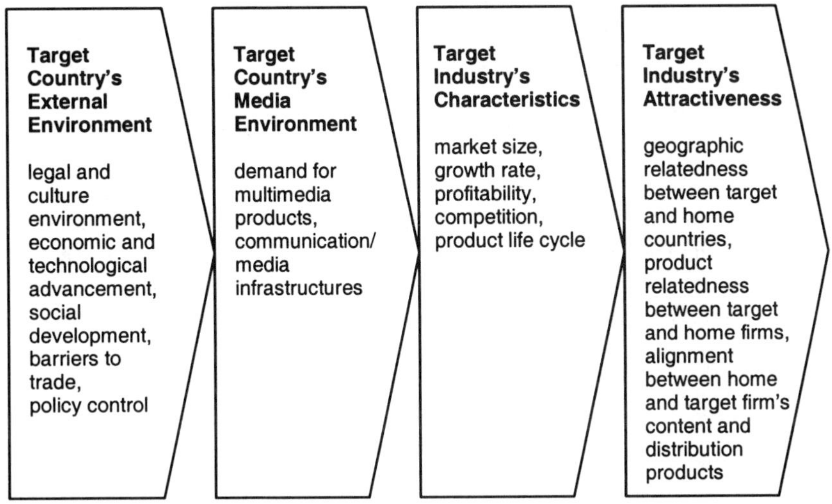

Target Country's External Environment	Target Country's Media Environment	Target Industry's Characteristics	Target Industry's Attractiveness
legal and culture environment, economic and technological advancement, social development, barriers to trade, policy control	demand for multimedia products, communication/ media infrastructures	market size, growth rate, profitability, competition, product life cycle	geographic relatedness between target and home countries, product relatedness between target and home firms, alignment between home and target firm's content and distribution products

Figure 9.2
Environmental Scan

consideration. They also need to choose the mode of foreign entries. Foreign entry decisions can be made through cautious consideration combining all the country-specific factors (cultural distance, institution, exchange rate, etc.), industry-specific factors (market size, market structure, industry type, etc.), firm-specific factors (firm capacity, firm size, etc.) and product-specific factors (product type, maturity, sales service, etc.). Some special attention needs to be paid to market size, extent of barriers and national policy control, the firm's size and capabilities, product characteristics, and level of transaction costs. Managers need also to be aware that the entry decision making for international media portfolios is often tailor-made, in response to a changing and dynamic international environment. To sustain an international position, firms can plan internal development and conduct strategic alliances. Both methods help to strengthen the competitive advantages of firms and their portfolio products, and both methods of development need to be based on the unique resources and core competencies. Finally, a strategy for portfolio decisions, a strategy for entry selection, and methods for development are formulated.

Following the completion of the above steps, firms would then move to the phase of implementing their strategies, which may involve issues such as resource allocation: how to allocate financial resources and human resources across different business units and different geographic markets. To implement these strategies successfully, managers are also required to have certain competencies, for example, to process large varieties of information, to understand the host country markets, to know and understand their portfolio products, and to handle complex organizational management.

The final stage in the process of management strategy is evaluation, by which the firm should make an assessment of whether the prior stages have achieved satisfactory results (see Fig. 9.3). Evaluation is not the terminus of the model. If any unsatisfactory performance is found here, managers should go back to either the implementation phase to tighten and enhance the control, or to the strategic choice phase to make other alternatives for their strategy, or even to the target country and market scan phase to restart a new cycle of steps in this model.

DISCUSSION

Some issues and strategies in managing international media portfolios across borders and cultures have been studied in this chapter. The internationalization of media portfolios is an irreversible trend, especially since the emergence of new communications and electronics technologies, which facilitate the delivery of media content and services across the world. Moving beyond national borders, media portfolio management is confronted with several unexpected questions and challenges.

In view of the external and internal issues that might influence the management of international media portfolios, media firms need to develop their cultural awareness of national cultural differences, align corporate culture with different geographic and product divisions, and understand local cultural concepts, such as language, religion, and attitudes to their media product portfolios. Because trade barriers and policy control constrain the internationalization of portfolios, firms must be aware of the barriers and policy conditions in the target country market. In addition, firms also need to conduct a careful environmental scan of the host country's media environment to ensure that the host country has real capacity to support and consume their media products. To manage international media portfolios which involve diversification in both geographic and product dimensions, managers are also required to be competent in processing complex information. They need to have explicit knowledge of portfolio products and the international target market, and tacit knowledge of multicultural management. International media portfolios bring about issues of resource allocation, and firms thus need to balance and analyze the importance of alternative products and international markets, and adjust the resource allocation to international product life cycles. International

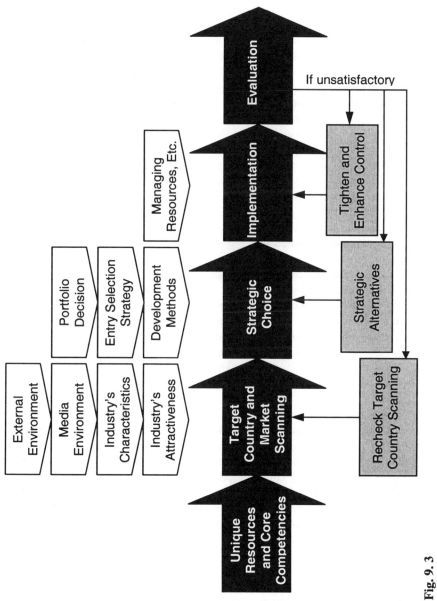

Fig. 9. 3
A Model for Portfolio Decision and Management Strategy

human resource allocation is also a challenge. How to recruit, retain, and allocate people across different product lines and international units is crucial to the success of the portfolio.

Several strategies can be applied to the management of international media portfolios. A strategy for portfolio decisions proposes a direction of related diversification for portfolio composition. After the creation of portfolios, the strategy for entry selection illustrates several factors that may affect the entry mode of portfolios. Due to the diversified features of products included in a portfolio and different conditions in the target market, the entry mode selection often needs to be tailor-made to prevailing circumstances. Upon entering the international market, portfolios can be developed and sustained through internal development and/or strategic alliances. While doing so, full utilization of firms' unique resources and core competencies can help firms to pursue competitive advantages and long-term development in a dynamic international environment.

The model for portfolio decision and management strategy presented in this chapter further illustrates this resource-based strategy planning and formulation process. Starting with the analysis of a firm's internal resources, the unique resources and core competencies of the firm are examined. Then the process turns to the environmental scan to explore the target markets and business areas where these unique resources and core competencies can be applied. Based on these, firms formulate strategies for their portfolio compositions and entry mode decision. They also make plans for portfolio development in an international environment. When they move to the phase of strategy implementation, issues such as managerial competencies and resource allocation need to be emphasized. And finally, if any unsatisfactory results occur at the evaluation stage, firms should go back to adjust appropriately in previous phases because the model represents an interlinked rather than a linear process of strategy formulation and implementation.

This chapter presented issues and strategies that have significant meaning to media portfolio management in an international context. However, further studies are required on a variety of issues. For example, this chapter has suggested that international media portfolios need to be established on the basis of unique resources and core competencies of firms, but the means for transferring these competitive advantages across borders are still a challenge. Moreover, the means for achieving synergies across different product lines in international markets is an important issue in the development of international portfolios. This will require greater study of issues of marketing and branding because effective means of transferring media brands into new international markets are relatively unexplored.

Media products face the conflicting logic of being public or market products, but most of the research on internationalization has been conducted with the assumption of the market model. For public media products or services to be internationalized, the approaches that should be applied to their portfolio creation, management, and strategy formulation need to be better understood. In this chapter, the related diversification approach has been assumed for media portfolios. However, success of unrelated (concentric) diversification is not rare. Thus, research needs to investigate conditions that could make unrelated diversification profitable despite the bias toward product relatedness in media industries. Furthermore, the international spread of media portfolios brings with it an exponential increase in the worldwide piracy of media products and services. Means by which firms can protect and manage the use of intellectual property rights in an international context need clarification. To answer these and other questions, a great deal of effort will have to be expended and future studies from a multidisciplinary perspective are required.

REFERENCES

Albarran, A. & Gormly, R. (2003). Strategic responses or strategic blunder? An examination of AOL Time Warner and Vivendi Universal, pp. in 35-46 in Picard, R.G., ed., *Strategic responses to media market changes.* Jönköping International Business School Research Reports, No. 2004–2.

Albarran, A. (2002). *Management of electronic media* (2nd ed.). Belmont, CA: Wadsworth Group.

Albarran, A. & Porco, J. (1990). Measuring and analyzing diversification of corporations involved in pay cable, *Journal of Media Economics, 3*(2), 3–14.

Anderson, E. & Gatignon, H. (1986). Modes of foreign entry: A transaction cost analysis and propositions, *Journal of International Business Studies, 17,* 1–26.

Ansoff, H. I. (1958). Strategies for diversification, *Harvard Business Review,* September-October, 113-124.

Aulakh, P. S. & Kotale, M. (1997). Antecedents and performance implications of channel integration in foreign markets, *Journal of International Business Studies, 28* (1), 145–175.

Barney, J. B. (1991). Firm resources and sustained competitive advantage, *Journal of Management, 17,* 99–120.

Bell, J. & Young, S. (1998). Towards an integrative framework of the internationalization of the firm. In G. Hooley, R. Loveridge & D. Wilson (Eds.), *Internationalisation: Process, context and markets* (pp. 5-23). London: Macmillan.

Bennis, W., Mason, R. O. & Mitroff, I. I. (1986). *Riding the waves of change, Developing managerial competencies for a turbulent world.* San Francisco: Jossey-Bass Publishers.

Bond, M.H. (1988). Finding universal dimensions of individual variation in multicultural studies of values: The Rokeach and Chinese value surveys, *Journal of Personality and Social Psychology, 55*, 1009–1015.

Chandler, A. D. (1962). *Strategy and structure: Chapters in the history of the American industrial enterprise.* Cambridge, MA: MIT Press.

Chan-Olmsted, S. M. & ., B. H. (2003). Diversification strategy of global media conglomerates: Examining its patterns and determinants, *Journal of Media Economics, 16*(4), 213–233.

Chan-Olmsted, S. M. (2003). In search of partnerships in a changing global media market: Trends and drivers of international strategic alliances. In R. G. Picard (ed.), *Strategic responses to media market changes* (pp. 47-64), Jönköping International Business School Research Report, No. 2004–2.

Chatterjee, S. & Wernerfelt, B. (1991). The link between resources and type of diversification: Theory and evidence, *Strategic Management Journal, 12*, 33–48.

Croteau, D. & Hoynes, W. (2001). *The business of media: Corporate media and the public interest.* Thousand Oaks, CA: Pine Forge Press.

Datta, D. K., Rajagopalan, N. & Rasheed, A. M. A. (1991). Diversification and performance: Critical review and future direction, *Journal of Management Studies, 28*, 529–588.

Devereux, E. (2003). *Understanding the media.* London: Sage Publications.

Demers, D. P. (1999). *Global media: Menace or messiah?* Cresskill, NJ: Hampton.

Dimmick, J. W. (2003). *Media competition and coexistence: The theory of the niche*. Mahwah, NJ: Lawrence Erlbaum Associates.

Dimmick, J. & Wallschlaeger, M. (1986). Measuring corporate diversification: A case study of new media ventures by television network parent companies, *Journal of Broadcasting and Electronic Media, 30*, 1–14.

Dunning, J. H. (2000). The eclectic paradigm as an envelope for economic and business theories of MNE activity, *International Business Review*, 9, 163–190.

Dunning, J. H. (1998). Location and the multinational enterprise: A neglected factor? *Journal of International Business Studies, 29*(1), 45–66.

Dunning, J.H. (1995). Reappraising the eclectic paradigm in an age of alliance capitalism, *Journal of International Business Studies, 26*(3), 461–491.

Dunning, J. H. (1988). The eclectic paradigm of international production: A restatement and some possible extensions, *Journal of International Business Studies, 19*(1), 1–31.

Dunning, J. H. (1980). Toward an eclectic theory of international production: some empirical tests, *Journal of International Business Studies, 11*(1), 9–31.

Dunning, J. H. (1977). Trade, location of economic activity and the MNE: A search for an eclectic approach. In Ohlin, B., et al., eds., *The International Allocation of Economic Activity: Proceedings of Nobel Symposium, Stockholm* (pp. 295-418). London: Macmillan.

Dunning, J. H. (1958). *American investment in British manufacturing industry*. London: Allen and Unwin.

Gershon, R. A. (2000). The transnational media corporation: Environmental scanning and strategy formulation. *Journal of Media Economics, 13*(2), 81–101.

Gershon, R.A. (1997). *The transnational media corporation: Global messages and free market competition*, Mahwah, NJ: Lawrence Erlbaum Associates.

Goold, M., Campbell, A. & Alexander, M. (1994). *Corporate-level strategy: creating value in the multibusiness firm*. New York: Wiley.

Grant, R. M. (1987). Multinationality and performance among British manufacturing companies, *Journal of International Business Studies, 18*, 79–89.

Grant, R. M., Jammine, A. P. & Thomas, H. (1988). Diversity, diversification, and profitability among British manufacturing companies 1972–84, *Academy of Management Journal, 31*, 771–801.

Griffin, R. W. & Pustay, M. W. (2002). *International business: A managerial perspective.* Upper Saddle River, NJ: Prentice-Hall International, Inc.

Hafstrand, H. (1995). Consumer magazines in transition: A study of approaches to internationalization, *Journal of Media Economics, 8*(1), 1–12.

Hitt, M. A., Hoskisson, R. E. & Kim, H. (1997). International diversification: Effects on innovation and firm performance in product-diversified firms, *Academy of Management Journal, 40*(4), 767–798.

Hitt, M. A., Hoskisson, R. E. & Ireland, R. D. (1990). Mergers and acquisitions and managerial commitment to innovation in m-form firms, *Strategic Management Journal, 11*(1), 29–47.

Hofstede, G. (1991). *Cultures and organizations: Software of the mind.* London: McGraw-Hill.

Hofstede, G. (1980). *Culture's consequences.* Beverly Hills, Calif.: Sage.

Hollifield, A. C. (2001). Crossing borders: Media management research in a transnational market environment, *Journal of Media Economics, 14*(3), 133–146.

Johnson, C. K. (1989). The role of finance in portfolio management, *Journal of Portfolio Studies, 9*(2), 122–149.

Johnson, D. & Turner, C. (2003). *International business: Themes and issues in the modern global economy.* Suffolk, UK: St Edmundsbury Press.

Johnson, G., & Scholes, K. (2002). *Exploring corporate strategy* (6th ed.), Englewood Cliffs, NJ: Prentice Hall.

Johnson, J. &. Wiedersheim-Paul, F. (1975). The internationalization of the firm: Four Swedish cases, *Journal of Management Studies, 12*(3), 305–322.

Kochhar, R. & Hitt, M. A. (1995). Toward an integrative model of international diversification, *Journal of International Management*, *1*, 33–72.

Kohut, B. (1984). Normative observations on the value added chain and strategic groups, *Journal of International Business Studies*, *15*, 151–168.

Küng, L. (2000). Exploring the link between culture and strategy in media organizations: The case of the BBC and CNN, *International Journal on Media Management*, *2*(2), 100–109.

Liesch, P. W. & Knight, G. A. (1999). Information internationalisation and hurdle rates in small and medium sized enterprise internationalization, *Journal of International Business Studies*, *30*, 383–394.

Litman, B., Shrikhande, S. & Ahn, H. (2000). A portfolio theory approach to network program selection, *Journal of Media Economics*, *12*(2), 57–79.

Lockett, A. & Thompson, S. (2001). The resource-based view and economics, *Journal of Management*, *27*, 723–755.

Lull, J. (1999). *Media, communication and culture: A global approach.* Cambridge: Polity Press.

Madhok, A. (1998). The nature of multinational firm boundaries: Transaction costs, firm capabilities and foreign market entry mode, *International Business Review*, *7*, 259–290.

Markides, C. C. & Williamson, P. J. (1996). Corporate diversification and organizational structure: A resource-based view, *Academy of Management Journal*, *39*(2), 340-367.

Markowitz, H. M. (1959). *Portfolio selection.* Oxford: Blackwell Publishers Ltd.

Mead, R. (1998). *International management.* Oxford: Blackwell Publishers Ltd.

Nevaer. L. E. V. and Deck, S. A. (1988). *The management of corporate business units: Portfolio strategies.* Greenwood, CT: Quorum Books.

Parhizgar, K.D. (2002). *Multicultural behavior and global business environments.* Middletown, PA: International Business Press.

Picard, R. G., ed. (2004). *Strategic responses to media market changes.* Jönköping International Business School Research Report Series No. 2004–2.

Picard, R. G. (2003). *Issues and trends in internationalization and globalization of media firms.* A paper presented to the Conference on Internationalization and Globalization of Media, Shanghai University, Shanghai, China, 1–5 December.

Picard, R. G. (2002). *The economics and financing of media firms.* New York: Fordham University Press.

Picard, R. G. (2001). Impediments to a global information society, *Global Media News, 3*(1), Winter 2001.

Picard, R. G. & Rimmer, T. (1999). Weathering a recession: Effects of size and diversification on newspaper firms, *Journal of Media Economics, 12*(1), 1–18.

Qian, G. (1997). Assessing product-market diversification of U.S. firms, *Management International Review, 37*, 127–149.

Ramanujam, V. & Varadarajan, P. R. (1989). Research on corporate diversification: A synthesis, *Strategic Management Journal, 10*, 523-551.

Rhinesmith, S. H. (1996). *A manager's guide to globalization: Six skills for success in a changing world.* Burr Ridge, IL: Irwin Professional Publishing.

Root, F. R. (1994). *Entry strategies for international markets.* London: Lexington Books.

Rumelt, R. (1984). Toward a strategic theory of the firm. In R. Lamb (Ed.), *Competitive strategic management* (pp. 556-570). Englewood Cliffs, NJ: Prentice Hall.

Sambharya, R. B. (1995). The combined effect of international diversification and product diversification strategies on the performance of U.S.-based multinational corporations, *Management International Review, 35*, 197–218.

Schein, E. (1992). *Organizational culture and leadership (2nd ed.).* San Francisco: Jossey-Bass.

Shank, J. K. & Govindarajan, V. (1992). Strategic cost analysis of technological investments, *Sloan Management Reviews, 34*(3), 39–51.

Smith, A. (1999). *The age of behemoths: The globalization of mass media firms.* New York: Priority Press Publications.

Sreberny-Mohammadi, A., Winseck, D., Mckenna, J. & Boyd-Barrett, O. (1998). *Media in global context.* Tunbridge Wells: Gray Publishing.

Tallman, S. & Li, J. (1996). Effects of international diversity and product diversity on the performance of multinational firms, *Academy of Management Journal, 39*(1), 179–196.

UNCTAD Source. (2003). *Audiovisual Services: Improving Participation in Developing Countries.* Retrieved on 10 May, 2004 from World Wide Web at http://www.unctad.org/en/docs//c1em20d2_en.pdf

Velten, T. & Ansoff, H. I. (1998). Managing business portfolios in German firms, *Long Range Planning, 31*(6), 879–885.

Young, S. J, Hamill, C. W. & Davies, J. R. (1989). *International market entry and development: Strategies and management.* Englewood Cliffs, N.J.: Prentice Hall.

10
Portfolio Internationalization:
The Case of a Successful Concept

Annette Risberg
Copenhagen Business School

Leif Melin
Jönköping International Business School

Although individual media products such as motion pictures and audio records can be easily sold internationally, establishing company operations for other media products requires significant strategic thought and structural development of the company, as the previous chapter has shown.

Periodicals, such as women's, home, and automobile magazines, are often published in several international versions. These magazines use some articles and material for all editions mixed with national material. This is not done in newspapers because much news does not travel well, even though it travels rapidly today. The content of a newspaper is difficult to use in another national context because the framing of the news, even of international news, is often national. International news typically needs to be domesticated and adapted to the local market (c.f. Clausen, 2001) and much domestic content is typically uninteresting elsewhere. Therefore advantages of internationalization and expansion into new markets for newspapers cannot be made in terms of large-scale economies.

But are there conditions under which newspapers can internationalize their operations and sell their product in several international markets? Some newspapers—such as the *Financial Times* and the *Wall Street Journal*—produce international editions published in English or translation versions. But newspaper companies are rarely international in the sense that they produce and adapt a newspaper for different markets. Instead, newspapers traditionally act on a local, regional, or national basis.

Bengt Braun, CEO of the Bonnier group, a Swedish publishing house, expresses the problem:

It is difficult for a newspaper to expand geographically and sell in another district. You cannot sell a local newspaper from town A in city B because it does not write about what happens in city B and therefore totally misses its target group. This is unlike many other kinds of products like a tape recorder or a coffee cup which you can sell in the same form in many places. But this is not for a newspaper that survives on being different everyday. Many newspapers seeking development have to buy into another daily newspaper in another region trying to find synergies (personal communication).

In the past decade several free newspapers have successfully been introduced globally, through the use of newspaper concepts that have been launched in multiple markets. Most notable among these have been *Metro* and *20 Minutes* (Bakker, 2002; World Association of Newspapers, 2000). Although based on a uniform concept and style, the content of the papers is particularly national and local to the city and country of publication.

This chapter presents a case study of *Dagens Industri*, a Swedish business newspaper in the Bonnier group, and its efforts at internationalization through the establishment of papers using the same concept in other nations. It is a rare case of internationalizing a paid circulation newspaper through start-ups of sister newspapers in several European countries. These international versions of *Dagens Industri* are not republished versions of the Swedish newspaper, and the Swedish editor-in-chief does not decide on the content of each newspaper. All local versions have their own editor-in-chief and editorial staffs. Thus, this case of internationalization is not about exporting a newspaper or its content, but about creating an international portfolio by exporting a newspaper concept.

According to the *Dagens Industri* management, the main parts of the concept are: this newspaper is *easy to comprehend*; is *a tool for managers*; and *takes a short time to read*. The articles in the newspaper are written so that people without a higher education in management and economics can understand them. The concept is aimed at a target group that is not just an elite group of top managers (the target group for e.g., *Financial Times*) but managers at many different levels in companies. In order to reach these managers, or decision makers as *Dagens Industri* calls them, the newspaper has to write about and explain complicated economic news in a way that is easy to understand. Therefore the newspaper contains short, simple headlines and easy diagrams that visualize the facts.

Dagens Industri wants to be a tool for the reader in his or her daily work, to improve his or her job performance, and to be a career development tool. The main focus of the newspaper is therefore on the business-firm level rather than on macroeconomic news. When macroeconomic issues are presented for the reader they are most often related to how they affect individual companies or entrepreneurs.

One important component of the concept is that *Dagens Industri* prefers to produce its own news instead of referring to news agencies or other newspapers. The journalists are told to search for exclusive news and to build networks of information sources to find out what is going on in the business world. *Dagens Industri* deliberately lets the journalists focus and slant the articles, which means that *Dagens Industri* is quite bold compared to other traditional newspapers. This concept, which allows writers to emphasize what they believe is important, was adopted from the practices of newspaper tabloids. The concept of *Dagens Industri* is built on the tabloid format, which former editor-in-chief and managing director Hasse Olsson brought to the newspaper in 1981 when he came from a large Swedish tabloid.

The tabloid format is perfect, according to the *Dagens Industri* management, because it means that the readers can avail themselves of the paper in a short time. *Dagens Industri*'s management emphasize that the paper should not take too long to read and no one should have a bad conscience for not having read the whole newspaper. The underlying assumption is that business people all over the world have a shortage of time and that they do not have the time to search for information but want it served. As a result, the *Dagens Industri* concept should be possible to export all over the world, company managers believe. This is the concept that *Dagens Industri* started to export in the late 1980s to the Baltic States and later to other parts of Europe.

This chapter describes and analyzes the internationalization of *Dagens Industri* and its concept, in order to determine how they became successful in their rather unique newspaper internationalization. In order to do so we will focus mainly on the entry mode used, a type of greenfield investment with specific characteristics, including an emphasis on control and knowledge transfer.

Dagens Industri's first international sister paper was started in Estonia in 1989. The Estonian start-up has been important for the company's subsequent internationalization. It was the learning case for *Dagens Industri* from which the company generated important knowledge for the following international start-ups. Therefore we will focus on how *Dagens Industri* entered the Estonian market and built up a new business newspaper, *Äripäev*. From this case we capture and conceptualize in more theoretical terms the emerging internationalization strategy of *Dagens Industri* for starting up newspapers abroad.

METHODS

This study is based on an interpretative method using the case study approach. The case study is based on semistructured interviews, participant observations, and available documents. The interviews were made at three locations, the Bonnier group, *Dagens Industri*, and *Äripäev*. Seven people in management positions at *Dagens Industri* and the Bonnier group were interviewed. Interviews were also made during a one week visit at the office of *Äripäev* in Tallinn. Eleven persons were interviewed, for about an hour each, and they represented both administrative and editorial management and staff. The first editor-in-chief of *Äripäev*, who no longer works for the newspaper, was also interviewed. Most interviews have been transcribed verbatim and detailed notes were taken during the interviews, summarized in written text straight after each interview. During the week spent at *Äripäev*, researcher Annette Risberg was assigned a desk in one of the newsrooms, where she spent the working days at site, making observations. Additional material such as company published material and newspaper articles on the topic have been collected as well.

All interviews, observations, and documents were analyzed to look for factors that give a trustworthy understanding of this internationalization process and why it became successful. The main theoretical perspective in use is internationalization theory.

DAGENS INDUSTRI ENTERS ESTONIA

The first sister paper started abroad by *Dagens Industri* was the Estonian paper *Äripäev*. Internationalization was a new experience to the *Dagens Industri* staff and Estonia was a market very different from Sweden. What follows is a detailed description of the start-up process of this Estonian business newspaper. The story is told by people from Estonia as well as from Sweden involved in the start-up. The section will end with an account of *Äripäev* about 10 years after the start.

In the midst of the revolution in Estonia that freed that country from the Soviet Union, the Swedish daily business newspaper *Dagens Industri* decided to start a newspaper there. It began with the editor-in-chief for *Dagens Industri*, Hasse Olsson, who had a vision for expanding the concept of *Dagens Industri* toward the East. Olsson tells his reasons to start a sister paper in Estonia:

> It was a personal interest that drove me to establish *Dagens Industri* in Estonia. I would say it was my heart rather than my brain that drove the

project. My interest in the Baltic States was founded when I was a child. I am of the war-child generation and grew up with classmates from Finland and the Baltic States. I have a historical interest in the Baltic States but my interest is also grounded in the fact that I am a sailor and I wanted to see the Baltic Sea opened up as a traffic route again after being closed for traffic for so many years. I also enjoy getting to know new people (personal communication).

In the summer of 1989, Olsson sailed to Tallinn during his vacation. He had arranged meetings with two Estonian consultants in Tallinn. One of them had been to Stockholm earlier that year to ask for Olsson's help in starting a newspaper in Estonia. The meetings resulted in an agreement to initially make a test edition of a newspaper.

Satisfied with the results of the meetings Olsson returned to Sweden and informed his paper's technical director, Kjell Wågberg, about the project. They decided that Wågberg should go to Estonia to find out more about the possibilities to start and print a newspaper in Estonia.

In Tallinn Wågberg tried to determine what the possibilities were to run a newspaper in Estonia. He met with the two consultants to learn the conditions for printing a newspaper in Estonia. One of the consultants, Hallar Lind, a former radio journalist, eventually became the first editor-in-chief for *Äripäev*. Lind tells about the first meetings with Olsson and Wågberg:

> In the summer of 1989 I was working for a consultant company called Mainor. At the time we were looking for the possibilities to publish a business magazine in Estonia. When Hasse Olsson came to Tallinn in 1989 he was looking for people who could tell him about Estonian economy and the Estonian newspaper market. He got the advice to contact Mainor and arranged a meeting with the director of the company. After their first meeting the director suggested that Hasse and I should meet. During this first meeting, which was over two hours long, he asked me about the situation in Estonia, the business market, the economical situation, trends and so on. He also asked me why there was no business newspaper in the Estonian market. After the meeting nothing happened for about a month, and then one day I got a call from Sweden, from Kjell Wågberg. He wanted to visit Estonia and learn about the printing plans of Estonia. So he came to Tallinn at the end of August (personal communication).

Because newsprint paper was distributed through a planned allocation process in the Soviet Union, printing plans were made each year so that each newspaper was allotted a specific amount of paper. Soviet newspapers were printed in large editions, up to 150,000 of each issue. The papers were rather thin, six to eight pages, and they were very cheap. The newspapers were run by the Communist Party and were tools for political messages. Articles were typically very long with no graphics. *Dagens Industri,* however, had short articles, lots of color and illustrations and was a very different type of newspaper compared to the Soviet-style newspapers. Wågberg concluded that it would be difficult to print in Estonia due to the paper quota and poor paper quality. Neither would it be possible to export newsprint paper from Sweden because it was too thin for the available printing presses. Furthermore, the printing presses in Estonia could only print in black and white and *Dagens Industri* needed a printing house that could print in full color.

When Wågberg came back he reported his findings to Olsson and other managers from *Dagens Industri* and the Bonnier group. They decided to go ahead with the project. Due to the paper quota and the poor printing quality it was decided that the Estonian newspaper would be printed in Stockholm. Lind was asked to come to Sweden to make further plans.

Lind spent a few days in Stockholm and met with people from *Dagens Industri, Affärsbolaget,*[10] and the Bonnier family. Lind said it would be possible to start a privately owned newspaper in Estonia because Moscow did not prohibit private companies any longer, but that a local partner was needed because foreign firms were not allowed to own more than 51% of a company. Further Lind told them that many people interested in starting newspapers in Estonia, so *Dagens Industri* would need to move quickly if they wanted to be first in the market.

During his stay in Stockholm, Lind learned about how to make a *Dagens Industri* newspaper. He met with different people who taught him about editorial and technical aspects, how to sell advertisements, and other things related to publishing a newspaper. Before the final decision to start the newspaper a dummy edition was made. They decided to go ahead with the plans, choosing *Äripäev* as the name of the newspaper. Just before Lind was to leave Stockholm he was asked how soon he could be ready to launch the paper. "In a month's time," he answered. The *Dagens Industri* representatives were surprised with his answer but concluded that they should try to have the first edition of *Äripäev* ready in a month.

In Tallinn Lind had a small office at Mainor (the Estonian partner) which was now turned into the editorial room. Four people were hired who together with Lind would be responsible for getting the first issue ready within a month. During this month they had a lot to do. They had to collect material and write

---

[10] *Dagens Industri* and *Affärsbolaget* were two subsidiaries within *Bonniers Affärsinformation,* a division in Bonnier Publishing Company. *Affärsbolaget* run weekly and monthly business magazines.

articles, set the layout, find ways to distribute the newspaper, and plan for the future if the test newspaper turned out to be successful. For this work they had a small office and one computer.

A couple of weeks into the project Lind got a call from Stockholm, telling him that Gideon Salutskij would come to Tallinn to help with the production of the first issue. Salutskij worked with *Dagens Industri*'s layout, was of Finnish origin, and could talk to the Estonians in Finnish.[11] "The Estonians don't speak very good English," Lind says, "but in the Northern area they speak quite good Finnish." Salutskij and Lind had earlier met in Stockholm where Salutskij had taught Lind publishing and printing matters.

> He gave us a lot of information and had a great knowledge. However, the two countries were so different at that time. We were at different levels in terms of thinking and traditions so we could not always use his or other *Dagens Industri* peoples' experience because the situation was so different (personal communication).

The launch date for the new paper was set for October 9, 1989. The printing plates were prepared in Estonia and thereafter Lind and a co-worker brought the plates, the computer disks, and all the material for the articles to Stockholm so the newspaper could be printed. Arriving in Stockholm the plates turned out to be of too poor quality for the Swedish printing presses. New printing plates had to be made. Upon inserting the computer disks into the *Dagens Industri* computers to make new plates they discovered that the files were not compatible with the computers in Sweden. The whole issue had to be rewritten and the layout had to be redone. It took two days and two nights before the material was in place again. Lind depicts:

> Even though this was a very interesting time, to work with all the people at *Dagens Industri*, it was at the same time difficult to work with them. It was an issue of languages. We made the newspaper in Estonian. As an editor it meant that I had to focus all the time on making stories short. It had to be a new newspaper and not an old Soviet-style newspaper. I had to focus on how to build up the stories and so on. And I think in Estonian. Then Mr Salutskij worked with us, and even though he was a great help to us, he did not always understand everything in Estonian. Then we had to start over and explain in Finnish what we had done. And he gave feedback in Finnish. Then everybody else got interested in what we were doing and how we were working. Hasse came and Kjell, as well as others. They were talking to

---

[11] Estonian and Finnish are both Finno-Ugrian languages.

us in English, and we had to explain everything again, in English. So I had
to use three languages at the same time. And there was a fourth language as
the Swedes spoke Swedish to each other. Sometimes I told myself: this is
crazy (personal communication).

Finally, the newspaper was ready to be printed. The first issue was sixteen
pages long. Late in the evening of October 4, 1989, the printing presses started
in Vällingby, a suburb of Stockholm. Pictures were taken of Olsson and Lind
starting the presses to immortalize the occasion. When Lind was asked how
many copies would be reasonable for the Estonian market he answered, "30,000
are quite normal." The *Dagens Industri* people thought that would be too much
considering the edition of *Dagens Industri* at that time was about 58,000, so they
settled on 10,000 copies.

A couple of days before the printing of the first newspaper, 3,000
newspaper placards were printed. When the two Estonians saw the placards they
could not understand how to use them as Estonian media did not use placards to
sell newspapers. Newspapers were sold in newspaper stands that had nothing
showing outside what was sold inside. Lind describes their reaction to the
placards.

It was strange that we had 3,000 copies of a placard for a country that
doesn't have the tradition of placards. And that was difficult to explain to
the people at Affärsbolaget, that one does not use newspaper placards in
Estonia. We did not know why we needed it, and they just said—No
problem, it's necessary to do it (personal communication).

The 10,000 copies of the newspaper had to be transported to Tallinn. A man
came over from Estonia in a small jeep-like car to ship the newspapers to
Estonia. Lind describes, "We had to pick the smallest man to drive, because the
car was so packed there was just a tiny space left for the driver." The
newspapers were shipped over to Estonia on the boat *Vireland* and on October 6,
the driver and the newspapers arrived in Tallinn. At the border control the car
was stopped. A soldier searching for anti-Soviet propaganda looked into the car
and asked about all the paper. The driver answered "it's just pink paper" and it
was allowed to enter.

The distribution of the newspaper could not be made in the same manner as
in Sweden, where *Dagens Industri* is very much a subscription-based
newspaper. The subscriptions system in Estonia was very different and was
handled by the post office. Once a year people registered their subscriptions at
the local post office and the postal service distributed them. *Äripäev* could not
profit from this system when the newspaper was launched. Instead one had to

build one's own subscription system and find a distribution company to distribute the newspapers. Such a system, however, was not in place when the first issue was launched. Instead they had to find another way to sell the first issue.

Äripäev was launched on a Monday, October 9, 1989. The day before, Lind appeared in a popular Estonian TV show.

Every Sunday afternoon there was a big television show in Estonia with about 400,000 viewers. It was a program covering what had happened during the week, and with the most popular artists. That Sunday, the day before the first issue would come out I had been booked on the show. There was an interview with me where I talked about the new newspaper that will be on the market Monday morning. I explained what the newspaper was about. This was interesting, because at that time there were no newspapers coming out on Mondays. There are many newspapers, all over the world that don't come out on Sundays. But in Estonia and the Soviet Union the six-day newspapers did not come out Mondays. Monday was a newspaper-free day (personal communication).

As *Äripäev* was launched on a day when no other newspapers were sold, there were no newsstands open. Eight o'clock Monday morning was the selling start for *Äripäev*. About fifty boys, dressed up in Estonian national costumes, were hired to sell the newspaper on the streets. Inside each newspaper there was an insert for subscribing to the *Äripäev*. By midday all 10,000 copies were sold. When Wågberg called later that day to see how things were going Lind told him to print 20,000 more copies of the issue. In two days the copies arrived from Sweden and they were also sold out.

Äripäev became a success and *Dagens Industri* decided to continue the project. In December that year the circulation was 40,000. In the beginning of December *Äripäev* signed an agreement with the newsstands to sell the newspaper. In January 1990, it had over 40,000 subscribers and the circulation was 55,000. During 1989, the paper came out monthly. From January to April 1990 *Äripäev* came out twice a month, and in May 1990, it became a weekly newspaper. In 1992 *Äripäev* came out three times a week and in 1996, it became a daily newspaper, publishing five times a week.

Success Factors During the First Years of Äripäev

Quite a few of the interviewees have stated that the quality of the newspaper was poor the first few years. Nevertheless the newspaper was popular. What was the reason for the success? First of all, *Äripäev* was a newspaper in a genre that did not exist in Estonia. Second, it represented something new coming from the West and people were curious about the newspaper. And everybody was hungry for news. Meelis Mandel, news editor in 2000, talks about how *Äripäev* was perceived by the readers when it was introduced:

> Ten years ago *Äripäev* was a hot paper that everybody read, from students to business men, to retired people, to government people. It was new, had different layout, with color and pictures. But it was also hot because it came from the West (personal communication).

Äripäev was so popular because it was different and represented something new. The layout was different, with pictures and colors, and the paper was of high quality. Moreover the marketing was very aggressive in the beginning. Igor Rötov, the current managing director and editor-in-chief, explains the circulation numbers:

> In the early years when *Äripäev* had an edition of 50,000 copies it was not a circulation that was paid for. It was a big marketing activity and *Äripäev* was cheaper than other daily newspapers (today it is quite expensive compared to other dailies). In 1993–1994 we started to raise the price to get a more correct price and then we lost many subscribers. Today we have 14,000 paying subscribers (personal communicaton).

One reason for the immediate success of *Äripäev* was that it entered a market that did not have anything like this kind of newspaper at a time when people were hungry for both news and products from the West. The high circulation numbers were the result of an aggressive marketing campaign. Even though the numbers went down after the price was raised, the low introduction prices had made it possible to carve out a part of the newspaper market. The competition at that time was not very hard and as *Äripäev* was first out it had a chance to establish itself in the market without fierce competition.

Problems Encountered During the Start-up Process

After the successful start during the first years of *Äripäev,* the situation became quite turbulent and troublesome for both external and internal reasons. The political situation was quite unstable in the Soviet Union during that time and in 1991 a revolt took place in Estonia by Russian troops called the Black Berets. The existence of all foreign companies was uncertain at that time and it was not sure that the paper would survive. It was even difficult to have frequent telephone contact between *Dagens Industri* and *Äripäev.*

A call could take several days before it went through, because of KGB that should listen to all incoming calls (personal communication).

Another problem was to find a printing house in Estonia that could live up to the quality demands. *Dagens Industri* found that suppliers tried to make an extra profit off the foreign owners and their demands for high quality. The problem was solved by writing very clear contracts with the printing houses and by *Dagens Industri* supplying them with the pink paper that the newspaper was printed on.

The lack of a distribution and subscription system for a non-Soviet newspaper was already mentioned as a problem during the start-up and it continued to create challenges. *Äripäev* had to build up a distribution system from the start, with support from *Dagens Industri*. Another problem was the newspaper placards. Despite Lind's protests, the newspaper came with placards and he had to find out how to use them. After some time he reached an agreement with the newsstand distribution company to hang the newspaper placards outside the kiosks.

The biggest problem experienced by Lind was the poor understanding of the local conditions by the Swedish management. Estonia was, in Lind's words, "wild" at that time and decisions had to be made very rapidly. He found that it took too long a time for the Swedish management to make decisions regarding *Äripäev*. One critical example was the decision to let *Äripäev* come out three times a week.

In May 1992, I decided that we had to come out three times a week. When the top managers in Sweden heard about this they were not pleased at all that I, the managing director and editor-in-chief in Tallinn, had made this decision myself. But I know this decision was correct (personal communication).

The decision to start publishing *Äripäev* three times a week eventually led to Lind leaving *Äripäev* in the autumn of 1992.

The Äripäev Company—Its Development and Objectives

Äripäev has, since its establishment, developed into a rather large company with many different products besides the newspaper. It publishes a weekly Russian-language newspaper and a monthly business magazine. Moreover, it produces and sells handbooks on different topics (e.g., IT, HRM, leadership) and in 1999 it started to arrange seminars for businessmen. In 2000, the newspaper had

1989	The newspaper is founded
1990	The newspaper is published twice a month and then weekly
1992	The newspaper comes out twice a week
1992	The newspaper comes out three times a week
1993	Change in management team
1996	The newspaper becomes a daily (five times a week) in February
1997	Mainor sells its shares to *Dagens Industri*, which becomes 100% owners
2002	Baltic Business News (BBN), a daily English-language news service covering business news from Estonia, Latvia, and Lithuania, is launched

Table 10.1
Important Events in *Äripäev*'s History

14,000 subscribers and the *Äripäev* company employed 185 people, 50 of whom worked in the telemarketing department.

In 1993, the management changed in *Äripäev*. Hallar Lind, the editor-in-chief from the start, left the company and Andrus Vaher and Rötov took over the management. They both started to work for *Äripäev* as reporters in 1991. When taking over the management, Vaher and Rötov decided to share the responsibilities and have done so ever since. Vaher is the managing editor and responsible for the editorial side of *Äripäev*. Rötov is the editor-in-chief and the managing director for the whole company. Even though they have divided the responsibilities between themselves, they lead the company together, and make all larger decision jointly. Besides Rötov and Vaher, the commercial director is also a member of the top management team.

The *Dagens Industri* concept is reflected in *Äripäev*'s business idea (see box on next page). The concept focuses on being a tool for decision makers in companies. *Äripäev*'s business idea is in line with this but focuses very much on entrepreneurs as it identifies its main readers as the heads of small companies (see the second to the last paragraph of the business idea).

The journalists and staff of *Äripäev* have adopted the concept. In most of the interviews made it was mentioned that *Äripäev* should be a tool for entrepreneurs. The notion of being useful for the readers is an idea that seems to permeate the whole organization. All the products developed are focused on being tools for decisions makers, from the newspapers and magazine to the handbooks and the seminars. They all have the aim of providing the consumer with necessary information and knowledge. This is in line with the first mission Olsson had when starting *Äripäev*:

In the Baltic States where *Dagens Industri* has established newspapers it has mostly been about teaching the readers about market economy, that is, we have a pedagogical purpose (personal communication).

ÄRIPÄEV'S BUSINESS IDEA

Äripäev offers heads of companies and entrepreneurs information they require for their work, and also serves as a channel for advertising between entrepreneurs.

In its other products Äripäeva Kirjastus has also focused on the production and sale of business and economic information. Private individuals who consume business information are also included in our target group.

A successful business advertising channel can be a media product only when its readership includes a sufficient number of decision-makers—people who are authorized to make decisions not only about the use of their personal money, but also about a company's money.

The dominant position of *Äripäev* among decision-makers is confirmed by the Decision-makers' Media Survey carried out by BMF Gallup Media in autumn 2002, in which it transpires that 65% of Estonian decision-makers read *Äripäev*.

Äripäev supplies its readers with both interesting and fresh news and also thorough and comparable information about the prices and quality of goods and services.

Äripäev does all in its power to protect the interests of its main reader - the head of a small company. Thanks to sharp criticism in editorials in *Äripäev*, officials and politicians have changed several regulations or laws that were harmful to entrepreneurs.

As a result of the work of *Äripäev* journalists, readers have obtained information that has helped many to save their company money or has opened up new, excellent opportunities to earn money (www.aripaev.ee, 2003-03-23)

Although *Äripäev* is a politically independent newspaper, it still has a political agenda. In its business idea it is stated that the interests of the heads of small companies should be protected. On its web page, *Äripäev* has a description of the newspaper (see box on next page) where it is stated that the objective is to promote a free market economy and to protect the interests of small business. This ideological view clearly comes from the owner *Dagens Industri* and Bonnier.

Äripäev has continued on this path and is today promoting a free market economy in order to protect and foster their readers' interests. This mission of *Dagens Industri*, was quite natural at the time for their entry as there was no developed market in Estonia for the type of newspaper product they wanted to sell. *Äripäev* had the purpose to report on private business and stock market activities but there were not much of those activities to write about. The Tallinn Stock Exchange, for example, did not open until 1996. It was therefore necessary for *Dagens Industri* to create a demand for its product and the educational objective was a way to create such a demand for *Äripäev*. One could question *Dagens Industri*'s transfer of this ideology to Estonia in 1989 (Risberg, 2002), but that discussion is however not part of this article.

Organization and Management at Äripäev

Dagens Industri usually hires young people rather than trained and experienced journalists for the sister papers. Olsson tells that they prefer to hire people under 30 as older people were "ruined by the Soviet system. By ruined I mean that they were afraid to take responsibility and risks, and moreover, they do not know how to work independently and they are afraid of being punished" (Olsson interview).

Instead of hiring experienced journalists and managers *Dagens Industri* chose to train young inexperienced people. Many of the journalists at *Äripäev* have no journalistic or media education. The news editor Meelis Mandel, for example, is a trained engineer. He started to work as a reporter and became news editor after a few years. In his spare time he is studying for a MBA degree at the university and many other *Äripäev* employees are also pursuing master's degrees.

Äripäev is described as a flat, open, and young organization. Much of the decision-making power is delegated to the department managers. In Rötov's words there are twenty people in the organization with the responsibility to achieve the common target for the organization. He believes that if there is a collective responsibility to achieve the goals of the company then each individual organization member will feel responsible for the target being met.

ÄRIPÄEV'S DESCRIPTION OF ITSELF

Äripäev, which is printed on weekdays, is Estonia's leading economics newspaper. The paper's readers are heads of companies and entrepreneurs. *Äripäev* offers them information they require in their work and also serves as an advertising channel between entrepreneurs. *Äripäev* does not compete with the daily papers in the area of general news, but does provide better Estonian business news.

Format and brief and clearly written stories make it possible to read the paper quickly before the workday begins. *Äripäev* supports a liberal organization of life, minimal state interference in the economy and citizens' private life.

The objective is to promote a free market economy, protect the interests of small businesses and assist in the development of a more prosperous, open and ethical society (www.aripaev.ee, 2004-03-24).

The staff and the management describe this as a democratic management style. Commercial director Raido Raamat says that the management team co-ordinate the activities in the company than manage them.

There is a handbook at *Äripäev* that includes necessary information regarding the company. In the handbook the company history is depicted, the company culture is described, job descriptions are specified, rules about what to do and not to do are set out, and the organizational structure is described. The handbook also contains the company's strategic plans. The delegation of the decision making is possible because of these long- and short-term plans. The long-terms plans are broken down for each department and department manager. The plans are frequently mentioned by the middle managers as something facilitating their work.

The company is also described as an open organization by the employees. It is easy to talk to the managers, to make suggestions and ideas, and to express one's opinions. The clear goal statements and the job descriptions are also seen as making the organization more open. The company has, however, started to experience some problems in communication. *Äripäev* has quickly grown from being a small company with about 20 employees to a company with almost 200 employees. Many employees have started to complain about a lack of communication and information in the company. However, compared to other Estonian newspapers, *Äripäev* still seems to be an open organization.

Äripäev's organization appears to be different from that of the average Estonian media company. A reason for this could be that *Äripäev* does not have the history of being a hierarchical and bureaucratic organization. Another reason for *Äripäev* being different could also be that the organization has a low average age among its employees and managers.

Äripäev has, of course, been greatly influenced by *Dagens Industri* during its development. When the managers and employees describe the *Äripäev* newspaper the *Dagens Industri* concept is easily recognized. Bonnier and *Dagens Industri* are represented on the board of *Äripäev* through two Swedish managers. During the first years the newspaper got much support from *Dagens Industri* regarding editorial issues and sales. Seminars and conferences were arranged to train the local staff in how to do things and how to run the newspaper. Today, the *Äripäev* management team says that the Swedish owners do not really interfere in the daily business, except when the company is performing poorly.

> As long as there is growth and profits no one seems to care what we are doing here—but when things got bad there was much interest from the owners on what we did in our daily business, like news, advertising sales etc. Otherwise we are quite an autonomous company but decisions still have to be approved by the board (personal communication).

The top management team does not have much contact with the Swedish owners in their daily work. The main contacts are the board meetings, and there are also some seminars arranged in which the top managers participate. *Dagens Industri* keeps control over *Äripäev* through the financial reports. The commercial director reports the sales numbers weekly. When new products are developed the contacts with *Dagens Industri* are more frequent. *Äripäev*, for example, took advantage of *Dagens Industri*'s experience when launching the monthly business magazine *Tuulu*.

Rötov expresses some concerns about having remote owners. He says that some changes wanted by the local managers do not take place because the owners, situated in Stockholm, do not always understand the local conditions and what is necessary in Estonia. On the other hand, the remote ownership and the relatively light control of the owners allows the local management to act rather autonomously.

FACTORS BEHIND THE SUCCESSFUL
ESTABLISHMENT AND DEVELOPMENT OF *ÄRIPÄEV*

Six reasons can be identified as influencing the successful start-up and development of *Äripäev*. The first reason is the organization and management of *Äripäev*. The organization structure is flat with few levels and with much decision-making power delegated to middle managers. The top management is accessible for the employees, and the working culture is perceived to be good. All this leads to an open atmosphere that also seems to have fostered the introduction of new products in the company.

A second reason is the competence of people working for *Äripäev*. The enterprise spends a lot of money on management and professional training, which, when combined with higher salaries compared to other Estonian newspapers, makes it an attractive employer. *Äripäev* has a good image and reputation in the society of being a modern and non-hierarchical company compared to most other Estonian companies. It is known to be profitable which makes it a safe employer. These factors taken together make *Äripäev* an attractive company to work for, which in turn enhances recruiting competent and skilled people.

A third reason that *Äripäev* is a leading company is that it is ahead of most of its competitors in terms of technology, journalism, layout, and management style and is considered the most modern media company in Estonia. Here the Swedish ownership, with *Dagens Industri* as the mother company, played an important role. When *Äripäev* launched its monthly business magazine, the responsible people could go to Stockholm to study the monthly magazines published by Bonnier. When launching the handbooks, they went to Copenhagen and the newspaper *Børsen* (also owned by *Dagens Industri*) to learn from its experiences in this area. *Dagens Industri* has also provided good training programs that have helped the staff to stay ahead. The international liaison manager, Vibjörn Madsen, has helped the management team a lot, especially during the first six years. His work has been important in the necessary transfer of knowledge when implementing the *Dagens Industri* concept in new start-ups.

Another success factor has been the financial support of *Dagens Industri* when needed. *Äripäev* has for many years been a profitable company, but during the first years there was some political turbulence in Estonia, which made the future insecure. While many other Western owners decided to leave the country, the Bonnier group decided to stay. At the same time the owners keep a distance from the company without interfering too much in the daily business and support *Äripäev* in developing its own profile.

However, *Äripäev* is still carrying on the ideology of the owner, inherent in the *Dagens Industri* concept. The greenfield approach has made it possible to control the realization of the ideology. By controlling the start-up process it has been possible for *Dagens Industri* to transfer its ideas about newspaper production and market economy driven societies to *Äripäev* and other sister companies. But it seems like *Dagens Industri* has been able to fulfill this control without reducing the autonomy given to the new local newspaper company.

The employees are proud of the products they are producing and they believe *Äripäev* is so successful because it helps its readers. The readers are, as mentioned earlier, identified as entrepreneurs. The newspaper *Äripäev* and its handbooks and the seminars are important tools for these entrepreneurs, who even call the company to ask questions because they regard the company as their consultant. However, *Äripäev* would not be a successful brand, with successful products, without the previously mentioned dimensions.

The *Dagens Industri* concept was important for the success of *Äripäev* because it provided something new and different to the Estonian market. *Äripäev* represented both "the West" and high quality. So the product was certainly a reason for success in the early days and *Äripäev* has, due to the success of the newspaper, been able to develop its other successful products.

The success also brings with it some problems regarding further growth. Ninety percent of the Estonian managers, almost their whole target group, are subscribing to *Äripäev* so there are difficulties with continuing to grow unless the number of mangers and entrepreneurs keep growing.

Dagens Industri's establishment of the newspaper *Äripäev* in Estonia became an important learning case for further internationalization by the company.

STARTING NEWSPAPERS IN FOREIGN MARKETS: THE BUSINESS RECIPE OF *DAGENS INDUSTRI*

The *Dagens Industri* management has used the experience and knowledge from Estonia to start several other sister papers in Europe. For these following start-ups, an international manager, Vibjörn Madsen, has functioned as liaison officer and each start of a new sister paper is led from Stockholm.

Besides the liaison manager, there are other *Dagens Industri* people involved in starting a sister paper. Madsen is in charge of transferring the general knowledge of how a newspaper like *Dagens Industri* works. Others have been in charge of transferring the editorial and layout concepts. The news editor of *Dagens Industri,* Anders Davidsson, has been involved in establishing sister newspapers in Latvia, Lithuania, and Poland, where he trained the local staff in editorial matters. The layout is another important matter because the concept implies that all sister papers should look more or less alike. The layout training has involved people from Sweden as well as art directors from foreign sister papers. The *Dagens Industri* representatives function as consultants at the local newspaper during the building up period. They help recruit people, find office space, and train the staff in the *Dagens Industri* concept.

In order to start a newspaper in a new country, *Dagens Industri* uses local contacts. In some countries they start the newspaper with a local partner, whereas in other countries they own the newspaper completely from the start, partly depending on local legislation. In Lithuania the local partner was the newspaper *Diena,* which was half-owned by the Swedish newspaper *Expressen* (also owned by the Bonnier group). The new business newspaper was accordingly called *Diena Bizness.* The editor-in-chief was recruited from *Diena's* business section and its layout manager became the art director for *Diena Bizness.* In Hungary *Dagens Industri* wanted complete ownership of the newspaper from the start and hired four journalists for the job.

The editor-in-chief and the art director are two key people recruited for start-ups. The editor-in-chief ensures that the *Dagens Industri* concept is followed and the art director makes sure that the new newspaper looks like a *Dagens Industri* newspaper. The layout of *Dagens Industri* is quite distinct and the sister papers look more or less alike; most distinct of all is the pink color of the paper. The next step is recruitment of key local staff to build up and run the newspapers. The editor-in-chief and the art director are trained in the concept so that they can in turn train the new journalists and other employees. The philosophy is that local people should run all foreign newspapers. However, there are always *Dagens Industri* people to support the staff in the start-up phase.

Davidsson and Madsen were in charge of starting up the Polish sister paper *Puls Biznesu.* Nine months before the paper was launched, a managing director, a marketing manager, and an advertising manager were hired. The planning started in May 1996 and the first number was planned for January 1997. The three local managers began to make a business plan and to work on the editorial concept together with Davidsson. In the meantime they looked for office space, planned for marketing, and recruited the local staff. Quite soon an editor-in-chief and a news editor were found. In September, there were five local people working with the project. During the fall they continued to recruit for key positions. During the fall the newly recruited managers started to hire people for their respective departments. The whole organization was built within a few months. Davidsson says it is necessary to work with such a short time frame because the newspaper does not make any money until it is launched. During the fall of 1997, several test editions of the newspaper were made. The local editorial staff practiced writing articles for the newspaper and making the right layout, and they tested the printing as well.

As mentioned earlier *Dagens Industri* does not always hire trained journalist when it recruits journalists and other staff members in the former Soviet states. The *Dagens Industri* managers have a specific criterion that the persons hired should not be too affected by the Soviet system (one interviewee said they should not have started their professional career before 1989). Therefore the management prefers recruiting young people without much experience and *Dagens Industri* representatives train the local staff in its way of doing business newspapers. Davidsson, for example, lived in Lithuania the first 6 months to support and train the staff and traveled back and forth between Poland and Sweden for several months to train the new local staff there. As soon as possible, however, the responsibility is handed over to the local staff.

Once the new paper has begun publishing, support from Sweden continues for some time with staff participating in the planning and commenting on the content, headlines, and graphics of the newspaper in order to improve the paper. In the start-up phase, the content of the newspaper is a joint decision between the local editor-in-chief, the journalists, and the *Dagens Industri* representative.

A problem experienced in the early stages of the different newspapers was that the journalists wrote mainly about macroeconomic news. But the *Dagens Industri* concept implies that macroeconomic and financial news should be framed from the perspective of the business firm or the individual entrepreneur. The journalists, however, did not always agree with this part of the concept but preferred to report macroeconomic news, influenced by the situation in former eastern European markets in which it was not accepted to report on business and companies.

All sister papers are built up in a very short time frame. Therefore the first employment period is very hectic for the staff, but the first year of the newspaper is somewhat of a training period for the editorial staff. Consequently, when a new newspaper is started, it is not a very good product for its first months and this creates a problem for the marketing people. The newspapers are sold very aggressively at the start but the quality does not really live up to expectations. This occurs because the editorial staff would lose interest if they were not allowed to make a "real" newspaper but only test editions for a longer period of time. In Poland it took 2 years before the newspaper became a good product with growing circulation and advertising sales.

Competition has been weak in most markets that *Dagens Industri* has entered. In Estonia, Latvia, and Lithuania the local *Dagens Industri* business newspapers soon dominated the market because they represented something new and sold quite easily. In Lithuania, for example, break-even was reached in a year and a half. The Polish case was a bit different because they did not enter that market until 1997, several years after Poland started its transformation to a market economy. The competition in the Polish market was hence quite strong, but the competitors mainly focused on macroeconomic news, without the specific business-firm focus that *Dagens Industri* sees as its signature. Eventually *Puls Biznesu* became the leading business newspaper in Poland.

A common problem experienced during the start up periods was the attitude of the companies and businessmen the newspapers wrote about in post-Soviet countries. *Dagens Industri* requires pictures of the persons who are the subject of articles. This tradition did not exist in the countries and the businessmen and managers did not want to have their pictures taken, as it was not *comme-il-faut* to talk about money and business.

Although there are broad similarities, the foreign sister papers differ from the Swedish *Dagens Industri* to some extent. Although the concept is the same, the focus of the content can be different. In its early days *Dagens Industri*, for example, published theme issues but abandoned them along the way. In a theme issues, the articles focus on a special theme such as cars and the staff seeks advertisers in the specific industry of the theme. This theme concept is something that is common among the new sister papers because it is a way to get a higher volume of advertising sales. The distribution systems for the new papers also differ from the original because of the special national conditions for distribution and subscriptions in each new market.

THE CHOICE OF ENTRY MODE
IN *DAGENS INDUSTRI* INTERNATIONALIZATION

It is quite common that media companies going international enter foreign markets through the acquisition of a local company because news cannot just be exported but needs to be adapted to or produced in the local market. In this concluding section we discuss *Dagens Industri*'s choice of entry mode in relation to existing theories in the field.

In theory *Dagens Industri* had three modes of entry to choose among: greenfield investment, joint venture, or acquisition. In 1989, only the two first modes were available for *Dagens Industri* because it was not possible for foreign firms to fully own a company in Estonia at that time. *Dagens Industri* chose to formally form a joint venture with a local company. The control of the company, however, was in the hands of *Dagens Industri* from the beginning, and it later became 100% owners of the company. In this discussion we will therefore regard *Dagens Industri* as full owners of *Äripäev* and we will also discuss acquisition as a possible entry mode for the company, as it could have been an alternative in Estonia if they had waited for a year with their entry. It was an alternative in the other countries they entered during the 1990s.

One of several motives for *Dagens Industri* to start a newspaper in Estonia was to get access to this emerging market. However, it was not possible to export a newspaper, like *Dagens Industri*, produced in Sweden for the Swedish market. It would also have been difficult to produce the newspaper in Sweden with the news coming from Estonia. But *Dagens Industri* had developed a special knowledge of producing a business newspaper and wanted to take their unique concept to other markets.

Several foreign media companies acquired existing local newspapers in the Baltic States as a means to get access to the market (Williams, 1997). Acquisitions have an advantage over greenfield investments because acquisitions come with an existing customer group, in this case the readers of an existing newspaper. Normally an acquisition would also bring with it an existing group of advertisers, but that was not really the case in eastern Europe at this time. If a company instead decides on a greenfield investment it needs to invest heavily in marketing (Gorg, 2000) both to learn about the new market and to become visible for the readers and advertisers.

Dagens Industri did not have much experience in other markets and definitely not in the Estonian market, which is why it would have made sense to acquire another company in order to get access to the market and existing readers. However, *Dagens Industri* defined the situation differently because its management was not interested in the local market the way it looked in the late 1980s. *Dagens Industri* wanted to export its concept, including the market economy ideology. If *Dagens Industri* had acquired an existing newspaper they would have had to invest a lot of money to change the journalism of that newspaper to fit the *Dagens Industri* concept. The best option for *Dagens Industri* was thus the greenfield investment, where they could have control of the process of building up the new newspaper company. Due to Estonian legislation in place at that time they had to form a joint venture with a local company but it was definitely *Dagens Industri* that was in control of the local sister paper. The arguments for the greenfield investment were that *Dagens Industri* had ownership advantages in the form of a higher level of technology than local competitors and it had a different product, a type of newspaper that did not exist in the Estonian market at this time.

These ownership advantages were competitive advantages in the Estonian market. Hennart and Park (1993) found in their study of Japanese investors in the U.S. that firms with weak competitive advantages used acquisitions while firms with strong competitive advantages used greenfield strategy. Buckley and Casson (1998) stated in their model of different types of foreign direct investments that an entrant with highly specific technology or skills would favor greenfield investment (see also Brouthers & Brouthers, 2000). It thus made sense for *Dagens Industri* to choose greenfield investment. It also fits with the general pattern of entry modes of Swedish firms entering eastern Europe in the early 1990s, in which 78% of all entries were greenfield investments (Rutihinda, 1996).

The competitive advantages, however, also proved to be disadvantages for *Dagens Industri*. Their high technology level brought with it problems to print the newspaper in Estonia. Initially, the Estonian printing houses could neither use the required paper nor print in colors. Because the newspaper concept was also new, they had to invest heavily in building up the market demand (Gorg, 2000). However, it was very useful that *Äripäev* at that time represented a product from the West, which in itself pushed up demand for the newspaper in Estonia.

A reason for *Dagens Industri's* decision not to acquire an existing newspaper was that they did not want the Soviet style management and workforce in their Estonian sister paper. With an acquisition the acquiring company inherits the acquired firm's labor force and corporate culture, whereas in a greenfield investment the firm can hire a new labor force and build up the culture from scratch (Hennart & Park, 1993). Because *Dagens Industri* outspokenly did not want Soviet-trained journalists and managers it was important not to take over an existing company culture and existing working routines. Greenfield investment was therefore the only choice for them as they then could mold the company and the workforce the way they wanted through training and control. Such control over foreign subsidiaries can best be gained through greenfield investments (Woodcoock, Beamish & Makino, 1994).

The control aspect of the entry mode can also be discussed in terms of the firm's business strategy. Harzing (2002), discussing how the firm's strategy affects the chosen entry mode, claims that firms with a global strategy would tend to use greenfield investments whereas firms with a multidomestic strategy would prefer acquisitions. A global strategy, focusing on strong internal integration, means that the parent company needs to have a high level of control of the production process in order to transfer the firm-specific advantages. A multi-domestic strategy, focusing on local adaptation, means that products are more adapted to the local markets, so important market knowledge and skills can most easily be acquired through an acquisition.

The *Dagens Industri* case reveals a mixture of these two strategies. On the one hand it has a global strategy to the degree that the newspaper concept is held constant in all markets. Therefore it is important for *Dagens Industri* to have a high degree of control over the transfer of firm-specific advantages. *Dagens Industri* has used its parent company staff in order to control this transfer of knowledge during the start-up processes. On the other hand *Dagens Industri* has a multidomestic strategy because the contents of the newspapers need to be adapted to the local market. For *Dagens Industri* the control aspect was more important than the adaptation aspect during the start-up phase. But in the long-term perspective *Dagens Industri* seems to have found a balance between the two strategies, with the local adaptation taking place via the hiring of local management and journalists with local knowledge.

Gupta and Govindarajan (2000) argue that the primary reason why multinational companies exist is because of their ability to transfer knowledge more efficiently and effectively in an intracorporate context than through external market mechanisms. In the traditional multinational company, knowledge flows out from the center to the units, and the parent company continues to serve as an active creator and diffuser of knowledge within the corporation. This fits with the *Dagens Industri* case, where the parent company wanted to transfer its specific knowledge on how to make a tabloid business newspaper to a number of new subsidiaries. Later transfer of knowledge also took place from the more experienced local newspapers to start-ups in other countries.

The greenfield entry (in the Estonian case slightly modified to be a technical joint venture for some years) seems to have been the right, if not the only, choice for *Dagens Industri,* considering its motives, its competitive advantages, and its strategy. Li (1995), as well as Woodcoock, Beamish, and Makino (1994), have found that greenfield entries perform better than joint ventures and acquisitions. *Äripäev* is today a successful and profitable company and was in 1999 listed as the fourth most recognized brand in Estonia.

In his study of Swedish entries in eastern Europe, Rutihinda (1996) found four different entry roles. The missionary role indicates that the goals the company has set for the domestic market are spread to all other markets. This role is characterized by a high degree of integration with the parent company and the exploitation of the parent company's competitive advantages. However, this entry role means a relatively low degree of value-added activities from the new local subsidiary. The next role, the contributor, has both very high integration controlled from the parent and a high degree of value-adding activities from the new subsidiary. The settler role involves low integration with the parent but a high degree of value-added activities by the local company. The fourth role includes both low integration with the parent and low value added, which implies an explorative phase during which the subsidiary is just monitoring the new market before further commitments are made. The internationalization of *Dagens Industri* initially had much of a missionary flavor, with the CEO at that time—Hasse Olsson—acting as the missionary himself, exporting the ideas of the market economy to countries in eastern Europe.

However, looking at the *Dagens Industri* internationalization as a whole, the company must be seen as a contributor, striving for high integration and control at the same time as each local newspaper produces added value, partly based on a rather autonomous local adaptation.

The success of *Dagens Industri*'s entry into Estonia builds on a tight control of *Äripäev*, mainly based on knowledge transfer from the mother company in Sweden. In the start-up phase, the implementation of the newspaper concept was tightly controlled through training of the recruited journalists and managers. In the following phases, local adaptation took place but the basic concept remained the same. The ideology of *Dagens Industri*, which focused on free markets, was transferred to the local staff as a way to control how the Estonian newspaper framed the published news. This transfer of knowledge from Sweden to the local subsidiaries deliberately ignored local journalistic and management experiences during the start-up of this and other sister papers. The control of knowledge has however been a base for the success of the sister newspapers.

The local management of *Äripäev* has executed the same type of control, especially through the company culture, explicitly communicated in the company handbook as a way to influence employees as to how to behave in certain situations. To conclude, knowledge transfer and training of local staff have been a way for the *Dagens Industri* management to both control the local staff and at the same time give them some autonomy. This seems to be a key aspect in the success of *Dagens Industri*'s international expansions.

The successful exportation of *Dagens Industri*'s newspaper concept reveals the ability of media companies to internationalize their product portfolios and that such expansion is not restricted to the world's largest media firms. Its experiences in internationalization, however, underscore the needs for firms to have clear visions, to select the proper entry mode, to establish supportive structures, and to create workable relations with knowledgeable local managers.

REFERENCES

Bakker, P. (2002). Free daily newspapers—Business models and strategies. *JMM—International Journal on Media Management*, *4*(3), 180–187.

Brouthers, K. D. & Brouthers, L. E, (2000). Acquisitions or greenfield start-up? Institutional, cultural and transaction cost influences. *Strategic Management Journal*, *21*(1), 89–97.

Buckley, P. J. & Casson, M. C. (1998). Analyzing foreign market entry strategies: Extending the internationalization approach. *Journal of International Business Studies, 29*(3), 539–562.

Clausen, L. (2001). *The 'domestication' of international news—A study of Japanese TV production.* Ph.d.-serie, nr.2001-21. København: Samfundslitteratur.

Gorg, H. (2000). Analysing foreign market entry—The choice between greenfield investment and acquisitions. *Journal of Economic Studies, 27*(3), 165-181.

Gupta, A. K. & Govindarajan, V. (2000). Knowledge flows within multinational corporations. *Strategic Management Journal, 21*(4), 473-496.

Harzing, A.-W. (2002). Acquisitions versus greenfield investments: International strategy and management of entry modes. *Strategic Management Journal, 23*(3), 211–227.

Hennart, J.-F. & Park, Y.-R. (1993). Greenfield vs. acquisitions: The strategy of Japanese investors in the United States. *Management Science, 39*(9), 1054–1070.

Li, J. (1995). Foreign entry and survival: effects of strategic choices on performance in international markets. *Strategic Management Journal, 16*, 333–351.

Risberg, A. (2002, July). Crossing the Baltic Sea in the name of the market—A post-colonial approach to the start-up of an Estonian newspaper. Paper presented at the 18th EGOS Colloquium, Barcelona.

Rutihinda, C. (1996). Resource-based internationalization: Entry strategies of Swedish firms into the emerging markets of eastern Europe. Ph.D. dissertation, Stockholm University.

Williams, D. (1997). Strategies of multinational enterprises and the development of the central and eastern European economies. *European Business Review, 97*(3), 134-138.

Woodcock, P.C., Beamish, P.W. & Makino, S. (1994). Ownership-based entry mode strategies and international performance. *Journal of International Business Studies*, Second Quarter, *25*(2), 253–273.

World Association of Newspapers (2000). *Free newspapers: A threat or opportunity? The case of the London Metro.* Paris: World Association of Newspapers.

Author and Subject Index

Contributors

LEONA ACHTENHAGEN is an associate professor of business administration (strategy and organization) and a faculty member of the Media Management and Transformation Center, Jönköping International Business School, Jönköping University, Sweden. Her research interests include organizations and strategy. She has had articles published in *European Journal for Work and Occupational Psychology*, *Zeitschrift für betriebswirtschaftliche Forschung*, and *Organization Studies*.

ETHEL BRUNDIN is an assistant professor in business administration (strategy and organization) at Jönköping International Business School, Jönköping University, Sweden. Her research interests include organizations, leadership, motivation, and conflict management.

MIN HANG is a doctoral candidate in the Media Management and Transformation Center, Jönköping International Business School, Jönköping University, Sweden. Her research interests are strategies of multi-national firms and organizational cultures.

THOMAS HESS is a professor in the Institute of Information Systems and New Media at the University of Munich, Germany. His research has been published in journal including *Wirtschaftsinformatik*, *Business Change and Re-Engineering*, *Electronic Markets*, and *International Journal on Media Management*. He is the author and editor of numerous books including *Netzwerkcontrolling: Instrumente und ihre Werkzeugunterstützung*, *Enabling Systematic Business Change: Integrated Methods and Software Tools for Business Process Redesign*, and *Medienunternehmen im digitalen Zeitalter: neue Technologien - neue Märkte - neue Geschäftsansätze*.

HUGH J. MARTIN is an assistant professor in the Grady College of Journalism and Mass Communication at the University of Georgia. His scholarship has been published in *Newspaper Research Journal*, *Journalism & Mass Communication Quarterly*, and *Journal of Public Relations Research*.

LEIF MELIN is a professor of business administration (strategy and organization) and manager of the family business program at Jönköping International Business School, Jönköping University, Sweden. His research has been published in journals including *Strategic Management Journal, Long Range Planning,* and *International Studies in Management and Organization.*

MARIA NORBÄCK is a doctoral candidate in the Media Management and Transformation Center, Jönköping International Business School, Jönköping University, Sweden. Her research interests involve organizational and marketing issues in media firms.

MART OTS is a doctoral candidate in the Media Management and Transformation Center, Jönköping International Business School, Jönköping University, Sweden. His research interests include business models and business development and marketing in media enterprises

ROBERT G. PICARD is Hamrin professor of media economics and director of the Media Management and Transformation Center, Jönköping International Business School, Jönköping University, Sweden. He is the author and editor of 20 books on media economics and management issues, including *The Economics and Financing of Media Companies,* was the founding editor of the *Journal of Media Economics.* He is currently editor of the *Journal of Media Business Studies.*

ANNETTE RISBERG is an assistant professor in the Department of Intercultural Communication and Management at Copenhagen Business School. Her research interests include international business and effect of mergers and acquisitions on employees. Her scholarship has been published in *Culture and Organization, Journal of World Business,* and *Leadership & Organization Development Journal.*

HANS VAN KRANENBURG is an associate professor of industrial organization and strategy at the faculty of Economics and Business Administration at Maastricht University, The Netherlands. He is a visiting research fellow at the Media Management and Transformation Center, Jönköping International Business School, Jönköping University, Sweden. His scholarship has been published in *Journal of Media Economics, Journal of International Business Studies, Journal of Law and Economics,* and *International Journal of Industrial Organization.*